The Happy Home for Ladies

Lilly Bartlett

A note on this edition

This novel was written and edited in British English, including all spelling, grammar, punctuation and figures of speech.

Chapter 1

'Well, Mum, I've really got to hand it to you this time,' I tell her, yanking at the snug waistband of my dress. My comment gets carried away, though, by all the chattering going on around us. My parents' friends can talk a mile a minute. 'You've outdone yourself,' I admit, louder this time. I *am* trying, though I sound touchy as touchy can be. On today of all days too. What is wrong with me?!

I guess she shouldn't really expect me to take the high road now, just because we're at a funeral. We've never let something as trifling as the spectre of death stand in the way of a good snipe. 'You were right. As usual.' And nobody in the entire history of angsty mother-daughter dynamics wants to admit that. Which just shows how much I've grown recently as a person.

If I'm being honest, Mum does deserve every bit of credit today. Dad would have chucked a few frozen sausage rolls into the oven and maybe ordered some portions of chips from the cheap chippy that's on his way home from work. 'It is the party to end all parties,' I admit, meeting her green eyes. The eyes that I didn't inherit. I got Dad's mud-brown ones instead. I missed out on her film-star legs too. My brother got those *and* her eyes. I've got her allergy to grass and dodgy karaoke voice.

'It's just a lot of money to spend on one day. A lot,' I can't keep from adding.

Not that she's listening. Which is typical. She's always been more interested in making sure everyone's overwhelmed by her generosity.

The house is heaving with people. I've never laid eyes on most of them. They're packed into the dining room and out back where the French doors lead on to the terrace and into the garden, and around the pool that Dad rushed to open early even though it's freezing out and nobody in their right mind would turn up with their swimsuit on under their clothes. People are huddling together in the living room, or the 'great room', as Mum makes us call it. I've got no idea what a great room is supposed to be, but I guess having a library full of books and a grand piano that's never had anything but 'Chopsticks' played on it qualifies.

Sighing, I say, 'I'll go check that Dad's all right.' I leave her grinning over another perfect party.

I don't mean to make my parents sound like nightmares. It's just that Mum drives me round the bend. And this *is* us on our best behaviour. You might have guessed that they throw lavish parties, and maybe you can tell that they live in a big house. But if I say it's Mum's mission in life to outshine absolutely everyone – which is totally true – you'll probably start thinking they're horrible. They're not, though. It's just that they worked really hard to start their own business and build themselves up from nothing. Plus, they're very generous. So hopefully you'll forgive them for wanting to flash a bit of their success.

I catch a glimpse of Dad through one of the six-foot-high lilac rose floral arrangements. Mum's got them all over the house. Lilac and deep green, that's the colour theme. She's coordinated everything: the flowers, tablecloths, serviettes, plates, foil-wrapped chocolates by the lorry load, and even the guests.

I tug again at the waist of my lilac gingham dress. I look like fat Dorothy, off to see the Wizard, but it was all I could find at such short notice.

Will wore gingham too. He's my older brother. He's also my only brother, unfortunately. We looked ridiculous standing beside each other. Tweedle Dee and Tweedle Dumber. I'm not surprised he's already scarpered.

Dad's not happy with his tartan purple shirt, either, but he knows which side his bread is buttered on. If Mum wants everyone to dress like their granny's kitchen curtains, then everyone is going to turn up in their granny's kitchen curtains.

He's deep in conversation with their neighbour. Valentina, I think she's called. Or Valentine. It's hard to keep all their friends straight. According to my parents, that's because I don't visit enough. I was here more when they first moved away, just after I'd finished school, when the two-hour journey to Essex was worth it to get my laundry done for me.

'Everyone's having such a nice time!' Valen-something says, kissing my cheek. 'I mean... under the circumstances. I'm so sorry.' Her face reddens to match her lipstick.

Dad squeezes her arm. 'It's exactly what Bev would have wanted, Valerie.'

Valerie, that's it!

We all stare across the room, over the friends' and neighbours' heads, past the OTT floral arrangements and beyond the long dining table, to Mum's photo leaning against the fireplace. It's one that Dad took last year on their cruise. She's smiling right into the camera, looking suntanned and happy. Dad's right. It's exactly the kind of send-off she'd have wanted.

Of course it is. She planned every last detail, because that's the kind of control freak Mum is. Was.

Everyone's finally gone and I'm dead on my feet. If you'll pardon the expression. You wouldn't think people would outstay their welcome at a funeral, but that Valerie just wouldn't take the hint. I was ready to flick the lights off and bang Mum's stew pot with the ladle to get her to go. And she and Mum weren't even that close.

'That went well,' Dad says, like he's just passed his driving test or something.

'Yeah, except for Mum being... you know.'

'Yeah. Except for that,' he says. Then he laughs. Of all things! 'She'd have loved the look on everyone's faces when the cake came out.'

The man's wife is dead and he's laughing over the cake? I'm no grief counselling expert, but that's not right. 'Dad, aren't you even a little bit upset? I mean, she and I had our differences, but I am sad that she's gone. Now I'm an orphan.'

His dark eyebrows draw together. They're only so startling because his hair is nearly white. 'What about me? Aren't I still your parent?'

'I'm half an orphan, then.'

His pat on my shoulder is awkward. Dad's not a great one for the touchy-feely. 'Now, now, there's no use crying over spilt milk, Phoebe. What's done is done.'

'It's not spilt milk, Dad, and Mum's not *done*, she's dead! Will you stop trying to make it sound like no big deal?'

I dash away the tears with my hand. Maybe I'm sad. Maybe I'm frustrated. All I know is that I do feel *something*. Unlike my father, the Dalek.

I look into his face, trying to remember whether I've ever seen him get emotional. He shouts at his football team on TV sometimes. 'How can you be so cold?'

'Phoebe, come on,' he says, running a hand over his five o'clock (yesterday) shadow. If Mum were here, she'd have made him shave this morning. She hates stubble. *Hated*. 'Just because I'm not falling to pieces doesn't mean I don't feel anything. People show their emotions differently, that's all.'

'Yes, but they show them, Dad. You're acting like you don't even care.'

'Let's not fight,' he says. 'Not today. Want a cup of tea?' Without waiting for an answer, he pulls out three mugs and chucks the teabags in. 'Oh.' He hesitates. 'Silly me.'

As he puts Mum's favourite spotty mug back in the cabinet, I catch the lost look skittering across his expression. I guess it is there, after all.

'I'm sorry, Dad.'

He'd rung me just after lunchtime. He never does during the day unless it's to tell me I've forgotten a birthday or an anniversary or something.

I'd just managed to wrestle four giant packs of chicken thighs out from the overstuffed freezer at work for the next day's curry. Care home residents might not seem like they'd appreciate food that's not bland or pureed, but our residents aren't what you'd call the norm.

'Who did I forget?' I answered with my mobile wedged between my cheek and shoulder.

'Hi, Phoebe. This is your father.'

'I know it's you, Dad. You come up on my phone.' Every conversation started like this.

'Your mother has gone into hospital.'

I felt my tummy sink to my knees. I clasped the phone to my ear. 'What's happened?' Horrible scenarios flashed through my mind: she'd been in a crash. No, it was a mugging. She's always marching around with a big expensive bag dangling off her arm. Or a random acid attack or a knifing or she'd lopped her fingers off chopping onions or confused arsenic for sugar in her tea. Though I'm not sure why there'd be arsenic in the cabinet.

'Heart attack, they think,' said Dad.

'Is she... okay?'

'Oh, yes, she's fine,' he said. 'She didn't want me to bother you. I just thought you might like to know.'

'How can she be fine, Dad, when she's had a heart attack? And, yes, I want to know!' Only my mother could think that a near-death experience wasn't even worth a phone call.

'I mean she's awake and feeling fine, so don't worry.' His voice was as calm as always. Unlike mine.

'Have you rung Will already?' I asked.

'He'll be busy with work. We don't want to disturb him.'

Of course, they'd never dream of giving him anything to worry about at work. Like the entire financial system would collapse if he were ever to take a personal call. I looked around my kitchen. In their eyes, Will was the one with the important job, not me. I'm 'just' a cook. 'I'm leaving now,' I told him. 'I can be there in two hours depending on traffic. I'll see you soon, Dad.'

'I'll meet you at the hospital in a few hours, then. Text me when you're off the motorway.'

'But aren't you at the hospital now?'

'Your mum wants me to stay at the office. The sealed bids are coming in today.' He gave me the hospital's address. Then he told me not to use the car park there.

'Parking will be expensive,' he said. 'There'll be spaces further along the main road and you can walk back.'

Honestly.

The drive there is a blur, but I do remember the feeling. It was all I could do not to scream and bash the steering wheel every time I had to slow down for traffic or lights. I just knew I wouldn't get there in time to see Mum one last time.

I found the closest spot in the car park, sprinted to the critical care unit and blurted my mother's name to the nurse, who calmly pointed me to her room.

'God, Phoebe,' said Mum when I skidded through the door. 'Where's the fire? You nearly gave me a heart attack. Ha ha.'

'Mum, what happened?!' She was sitting up in bed with a blue hospital gown draped loosely across her front. Wires trailed from under the covers to the machines that beeped and chirped beside her.

She had her mobile to her ear. 'Sorry about that,' she told the caller. 'I'll have to ring you back.'

She kept her phone clasped in her hand as she waved away my question. 'It's a lot of bother over nothing. The doctors aren't even sure it was a heart attack. They're making me go through tests to check. Your father didn't need to bother you.' She looked me up and down. Then she sighed. 'Isn't there *something* better that you could wear to work?'

I glanced down at my black checked chef trousers and short-sleeved white tunic.

'And those clogs. I wouldn't wear them around the house, let alone out of it. Why can't you try a bit harder, Phoebe? Don't you care what people think?'

I ignored the jibes. Only because she could be dying. 'Tell me what happened, Mum. Did you have pain?'

'Of course I had pain,' she snapped. 'It was a heart attack. Or something like it anyway. I feel fine now, though. I need to get back to the office. The sealed bids are coming in today. I can come back after for the tests if they're so keen on them.'

'I'm sure the office understands that you're here.'

'Pah, I didn't tell them! And don't you, either. They think your dad gave me a surprise spa day.' Then she muttered, 'As if I'd tell them about something like this.'

What was *wrong* with my mother? 'Mum, that's nuts. You can't cover up a heart attack with a spa day. You're ill. You could be here for some time. Everyone at the company cares about you. They'd want to know.'

'I just bet they would,' she said. 'Phoebe, how many times have I told you that people will exploit their advantage. I'm not about to give them an excuse.'

'These aren't just people, Mum, they're your friends. Your employees. You've worked with them for years.'

She waved away my protest. 'You'd hope that friends wouldn't use something against you, but why would I take the chance when I don't have to? If you've learned anything from me, darling, I hope it's that.'

Then she pulled off the covers and started to swing her legs to the floor, sending the machines into a meltdown.

'Mum, don't!'

A nurse hurried into the room, probably expecting cardiac arrest. What she found was the world's worst patient peeling off the tape holding the monitors to her chest. 'What are you doing?' the nurse demanded. 'Get back into bed. You've got to rest. And keep these on.' She pulled off another length of tape with a furious tear and stuck it to my mother. 'If you need the loo, push the button and someone will help you.' She glared at Mum. 'Do not leave this bed.'

'I'm sorry,' I murmured to the nurse as she left. 'Mum, why can't you behave?! You need to stay here until they know what's wrong. These people are trying to help you.'

'I know that, Phoebe, but I've got things to do. I'm very busy. We didn't build our business by sitting around on our bums, you know.'

How many times had I heard that over the years? Whenever I didn't do things the way she thought I should. Which was almost always. 'Being in hospital with a heart attack is not just sitting around on your bum,' I reminded her. 'Besides, you've got Dad looking after the bids, so you don't need to worry about anything.'

She rolled her eyes. Then she zeroed in on my hair which, I remembered too late, was still in its ponytail from work. 'Couldn't you have done something with that?' She patted her own perfectly coiffed gingery head. She looked like she'd had it styled on the way over in the ambulance. 'You only have one chance to make a first impression. You could look so much better, you know, if you tried at all.'

Despite my mother being mortified by a hair tie, I actually think it looks all right, thank you very much. It might not be as shimmery and because-I'm-worth-it as Mum's, but it's a nice brown, long, straight and thick.

'You made a great first impression with that nurse,' I said. 'You'd better be careful or she won't give you the good biscuits at teatime.' I heaved a great sigh. 'Do you need anything? I can run downstairs to the shops.'

I was desperate to get away for a few minutes to catch my breath. Besides, my tummy had been twisting into knots since the drive.

She always did that to me. My mother didn't get ulcers, she gave them. Which said everything about our relationship, really.

Chapter 2

By the time I got back with all Mum's shopping, Dad was there, sopping wet from the squall that had whipped up outside. His dress shirt was stuck to his chest and little rivulets dripped down the sides of his face from his flattened hair. His whole head had gone grey early, but at least he's still got it, and despite the stress of being an entrepreneur, he doesn't look his age (fifty-eight). He does look like a builder, which he is, even though he spends more time on email now than on building sites.

'You really didn't park in the garage?' I asked him.

'You really did?' he shot back. 'I told you it was a waste of money.'

That's pretty much what passes for a friendly greeting in our family.

Dad wasn't offended because he's cheap. We're talking about the man who drives a £60k car. He and Mum went on exotic holidays. He's not afraid to spend his cash. He just hates feeling ripped off. That's why he buys own-brand baked beans if the good ones aren't on sale. Tesco won't ever put one over on him.

Not Mum, though, aka Spendy McSquillions. She'd never met a purse she couldn't empty. It was a good thing their business had done well.

'I'm only supposed to have one visitor at a time,' Mum said when I gave her the carrier bags from downstairs.

'I'm sure it's fine, Bev,' Dad said. 'Phoebe's driven all the way here.'

'I know, thank you,' she said to me. 'But really, you don't have to stay, now that Dad's come. I'm fine, don't worry about me.'

I could tell that she was fine by the way she was just as critical as usual.

'Mum's right,' Dad added, glancing at his phone. 'You've got to get out of that garage,' he said, like the parking attendant there was holding my car hostage.

'I don't care about the money, Dad.'

But I let them convince me to go back to their house. He'd only keep going on about the expense anyway, and clearly Mum wasn't in any danger.

I couldn't say I was completely at home at my parents', but it felt comfortable enough. Like I said, it wasn't where I grew up. They sold that when they decided to make their fortune a hundred miles south. Still, I flattered myself that the guest bedroom where I always stayed was 'my room', and that I'd at least get first dibs over any Tom, Dick or Harry who came to visit.

Dad didn't stay at the hospital very long after me, but he went back to work and then out for some dinner meeting that couldn't be moved just because his wife and business partner was dining in Critical Care.

When I got to Mum's room the next morning, all I saw was a lump in her bed with a sheet pulled over it. Exactly like they did in films when the paramedics had done all they could to save the patient.

She was dead! 'Mum!'

'What!' snapped the voice under the bedding.

'What are you doing?'

Mum appeared with an angry yank of the sheet. She had her phone to her ear.

'You're not supposed to use that in here!'

'No kidding, Phoebe, so stop shouting about it or the nurse will hear. Shush.' She waved me away as she continued to talk and scribble in the notebook I'd picked up for her in the shop.

'That could interfere with the machines, you know,' I said when she'd hung up.

'Don't be such a worrier,' she grumbled. 'It's my machine, so it's my risk.'

'There are other patients with machines on the ward, you know. Do you really want to kill one of them with a phone call?'

Mum rolled her eyes. She was a famous eye-roller. 'Don't believe everything you read, Miss Health and Safety. If it was such a problem, then they'd block mobiles.'

'If it's such a problem, then they'd put up signs.' I pointed to the warning posted by the door. 'Oh, look, they have.'

Then, right on cue she said, 'Are those the same clothes from yesterday?'

'I was at work when Dad rang,' I reminded her. 'I can pick up some things later if it's so important to you that I dress for the hospital.' I knew I should have at least borrowed one of Dad's shirts. Though the checked trousers were still a problem.

I didn't usually take Mum's image critiques to heart. I'd never leave my flat if I did that. Instead, I tried not to give her too much to work with. It was easier emptying the gun than trying to keep the bullets from hitting their mark when she spotted an easy target.

'Standards,' Mum said. 'Anyway, did you have a nice breakfast with Dad?' We'd gone out to the builder's caff before he left for the office. 'The food here is vile. They couldn't make a decent fry-up with guns to their heads. You could teach them something. Maybe you should work for the NHS. I bet it pays better than what you're getting now.'

Not wanting our possibly last conversation to be an argument, I ignored her career advice. 'Maybe you shouldn't be eating fry-ups, Mum,' I said instead. Although she *was* generally one of those women who kept fit and ate well-ish. If she started filling out a bit, she just cut back, as she loved to say. Simple as that. The implication was that anyone could do it. But I'm no supermodel and there's no 'just' cutting back. I'm rounded, like any good chef worth her salted butter should be.

'At least put on some decent clothes if you're going to stay,' she said. 'I don't want people thinking my cook is visiting me in hospital.'

'Sorry I didn't think to pack a ball gown for your heart attack,' I said. I'd gone from worried about my mother to rowing with her in less than twenty-four hours. In other words, totally normal.

She glanced at her phone. 'The shops are open now.'

'I'll stop back after lunch, then,' I told her.

My mobile rang a few hours later. 'I'm sorry I snapped at you,' she said, and she meant it. She usually apologised for her outbursts. Not for thinking what she thought, but at least for saying it out loud. 'You don't have to bother with new clothes. I'll be out of here soon anyway, as soon as the doctors tick all their silly little boxes. They're only covering themselves. I've been through most of the tests now, and they're saying it probably wasn't even a heart attack. I don't want you to worry, okay? Honestly, Phoebe, you don't have to stay. There's nothing wrong with me. Ask your dad if you don't believe me.'

'Well, if you're sure.' I didn't need too much convincing, because everyone knew that my mum was invincible. She'd probably be back at the office bossing everyone around before I got to work on Monday.

My jaw started to unclench as soon as I got onto the motorway toward home. Please don't get me wrong. I love my parents. It's just sometimes hard being their daughter. Maybe all driven people are like that, setting the same high bar for everyone else that they do for themselves.

I didn't strictly have to go past work on my way home, but I drove that way anyway. The care home is a grand old building and would practically be stately if there was anything aristocratic about the residents. It used to be the owner's family home – also not aristocrats – and there's a portrait in the entrance of the card-happy ancestor who won it gambling. He lost everything else the same way, though, so it's never really been looked after beyond the minimum of upkeep.

The house is set back from the road with wide, sloping lawns running on either side. Our boss, Max Greene, had the drive widened a few years ago, but other than that it hasn't changed since his mother owned it. That's both a blessing and a curse.

June's car was parked out front. She wasn't supposed to be working on a Saturday. We're the weekday staff. We've got night and weekend cover and she promised me no more overtime. She had the nerve to get snappish just because I pressed her on it.

I pulled into the drive behind her car.

'You didn't answer your phone,' my best friend called down the corridor as soon as she saw me come through the side door where the office is. 'How's your mum?'

So she wasn't going to make it easy for me to bollock her about the overtime.

'As frightful as usual,' I said, throwing myself down on the extra chair in front of her desk. June's mind might be ultra-organised, but her office isn't. There are binders stuffed full of receipts and records teetering all over the top of the cabinets, and her desk looks like she's been shredding evidence. 'I was driving when you rang,' I said. 'And you were working while I was driving.'

But June didn't rise to the top of senior management (also the only management) at the Jane Austen Home for Ladies by caving in at the first sniff of trouble. She ignored me. 'Frightful is good,' she said. 'That means Bev's back to normal. She's out of hospital now?' She stretched her arms above her head and leaned back in her office chair, like she hadn't a care in the world. The hem of her top rode up to flash a few inches of tummy, but she didn't notice.

'No, but she'll be home soon. It doesn't sound like anything too serious.' Of course, June knew this already. I rang her from the hospital just after I first saw Mum. Was that only yesterday? 'She sent me home.'

June nodded. I didn't have to explain. We'd spent our entire childhood at each other's houses. She knew all about my parents first-hand.

'Nick's gone home,' she said with a smirk. 'He only came in to do an hour with Laney.'

'Hmm? That's not why I'm here.'

It was exactly why I was there. Even though my dreams about Nick were quite hopeless by then, I couldn't stop wishing. It's not easy getting over someone when you're around him every day at work.

'I only came in to get you out of the office,' I lied. 'You're not supposed to be working on your day off.'

'And you're not supposed to be stalking on your day off.'

Touché. We should both have been away from work doing better things.

She closed her laptop. 'Do you want to do something? I told Callum I might meet him later, but it's not set in stone. We can get a drink if you like.'

'June, you cannot keep blowing Callum off,' I said. 'He'll get sick of it eventually, and then he'll dump you.'

But she shook her head. 'The less I see of him, the more he likes me.'

'By your logic, he'll be in love with you if you never see him again. Doesn't it seem a little bit, I don't know, *unhelpful* to your sex life never to see your boyfriend?'

I could never do that. When I'm mad for someone I can't keep away from him. Well, obviously, because there I was at work on a Saturday, on the off-chance that I might see Nick.

And June was mad for Callum. Mad like I'd never seen her before. It was easy to see why. He was gorgeous and fit and loads of fun, and they were really going for it, hot-and-heavy-wise, when they first got together. But then he made one little joke about her trying to handcuff him when she suggested a weekend break, and she started playing so hard to get that he had more chance of winning the lottery than seeing her.

He was still keen, so far, but for how long?

'Come on, I'll walk out with you,' she said.

I might not have seen Nick, but at least I got her away from work. 'Go see Callum,' I urged her when we got to our cars.

'Maybe.'

Dad rang me around midnight. 'Phoebe, this is your father.'

'What's happened?'

But I knew, even as I asked the question. Mum wasn't invincible after all.

The doctors were baffled. None of the tests had shown that cardiac arrest was imminent. But then, Mum always did love to surprise people.

She left behind pages and pages of notes in her sprawling handwriting. Like she couldn't get the words on the page fast enough. That's what she'd been doing on her mobile all the time. Planning her last hurrah, just in case. She'd probably spent her final hours on earth trying to figure out which canapes would most impress their neighbours.

At twenty-eight, I was half orphaned. I was also stuck with such a confusing mishmash of feelings about Mum that I didn't have the faintest idea what to do with them. All I could do after the funeral was to throw myself back into my life and hope for the best.

MICHELE GORMAN

Chapter 3

Three months later…

We've lost Laney at work. That's no euphemism, though I can see why you might think so, what with me recently 'losing' my mother, plus us being in a care home and all. *I'm sorry, madam, we did everything we could, but we've lost Laney.*

We actually can't find her.

It's not the first time, but it is the longest that she's been missing. Even June is starting to get nervous. Not that anyone but me would be able to tell. She's the most famously unflappable person here. The worse things are, the calmer she gets. That's how I know she's worried, when she starts speaking like she's convincing someone to put down the knife. But I would never let on. Everyone's got their coping mechanisms.

Laney was last seen at breakfast, sitting with her usual friends at their usual table. Not the one directly next to the big sash windows in the dining room, because Laney doesn't like to squint when it's sunny, and besides, Sophie thinks the light fades her hair colour. Which is already the colour of wholemeal bread, so I don't know why she's so worried. Sophie says she and Laney were going to do Zumba together, but Laney didn't turn up for it.

That wouldn't normally raise any alarm bells, since Laney isn't much of an exerciser. She is a joiner-inner, though, who doesn't like to disappoint people. Plus, she doesn't usually go off on her own, so we're getting worried.

'I didn't think much of it,' Sophie continues, pulling her navy-blue legwarmers back up over her sturdy calves. 'It's not the first time she's stood me up. She *will* skimp on her exercise.' Her deep brown eyes are huge behind her thick glasses. I can never look at her without thinking of a barn owl. Now I'm tempted to say 'She whoo?' It's as much because she's owl-shaped and has a beakish nose as because she powders her round flat face with a shade that's so light that we could use her as a road-marker post at night.

Sophie has been a Jane Fonda workout devotee since 1982, as she reminds us every chance she gets. Hence the legwarmers. She also makes everyone feel guilty for eating donuts, so she's that kind of person and we do try to overlook her faults.

If we weren't so chronically understaffed and overworked, we might not have lost Laney. It's a wonder we don't lose more residents. Max will be furious. He's edgy about his business as it is.

Nobody would call him a good boss, except in the sense that he's not generally around to bother us. When he does visit, he always rings first as a warning. That's because he knows he's not popular.

Not like his mother, the founder and previous owner of the Jane Austen Home for Ladies. That's its official name now, though everyone in the village calls it Friendship House, because of the plaque beside the front door, from when people named their houses instead of numbering them. That must have been a nightmare for the postie.

We all call it the Happy Home for Ladies though. Sounds nice, doesn't it? It was Max who made his mother drop the Happy, in case anyone ever sued us for false or misleading advertising. It's not, though, because the residents are happy. Plus, they're women. Max was just being his usual miserable self.

'He's here,' June calls out, speaking of the devil as she glances out the window. 'Everyone, act normal. It's not like he's about to do a headcount.'

But this is the biggest kerfuffle the residents have seen since Dot fell out her bedroom window. They're all gathered in the dining room making plans for Laney's rescue, wherever she may be. Fat chance of acting normal.

'Has anyone checked the greenhouse?' Nick wonders. 'I could go look.'

Nick is the only one who ever goes in there, and then only to get out the lawnmower. I can't see Laney suddenly wanting to become a garden expert, but you never know with her. Any throwaway comment can send her mind skittering off on some obscure trail. Then, down the rabbit hole she goes.

'Let me go with you,' I tell Nick. 'I mean, if she's there, she could be hurt. There should be two of us.'

That sends the residents into another flap. I should know better than to mention getting hurt to residents in a care home. Now I feel bad for upsetting them for my own selfish ends.

And they are totally selfish. I'll latch onto any excuse to be with Nick, even if it's only in a draughty old greenhouse that stinks of fertiliser.

I'm sure my feelings would be easier to ignore if we didn't have so much fun together. If only he'd get grumpy once in a while, or develop an annoying habit or at least a bad case of halitosis. But he remains stubbornly fanciable. There isn't even any hint now of the awful weirdness that almost ruined our friendship. Those were terrible weeks, but at least if they'd gone on then I wouldn't still be pining for him. Maybe I'd be satisfied with never sharing anything more than a friendly laugh in the shed together.

When Sophie puts her arm around Dot's bony shoulders, I say, 'I'm sorry, Dot, I'm sure she's not hurt!'

If Sophie is a sturdy barn owl then Dot is a sparrow, reed-thin and restless. She doesn't seem like the type who'd say boo to a goose.

She waves away my protest, sending her bracelets tinkling merrily. 'It's all right. There's no need to fuss over me.'

How thoughtless can I be, when Dot's only been off crutches for a few weeks?

We thought we'd lost her a few months ago. And I do mean that in the scary sense of the phrase.

Thank goodness for the rhododendrons that cushioned Dot's landing when she tumbled from her window. Otherwise she might have broken a lot more than her leg and her arm.

I still don't know what made her think she should try washing her own windows. Granted, we've had storms lately and they're not as crystal clear as they might be. But she could have asked for someone to give them a wipe. Nick would have been the first one up that ladder.

Dot's independent streak is a mile wide, though. Plus, she's super polite and hates to put anybody out. Which was why she climbed out her window with a roll of kitchen towel and a squirty bottle of Windex.

'I didn't think anything of it,' she'd said, once the plaster casts had set and she was safely back from A&E, resting at ground level in one of the wing-backed chairs in the living room. 'I've always washed my own windows. Though I did live in a bungalow then.'

She bought that bungalow herself by saving every bit possible from her teacher's salary – whatever was left over after paying the rent and the bills and single-handedly raising her two sons.

This place is full of very capable women like Dot, there's no doubt about that. But some aren't as agile as they once were. If Dot – who's got all her marbles and then some – thinks nothing of freestyle window cleaning, then I'm afraid to think where Laney might be right now.

'I'm sure Laney's not hurt!' I tell everyone again.

'We'll just check the greenhouse,' Nick adds, flashing me a smile that sends my downstairs aflutter. 'Meanwhile, maybe someone could check out front? Look at that sun. She might have put her bikini on to work on her tan.'

This launches the women into hysterics, but Nick manages to keep a straight face. That's more than I can say for myself. I'm such an easy audience.

'That'll keep them occupied for a few minutes,' he says as the entire room clears. He holds open one of the French doors leading off the living room. 'After you,' he says as I step onto the wide patio that runs along the entire back of the house.

It's a big house, with nearly thirty bedrooms. Proper *Downton Abbey* proportions. It rambles off on both sides from a three-storey central building where the grand entrance, dining room and two living rooms are. There's even room in the middle of the entrance hall for a pedestal table with a giant urn of lilies or sunflowers or that curly bamboo. A wide oak staircase winds up one side of the hall to the bedrooms upstairs and further on into the eaves, where the staff would have lived in olden times. More bedrooms pack the wing on one side, with my kitchen on the ground floor of the other and bedrooms above.

Max, our boss, didn't grow up with a silver spoon in his mouth, despite living in this place. His father, Terrible Terence, worked in accounting and his mum, Mrs Greene, was the town's librarian. It was her family who passed down the house from days of yore, but she moved herself, Max and Terence out to the cottage at the back – which is still the size of a normal house – when she opened the care home.

That was nearly two decades ago. June says that applications have been pretty sporadic these past few years, and that's got Max worried. He has tried advertising outside the area but, unless their parents are like Terence, most people want to keep their family nearby.

I glance over at Terence's cottage as Nick and I walk towards the greenhouse. There's no sign of him. Good. The residents are worried enough without him stirring the pot.

Nick is walking slightly ahead of me. Not because he's rude. He's just worried about Laney being out here, though I doubt she is. Laney might be daft most of the time, but she knows what she likes, and she likes her creature comforts. She wouldn't sit in a draughty greenhouse full of spiders. She's in the house. Somewhere.

Nick's keenness gives me the chance to watch him as he strides across the lawn. I haven't passed up that chance once since he started work here six months ago. You'd think I'd have him memorised by now.

Who am I kidding? I do.

I'm still amazed that Nick is working here. June would normally handle all our hiring, but Max was the one who found Nick for us. Our old occupational therapist left when her husband got sent to Germany for work. Unsurprisingly, June didn't get a huge queue of candidates looking to work for a care home in a little market town in Suffolk.

That's where we are, in Framlingham. We're not that far from Norwich or Ipswich, but it feels a million miles away. It's pretty and it's home, but it doesn't exactly scream 'career opportunity' to many people.

Also, because Max never passes up the chance to stretch his staff's duties where he can, the job wasn't strictly related to occupational therapy. You should have seen the brief June had to work with. The job description read like a holiday camp brochure. Our boss reasoned that OT wasn't miles different from physical therapy (it is), and physical therapy includes exercising and stretching – which may as well be aerobics and yoga – as well as brain-sharpening activities. Scrabble uses the brain, so he wanted his new hire to run games nights too.

June didn't waste any time ringing Nick for an interview when Max gave her his CV.

'Wow, he's fit,' I'd whispered when he turned up. I was glad June was doing the interview. I wouldn't have been able to concentrate. My unprofessionalism was boundless from day one.

'Plus, he's got a first,' she answered. 'Plus, the perfect qualifications.'

Plus, look at him, I'd thought.

You know those adverts where the tanned, shirtless guy tantalisingly licks the yogurt pot lid and makes you want to eat *Bifidus activertium*, or whatever it's called, every day? That. Only he didn't need any props to lick.

He'd strode right up to us. Blimey, what confidence he seemed to have. It was a bluff. Best foot forward for an interview and all that. He's no peacock, but a shy bird like me. 'I'm Nick Parsons. I have an eleven o'clock interview?' He glanced at the clock on the wall. 'Sorry, I'm early. That's annoying, isn't it. I did wait outside for a bit, but it started raining.'

When he smiled apologetically, I wanted to hug him.

'How long have you been out there?' June asked. Nick's hair was soaked. Even so, it was a thick wavy mop.

'About an hour. Hour and a half, tops.' Then he laughed at himself. 'I nearly camped overnight in your garden. My own sad little Glastonbury, without the music.'

'And not even Portaloos,' I said. 'I'm glad it didn't come to that.'

'I wanted to make sure I wasn't late. I'm… keen for this job.'

June hired him in the interview. She got her perfect employee, and I got a blinding crush that I still haven't recovered from.

Within about a week it seemed like Nick had always been here. He's so easy-going that he's doing everything in Max's unreasonable job description, and then some. Aside from being the occupational therapist, Scrabble organiser, exercise and yoga instructor, he's also the part-time gardener, driver and handyman. No matter what Max asks him to do, Nick throws himself into it without a grumble.

This is great for me, since we haven't got a dedicated games table, therapy room or exercise studio. There are TVs in each of the two living rooms, and woe betide anyone who disrupts the viewing schedules, so Nick uses the large dining room that's just off my kitchen. Which means we spend most of our days together. Or at least separated by only a wall.

To say we don't get much eye candy around here would be an understatement. Aside from our boss, Max (mid-fifties, not bad-looking if paunchy baldness turns you on), and his horrid father who lives in the cottage at the back of the property, and Davey, the Morrison's delivery bloke, we're all women here. Even the half-dozen carers who are on hand to help everyone with their day-to-day needs. The residents like it that way. That is why they live in a women-only home.

They love Nick, though. Who wouldn't? He's fifty per cent Greek and one hundred per cent Greek god. He is well over six feet tall and built like a swimmer, and somehow his features combine into the most beautiful face I've ever seen in real life. They shouldn't, really. He might have a finely chiselled jaw and high cheekbones, with a smile that's absolutely impossible not to return when you see it, plus heart-meltingly deep brown eyes. But his eyebrows are caterpillar-thick and his nose is definitely Grecian so, objectively, I know he's not really perfect.

Just perfect to me.

What I wouldn't give to run my fingers through his silky-looking nearly black hair, preferably while we're in a passionate clinch and he's telling me how gorgeous I am.

If only he were dim, or mean or boring. Then my life would be loads easier.

But he's not, and it isn't. Nick hit me like a triple shot of ouzo, with all the fire in my tummy but none of the nasty after-effects… well, at least not right away. Let's just say it was a delayed hangover.

The sad fact is, I love him and there doesn't seem to be anything I can do about that.

'You don't really think she's out here, do you?' Nick says accusingly as he slows down for me to catch up.

Of course he knows this is just another attempt to be near him. 'She could be.'

'Uh-huh. When was the last time Laney went outside for anything other than tea on the lawn? Admit it, this is just an excuse.'

I'm admitting nothing. 'Mmm?' I should have expected this. I've been about as subtle as a sledgehammer.

'It's too nice to be inside,' he goes on with a sly smile. 'Look at that sky. How can we not want to enjoy it? You've got spring fever.'

'This is August.'

'It's overdue, then. This is my favourite month.'

'You said that in March when the clocks went forward. And in June when the roses came out.'

He shrugs. 'I'm easy when it comes to my calendar affections. Let's get outside for lunch today. Even for half an hour or so. It's supposed to rain all weekend. What do you say? I don't have yoga till two.'

I nearly laugh with the relief. 'Right, yes, great idea. I'll put together some bits. There's leftover quiche, and I can do that smoked aubergine dip. It doesn't take long. And the sourdough will be out of the oven in half an hour.'

When he grins, the laugh lines crinkle from the corners of his eyes. 'You know the way to a man's heart.'

If only that were true.

'I'm sure Laney will turn up,' I tell him as we near the greenhouse. 'If she's not in there, we can have another look through the house together.'

I told you I was shameless.

And just to show that no evil deed goes unpunished, my tummy twists as Nick opens the glass door.

'Ooh.' That hurts.

He turns back to me. 'Are you okay?'

'Just my tummy. I'll be fine.'

Leave it to my ulcer to ruin the moment. Not that standing around in a dirty shed is much of a moment, but I'm working with what I can get. 'She's not in here,' I say, peering at the compost bags like she could be hiding in one. 'I think we should check inside again.'

What did I expect to happen here, anyway? That overcome with emotion and the smell of damp, Nick would leap over the strimmer and declare his love?

That ship sailed months ago.

June catches my eye as I hurtle down the hall towards the kitchen and my medicine. Her look is pure sympathy.

When it first started happening, I assumed it was just indigestion. That can be an occupational hazard as a cook. But eventually, when the pain went on and on, I had to look for another diagnosis.

I found it, but not before I'd humiliated myself in front of Nick and ruined any chance of him ever asking me out again.

'Feeling better?' June asks when I get back to find that Laney still hasn't turned up. 'Max left. He didn't notice anything amiss.'

'Fine, thanks.' Or at least I will be in a few minutes, once the pain relief kicks in. To be fair to Mum, she didn't really give me an ulcer, as much as I like to claim otherwise. Doctors used to think that stress and hot food cause them, but they don't. They just aggravate ones that are already there thanks to too many anti-inflammatory drugs or, in my case, a weasely little bugger of a bacteria. *Helicobacter pylori*, to give it its official name. It's supposed to clear up now that I'm on antibiotics.

'Have we checked everyone's room?' I ask June. 'Maybe Laney is upstairs.'

She nods. 'I sent everyone back to their room to look for her. They've all come back now and still no sign.'

Nick had set up the Scrabble boards before we noticed Laney's disappearance, and some of the residents have started their games.

As we scan the large dining room, June says, 'What about Maggie?!'

Of course. Maggie's not down here. Hers is the only room that hasn't been checked. 'I don't suppose you want to go look?' I ask June.

When she shakes her head, her blonde curls bob around her face. Growing up, I wanted her corkscrews. Unlike the rest of us, she never played the I-hate-my-hair-I'll-trade-for-yours game. She knew she got lucky there.

'Draw straws for it?' I offer.

'I was the one who brought up her bill yesterday.' She rubs her bicep like she's been punched.

As if Maggie would deign to actually touch another person. 'Fine. Coward. I'll go.'

'Nick?' June calls over, innocent as you please. 'We think Laney might be in Maggie's room. Do you want to go with Phoebe to check?'

She flashes me a smile as the residents fall in behind us. No one wants to miss an excuse to see Maggie.

She's going to love this.

Maggie lives in the only occupied room at the top of the house. None of the others want to trudge up all those stairs every day.

There is a lift – Max's mother had it installed – but it's tiny, slow and makes a worrying jolt when it stops, so nobody goes in it unless they have to.

'Maggie won't like the invasion,' I murmur to Nick as we head the senior parade up the stairs. 'I wish she'd use her mobile like everyone else.' It's no use ringing ahead to warn her.

We try to keep everyone connected by mobile. Most of the residents love their phones and a few of them are better at text-speak LOLs and LMFAOs than I am. They're no substitute for face-to-face friendships, but they do mean that no one has to be isolated if she's not feeling well enough to be downstairs with everyone else.

Maggie's not interested in being with everyone else. She lives in her room. Which is why the women are creeping towards it like they're about to spot a unicorn.

Nick knocks gently on the door. 'Maggie? It's only Nick. May I come in?'

When he puts a steadying hand on my shoulder, I want to lean into him. Of course, I don't do that. I'm sure he wouldn't mind. It's just not appropriate anymore.

'Come!' Maggie orders.

With the ladies so keen to get a good look at Maggie, we all nearly fall through the door.

'To what do I owe this… visit?' she asks from her deep blue velvet sofa. Though her voice isn't loud, it won't be ignored. She holds herself so upright that she could be wearing a back brace. Her narrow, regal face barely moves when she speaks. It's unnerving, like suddenly having a marble statue demand what you think you're doing in its museum.

She's dressed as usual in swingy black wide-legged trousers, like they used to wear in the seventies. As a rare fashion concession to Mum, I once tried on a pair of M&S ones. I looked like an extra-wide loft board standing on end, but Maggie has the tall, slender figure to pull them off. They swirl around her legs as she re-crosses them. Her blouse is perfectly pressed, white and stiff. Much like the woman herself. Everything about Maggie seems metallic, from her short iron-grey hair to her steely blue eyes to her cold, imperious voice that can cut you in half.

The only hint that she might have a softer side – possibly only seen under a microscope – is the selection of long, flowy brightly patterned silk cardigans that she always wears over her trousers and top, with the most gorgeous floral lapis lazuli brooch pinned on. It's always the same blue one.

Laney is sitting in the stiff reading chair facing the sofa. 'Oh, hello,' she says. When she smiles, a few of the women wave back at her.

'Maybe you should wait outside?' I suggest, gently pushing them back over the threshold. Maggie's fridge face has turned to deep freeze. 'We were just looking for Laney,' I say to Maggie.

'I'm here!' Laney sings, grinning and squeezing her shoulders to her ears. Her tawny brown eyes are creased in a smile, as usual, as if she's eager to hear the most hilarious punchline. She and Maggie couldn't be more opposite. Where Maggie is sharp-edged, Laney is soft, though she's not fat. Everything about her oozes warmth, from the top of her head – she wears her hair in short wavy golden-brown layers – to the tips of her toes, poking out from the bottoms of her frayed jeans and shod in shiny blue Converse high-tops.

'You've got your mobile off, Laney,' says Nick. 'We were getting worried. We thought you might have run away.'

Her smile disappears. 'Oh, is my phone off? I'm so sorry! I didn't mean to worry anyone. I'd never run away from here! Not in a million years.'

The women behind us, who are still jostling in the doorway for a good look, all start murmuring.

'Run away from *here*? Who'd want to do that?'

'All my friends… Love you—'

'I can't imagine—'

'They'll take me away from here in a box—'

'I was just…' Laney's eyes search the ceiling for the answer. 'I guess I got distracted. I am sorry.'

'But why would you…' *want to be with Maggie?* I start to ask. I can't keep the surprise out of my voice, but Maggie is tetchy enough without hinting that it would take wild horses to drag me to her room, so I don't finish. 'As long as you're okay,' I say instead. 'We'll leave you to your visit.'

'I'm quite tired, actually,' Maggie says, as something catches her eye out the tall sash window beside her. 'That man! You!' She raps on the window. 'You there, stop it!'

I go to see what's wrong, even though I think I know. 'Terence!' I fling open the window. 'Terence, we see you.'

'Not again,' Nick says.

'In the rhododendron bushes this time,' I say. 'We've warned you, Terence. I'm telling Max! That's not hygienic.'

'I was going to give those a trim today too,' Nick grumps.

Terence flips me two fingers from where he's standing in the border. He doesn't even bother doing up his fly first. Then, relieved, he saunters back to his cottage. His thick, beige button-up cardigan hangs loose from his shoulders and goes nearly to his knees. I often wonder whether it originally belonged to his wife. He's always in rumpled beige cotton trousers, one of those checked shooting shirts and scruffy trainers. A casual observer (who hadn't just seen him wee into the bushes) might mistake him for a kindly grandad.

'That man needs to be put down,' Maggie says. 'It would be the kindest thing.' Then she rubs her temples. 'Laney can go back downstairs with you now.'

Just like that. I'd like to tell Maggie where to get off, dismissing Laney like the dog she just called Terence. But Laney isn't offended, so I keep my mouth shut. 'Oh, right, well, Maggie, I'll see you later.'

'Cook,' Maggie says as I turn to leave. She knows my name perfectly well. But no, I'm just the domestic help to her. She calls June 'Manageress' and Nick is simply 'you'. 'Don't bother with supper tonight,' she continues. 'I won't be hungry. I'll have breakfast as usual tomorrow. One hard-boiled egg, please.'

I bob my usual curtsy. It's completely ironic, but it doesn't faze her.

Everyone sucks up to Maggie around here. That's because she's the only resident who pays full price. That also means she gets the biggest room, since the servants' quarters were turned into suites before I started work here. Although in an old house like this, all the bedrooms are spacious enough for a bed and a little seating area. Maggie also gets to have her meals in her room instead of down in the dining room with everyone else. We'd kick up a fuss about it, but that would only backfire. Then we'd have to spend more time with her. This way, everyone is reasonably happy. Max gets his money, Maggie remains a recluse, and the residents don't have the Ice Queen with them at mealtimes.

We might never know what made Laney want to go see Maggie when, for everyone else, facing her means drawing the short straw. Laney's mind works in very mysterious ways.

It's not dementia or Alzheimer's. Otherwise Laney might have to go to a nursing home, where they've got specialist medical care. We're more of a tea-and-sympathy type set-up around here. There is round-the-clock help with cleaning, dressing and that sort of thing for those who need it, and the carers keep track of everyone's medication. Though personal care assistants aren't exactly sought-after well-paid jobs, so there's a high turnover amongst the staff. It's June, Nick and I who really try to make it feel stable and homely here.

At first glance we probably look like an ordinary care home. We've got handrails, call buttons and shower seats, but the residents don't all need care in the traditional, council-approved sense of the word. The women range in age between a sprightly sixty-eight (Laney) to around ninety. I'm pretty sure that's how old Maggie is, though she wouldn't let June put her age in her file. Some, like Dot and Sophie, moved in because they wanted the company. That's a big reason that Mrs Greene, the founder, set up the home. She understood that some women, having raised their children and buried or divorced their spouses, or not having had children or spouses (buried or otherwise), might get lonely as they got older.

It's much more fun being here as part of a community. Plus, they don't have to cook or clean.

Nick's carrying a couple of yoga mats under one arm when he comes into the kitchen to get me for lunch. His other hand is behind his back. 'These are just in case the grass is wet,' he says, hoisting the mats.

'Why, sir, you are so gallant,' I say in an atrocious southern belle accent, 'to think of my comfort.'

He laughs. 'But of course, madam, that's what gentlemen are for. I'd even strip off and throw my shirt over a puddle to keep your delicate feet dry, should the need arise.'

'… or you could just use the yoga mats and save your shirt,' I say, distracted by the idea of Nick stripping off.

'Oh, right.'

Way to kill a flirty mood, Phoebe.

Then he hands me the three huge white pompom hydrangeas he's been hiding behind his back. 'Thanks for doing this. I know I've made more work for you. Though I did cut these off the bush out back, so technically I'm thanking you with stolen property.'

'It's very pretty stolen property, though, I'll take it!' I squeak. I know he's not trying to be romantic and I'd love to sound calm, like I get flowers from gorgeous blokes every day. I'm not so sad that I'll save them forever. I am thinking ahead to how I can dry them so they don't turn brown when they die, though. I'll probably keep them for a little while – a year or two, definitely not longer than a decade – and then toss them when they've all but turned to dust.

'Get a tall vase from the cabinet, will you please?' I say. There's a full cupboard to choose from. Our residents usually get celebration flowers for their birthdays and Mother's Day, and sometimes guilty ones when their children skip a visit. 'No worries about the lunch. It is what I do.'

Grabbing the bag that's already packed with the food and plates – I've been ready for an hour –we start for the back garden. It was thoughtful of Nick to bring the yoga mats for the grass, but I've got my eye on the wooden bench right at the far edge of the lawn. Not only will it save my legs going numb from sitting cross-legged, it's not too close to Terence's cottage, and it's tucked away from the house down a gentle hill.

Not that we need seclusion to have lunch. I know this isn't a date. I'd just like to pretend, so I'll have a double helping of delusion with my quiche, thank you very much.

'This was a great idea,' he says, following me towards the bench.

I laugh. 'You're not supposed to compliment your own idea!'

'Then let's say it was your great idea. I do appreciate it. I know you don't usually cook extra for your lunchtime. If there's anything I can do in return…'

I catch his eye, but I can't tell if he means anything by that. He's not so much as cracking a smile or raising an eyebrow to give me a clue.

I can't take the chance. It would be too mortifying to proposition him when he's only being nice. Instead, I say, 'If I ever want to brush up on my professional yoga certification, then I know who to ask. That's right, kill yourself laughing.' Just because Nick could run a marathon before breakfast and not even break a sweat.

'Sorry. Sorry. You *could* exercise if you wanted to,' he says.

That's a big *if*.

He notices my look. 'I only mean for health reasons.' He knows how annoying it is to come off as fit and preachy. 'You look great.'

The sun peeks out from behind a fluffy cloud just as we get to the bench. 'I very much appreciate your compliment.'

'No, Phoebe, I'm completely serious. You shouldn't put yourself down. You do look great.'

My face goes warm. He's mistaking my comment. I think I look just fine. Do I not? 'I wasn't putting myself down. I'm saying thank you. Some people might be built for speed. Some are built for endurance. I'm built for comfort.'

'And beauty,' he adds.

How am I supposed to get over him when he keeps saying nice things like that?

Chapter 4

Nick can't help being nice. He's the kind of person that you naturally want to like. Maybe that's why, within days of him starting work here, we had the smooth banter of old friends. He made it simple. He definitely gets me, a lot like June does, so going from nought to sixty was so easy. Maybe too easy, because I was mad about him by the time he got his first pay cheque. It took him a little while to catch up but, looking back, I think he did. I only wish I'd realised it at the time. Then things would have turned out so differently.

We're standing together with June on the back lawn, but he's got his eye on Terrible Terence, who's pacing along the border between his property and ours. Terence is watching our waitresses, Mary and Amber, set up the tables in the garden. He knows perfectly well that the visitors come today. And he knows we serve lunch outside on sunny days.

It's my Saturday to work. Just a half-day, though, and it's only every two weeks. There's a weekend cook who does the shifts when I'm off.

Today is when most of our residents' friends and families come to visit. Not that they couldn't come any day they like. We run a home for women here, not a prison. But we put on a special programme at the end of each week, so that's when we're busiest with visitors. The free lunch probably has a lot to do with their timing.

That's where I come in, and it might sound simple to feed a bunch of mostly older people, but I promise you, it's a challenge every single time. I never know how many visitors will turn up, even though we do ask for numbers. And Max, the tight arse that he is, loses the plot if I cook so much as an extra potato. So, getting the amounts right is hard enough.

Throw in everyone's preferences, allergies and pseudo-intolerances (*My psychic says purple food blocks my spiritual healing*), plus having to cook for grandchildren right through to octogenarians, and even Prue Leith might struggle.

At least I know by now what our residents like, and what they don't. Laney won't eat anything that's too potatoey. That's a texture, not an actual food group, which so far includes potatoes – mashed, fried, chipped, baked, roasted, fondanted or skinned – nearly all beans and pulses, polenta and under-ripe bananas. And Sophie has more food-combining rules than she probably has legwarmers.

Where was I going with this? Oh, yes. Visiting Day lunches. Volume isn't a problem. I was trained to cook three courses for a hundred at a time during catering college. I can make a shepherd's pie the size of a bathtub and still get the spices perfect, with just the right amount of gravy. That's why Mum and Dad always had me cater their parties. Not that they wanted shepherd's pie. Their friends are more tiny food people, mini burgers and one-bite chocolate eclairs and the like. Which I can also do, although not here.

The residents don't mind trying new things, but God forbid I try anything funny with their desserts.

If there's anything I miss about my old job at the bistro, it's trying funny things with desserts. But I don't like to dwell too much on the past. The restaurant doesn't even exist anymore. It went up in a puff of smoke, along with my restaurant chef career.

This is more stable work anyway, and even though it's a madhouse when the families visit, I do enjoy the extra buzz.

Not that it's God's Waiting Room on the other days. Between the activities calendar, Nick's occupational therapy sessions and Sophie's Zumba classes, these women have more of a social life than I do. Plus, they get trips out in the town and all the dramas you might expect from twenty-two independent-minded women living together.

But it's at the end of the week that the grandchildren come, and that gives the home a special vibe. It puts everyone in a good mood.

Well, nearly everyone.

Terence is still glowering from the shrubbery.

Technically, as he's not in our garden, he's doing nothing wrong. He's right on the border, taunting us. I just know he's going to do something. He always does. We never know what, so we have to play cat-and-mouse until he makes his move. And then we try to head him off.

June's watching him too. 'If that dirty old bloke gets his todger out again, I'm ringing the police this time. We've been way too easy on him lately.'

As the head of HR (as well as office manager, accountant and unofficial Agony Aunt), she takes things like harassment seriously. There was a real ding-dong between her and Max a couple of months ago when he tried to convince her to go easy on Terence. Sometimes I do feel sorry for Max. He's an incompetent twit, but he doesn't deserve a father like that.

'I had hoped the hospital stay might mellow him out,' Nick says. When Terence came down with pneumonia last year, it was touch-and-go for a bit. He ended up in Critical Care on a respirator. You'd think a thing like that might make him mend his ways. But no. He's worse than ever.

'I hoped it would kill him,' says June. With an impatient swipe, she brushes her blonde curls away from her face. It's as much a nervous habit as because the wind has picked up. Clouds are scuttling across the sky now. We might have to serve lunch inside after all. 'But he's too mean to die.' Then she glances at me. 'Sorry, that probably insensitive, with your mum and all.'

I shake my head to let her know I'm not offended. My emotions have been all over the place since Mum died, but they're not the ones I expected. I can't seem to find a manual about how to grieve properly for her. And I need one because I'm doing it all wrong.

Everything I read online says I should let myself feel sad. That would be fine, except that I'm not feeling sadness as much as rage. And it's not normal grieving anger, either. It would be normal to be furious with Mum for dying and leaving us. Or for not taking care of herself enough to stay alive.

I'm livid with her because she's not here to be livid with in person.

That doesn't seem right.

June has been my rock throughout everything. Well, that's what best friends are for, right? Even so, I really appreciate it. Some people get too uncomfortable about death or sadness to get down and dirty in the emotions with you. Like my dad, for instance.

I worried constantly about him after the funeral. Which is why I *may* have rung him more than usual. He started avoiding my calls. He's not being malicious. He's just tired of me asking how he is, which makes him think about Mum and then he gets sad (he claims, though I've still not seen very much evidence). Dad's always been a stiff upper lip person.

Dad did actually answer my call this morning. Only because June showed me how to block Caller ID. I've sunk to stalking my own father.

'Has Will been to see you?' I'd asked, even though I knew the answer.

'Your brother is very busy with work,' Dad said.

'Well, so am I, and I'm happy to come see you whenever you like. He could find the time, you know.' Will works in a bank, not sequencing the human genome or curing cancer. But he's always thought the world revolved around him, and our parents didn't help.

'Your brother is successful, Phoebe,' Dad explained, like that was any excuse for ignoring your parents. 'It stands to reason that he'd be married to his job. That comes first.'

'And that's okay with you? It's a double standard, by the way.'

'No, it's not,' he said.

'Oh, really. I'm successful. I run my own kitchen, I've won awards. Yet you don't expect me to be married to my job.'

'That's because yours is an unsuitable match.'

It was like my mother had come back from the dead to insult me. It's not fair. She shouldn't still be able to upset me by proxy. 'I was just checking that you're all right,' I murmured. 'Tell your son to visit you. He owes you for putting him through uni.'

June and Nick are clearly worried by my silence. 'It's okay,' I tell them. Nick is rubbing my arm, sending tingles all up and down. That shoves all thoughts of my parents from my head. 'I thought maybe Max would move his dad somewhere else when he got out. He's really not all there anymore. He should probably be in a home. He's always at his worst on visiting day.' And he's no picnic the rest of the time.

But the sun is still shining, so far, and the tables that the waitresses have dotted all over the lawn look gorgeous and very stately-homey.

That's one of the best things about this place for the women: the space they get without having to be alone. Most of them could live pretty well on their own, as long as they had someone to check in on them, and maybe help with some cooking and cleaning. But if they didn't live here, then they'd either be tripping over themselves in a one-bedroom flat or, maybe worse, be rambling around their family house with nothing but memories for company. My gran got terribly lonely after Grandad died, even though she lived near Mum and Dad and they visited a lot. Her whole world shrank to Mum's visits. If I'm lucky enough to live into old age, I just hope the Happy Home for Ladies is still here for me.

We all go back inside to finish getting ready for the visitors. The women are always excited on Saturdays, even when it's not their own family who'll be stopping by. They've been living together for so long that, in a way, they've pooled their loved ones together. Anyone can dip into the mix of visitors and come up with a friendly face to enjoy.

I'm just getting the warming trays out for the buffet when Davey arrives with our Morrison's delivery.

What can I tell you about Davey so you can picture him but not think he's a prat? If you saw a photo of him, you'd probably think he was fit, and he is. His hair isn't as dark as Nick's, but it's wavy like his, and he uses some kind of wax or putty to make it stand up all over. He's got a nice smile and pretty green eyes, and he is in good shape from lifting delivery boxes all day long. The problem is when he speaks. Aside from what comes out of his mouth, he's got this weird way of shimmying his head, like one of those bobble-headed dogs. It makes everything he says seem like an innuendo. So, imagine an okay-looking shimmy-headed guy with muscly arms. That's Davey.

'They didn't have your cod fillets so there's haddock instead,' he says, consulting his list. 'Whose birthday is it? You've got candles.'

I snatch the sheet from him. 'You're only supposed to deliver the order, Davey, not inspect it. What if there were personal things on there?'

'Like tampons?' he says. 'I don't mind. You should see some of the orders I deliver.' Head shimmy. 'Condoms. *Super size.* Let's just say I know who's getting lucky in this town.'

'Let's not say that, okay?' I sign his scanner.

'Do you want me to fill your shelves for you?'

He always asks this. He probably makes the same cheesy offer to every woman under the age of fifty on his route. Our orders are always on time, though, so I guess he's not one of the ones getting lucky in this town. 'I'm fine, thanks.'

'Well, then how about a quick shag instead?'

'How about if I make a quick official complaint to Morrison's instead?'

As usual, my rebuff doesn't put him off. 'You know you love my banter. It's the highlight of your day… you could have it all the time if you'd ever say yes to a date.'

He's not shimmying his head now. I *can* see the nice bloke beneath the bluster when he acts normal. 'I'm okay, thanks.' Why can't someone I *like* pester me like this? 'Besides, you're not really interested in me, Davey. You only like the challenge because I always turn you down.'

He rubs his chest beneath his hi-vis vest. 'Ah, you could test your theory and say yes.'

'Or I could say no, and we stay the way we are.' I shift a few things around in the giant freezer drawer to make room for the haddock. I'll do fish and chips next week, with minted mushy peas. Sophie's been on at me about superfoods lately. It's always something.

As if my thoughts of mushy peas have conjured her up, she marches through the kitchen door. 'Phoebe, may I have a word?'

She's got on her red and white stripy legwarmers today, with her usual black spandex leggings beneath a purple and green skirt.

'The blokes in this place are lucky to work here!' Davey announces. 'I don't know how they get any work done.'

Sophie smiles coyly, even though she knows perfectly well that Davey says the same thing to everyone here. 'Well, I do like to keep fit,' she says. 'That's why I'm here, Phoebe. Are you putting more butter than usual in the food?'

'No, I don't think so. Why?'

She shoots a dirty look at the ricotta that I'm just about to season for the lasagne. 'That's not low fat, is it? You're killing us, you know, with your fat and your butter.'

I do admire Sophie's dedication to her health. A little of the discipline she has would probably do me good. But it's too much. 'We've been over this already, Sophie. Fat isn't the villain you think it is. Our bodies need it to be healthy. You know that I balance every meal so there's not too much fat or too much carbohydrate or too many calories.'

Lasagne has cheese in it. Get over it, I want to tell her.

'Can you at least use less butter in the mashed potatoes?' Sophie especially worries about those.

'Yes.' Give me patience. 'I could use chicken stock, but you objected to the salt. I could use yogurt, but you didn't want the extra dairy. And speaking of which, why do you care about the lasagne anyway? You never eat it.'

'Excuse me for worrying about my friends' hearts.'

More gently, I say, 'I know you've got everyone's best interest in mind, Sophie. This should cheer you up. I'm making mushy peas with mint next week.'

Her owlish eyes shine behind her glasses. 'Mint is a superfood!'

'I know, you told me.'

She smiles, forgiving me my buttery trespasses.

'I don't know how the blokes in this place get any work done!' Davey announces again as June comes in. When I roll my eyes at him, he gives me a cheeky grin. 'Don't bust my game.'

'I don't know how you get any work done,' June says to him, 'when you're always hanging about bothering us.' But she's smiling. It's hard to be really offended by Davey.

'Want to go for a drink after work?' she asks me.

'Sure,' Davey says.

'Not you. Phoebe.'

At first, I nod. 'Actually, no, I won't if that's okay,' I tell her. 'We're having dinner tomorrow, right? I'm broke till payday.' I get by, with a little left over to save for a rainy day or, more often, the occasional holiday. But I'm no celebrity chef.

'How come you'll go out with her, but you won't go out with me?' Davey asks.

'I'm cuter than you are,' June says.

Suddenly, we hear shouting and screaming from outside. We all stare at each other. 'I hope nobody's…' I start to say.

'So do I,' June says as we rush out to the lawn. We might not be a nursing home with properly ill patients, but the women are older. There's always a chance one of them will keel over.

But nobody's dead. At least not yet.

Nearly all the residents are gathered together, but I can spot only a few visitors with them. It's still early so, whatever's the trouble, at least we don't have to air our dirty laundry too publicly.

That thought catches me squarely in the gut. It's what Mum would have said. A weird mix of sadness tinged with horror wells up in me. Sadness because, well, she's not actually here to say it. And horror because no matter how much you promise yourself that you won't become your mum, eventually it's bound to happen.

It's Mary, one of our waitresses, who's screaming the house down. 'What's wrong?' I shout over to Nick. He's got his forearms looped around her waist, trying to keep her from reaching Terence. Every time she lunges for him, her sleek ponytail whips her in the face as Nick pulls her back.

Terence is standing impassively just out of reach with his hands in his chinos pockets. Why am I not surprised that this involves him?

'You want a piece of me?' Mary keeps shouting as she flails her arms at him. 'Do you? I'll give you one!'

'Mary, will you please calm down!' I say over her protests. 'What is wrong with you?'

'There's nothing wrong with *me*. It's him, the dirty bugger. He groped me,' she says. 'Right there on the lawn.'

'Technically, you mean right there on your bottom,' Terence points out. 'Precision in language is important, my dear.'

'Terence! You've been warned about this before,' June says.

'What will you do, fire me?' he shoots back. 'Throw me out of *my* house?'

'I'd like to clock you, is what I'd like to do,' Mary says. Then she sees our boss stalking towards us. He must have heard the commotion from the office. This is just what we need.

'Max, I am not taking any more of this,' Mary says. 'Your father has groped me. I've got a good mind to ring the police.'

Max's expression is resigned as he turns to Terence. As annoying as it is for us to have to deal with him, it's harder for Max. He's actually related to the old man. He can never get rid of him. 'Dad, did you?'

Terence waves his hand. I'm just glad it's out of his pocket now, given what he's done. 'She's overreacting. It was only a friendly pat. I was telling her she's doing a good job.' He looks at Mary. 'You should be grateful for the attention, frankly.'

Her frustrated scream doesn't need any interpretation. 'I quit. Max, that's it. I'm not going to be harassed by that man. Find yourself someone else to deal with him.' She yanks off her apron and shoves it into the other waitress's hand. Amber looks like she's not sure whether to follow her colleague or not. Then she goes back to her phone.

This is a disaster. There's no way that Amber can handle service on her own. She barely does any work as it is. 'Wait, please, Mary! You can't quit. We need you!' I say. 'Max, tell her!'

But it's no use. She's already striding across the lawn towards her car.

Now what am I going to do? 'Max, I can't run the restaurant all by myself. No offence, Amber.'

Amber looks up from her phone. 'Hmm? Oh, none taken.' She goes back to crushing candy or whatever she's doing on that thing.

'Well, Max? What are you going to do?' This is his fault, after all. If he'd shipped his horrid father off after the hospital, Mary mightn't have quit.

Max's jowly face flashes several expressions as he works out an answer. He's not great at thinking on his feet. 'Well, we can always microwave ready meals,' he finally says. 'That would free you up to take over for Mary.'

He sees the look on my face. 'Or put them in the oven?' he tries. 'I don't know. Whatever you do when you cook.'

Whatever I do when I cook? 'Max. I prepare three meals a day, carefully balanced for the residents' nutritional requirements. Not to mention their weird phobias and dietary whims. You really think you can replace all that with a few ready meals?'

I can't keep my voice from shaking. I've worked here for three years, and this is all he thinks I do?

'They have some very good ready meals now,' he answers. 'I'm only trying to make a suggestion.'

Everything I've done, the exacting planning, budgeting and bending over backwards to make food that the residents will love, has made no difference in my boss's eyes. I'm nothing but a glorified takeaway delivery person to him.

'Hey, don't get upset,' Nick says. 'Please don't.' His voice is so full of concern that I just choke up more. When he puts his arm around me, it squeezes out a very unladylike sob.

To be clear, though, this isn't sadness. It's fury. How dare he.

'I'm sure he didn't mean to offend you.' Nick's eyes search Max's, looking for an apology. Meanwhile, I can't stop thinking about being in the crook of Nick's arm with his lips inches from mine.

'Well, he bloody well did offend me,' I mumble. I haven't worked this hard to be dismissed by someone who thinks the supermarket sells haute cuisine.

'God, no, I didn't mean to upset you, Phoebe. I'm sorry. We'll get another waitress for you, I promise. We can get a new one tomorrow, right, June?' He sounds like he's replacing an ice cream cone that I've dropped on the floor.

All this rage can't only be about Mary quitting, or Max's insensitivity. Deep down it must be about Mum too, because she put this soundtrack in my head in the first place. 'You're Not Living Up to Your Dreams' was on the greatest hits album, but the B-side included classics like 'Why Can't You Be More Like Your Brother', and everyone's perennial favourite: 'If Only You'd Try Harder'. She didn't want to hear that I was living up to *my* dreams and doing the best that I could. Maybe I haven't dealt with that as well as I'd thought.

'We'll get a temp to fill in for Mary till we find a replacement,' June says, enveloping me in her arms. 'Don't worry.' Nick passes me off to my best friend like a relay baton. 'Want that drink later?' she asks. 'I'll buy.'

'God, yes, thanks.'

Nick offers to bring Terence back to his cottage. I'm surprised that the old man agrees to go. Whenever Max tries getting him to do something, he unleashes a tirade that would make a sailor blush. Nick definitely has a way with people. As they walk off, I can hear him speaking quietly to Terence. He's a perv-whisperer.

'He really is good, isn't he?' I say.

'That's the best hiring decision I ever made,' June answers. 'Aside from you, of course.'

MICHELE GORMAN

Chapter 5

It's thanks to my lucky stars that June hired me. Otherwise I'd have had to leave our little home town to find work after the bistro closed down.

The bistro was my first job out of catering college. It wasn't overly fancy, at least not when I first started working there. It teetered somewhere between a builder's caff and someplace that served food *au jus*. Set in the old town fishmonger's shop, its walls were tiled white with a pretty Victorian green border running around the whole room. We only had seating for twenty-eight, with the open kitchen behind the old fish counter. Jen, my boss, kept as many of the original features as she could. Pale green ironwork surrounded the huge plate-glass front windows and door, which rattled awfully in winter, so we had a heavy velvet curtain in front to keep the customers from blowing away whenever someone came in.

There were fishy touches all over the restaurant: some of the original adverts for jellied eels and pilchards in old money, weighing scales with their enamelled dish on the battered sideboard. Fishhooks hung from the ceiling and the old barrel by the door held customers' wet umbrellas. We even used the display counter – once upon a time piled with ice and seafood – for our desserts.

Jen had upmarket ideas when she hired me. Best of all, she believed in me. But, being fresh from catering college, I had yet to believe in myself.

I don't mean that I didn't have the skills. I knew my pâté from my parfait. I just didn't have the confidence. Yet there I was, the new cook in a newly reopened bistro – Jen had the word 'café' prised off the front of the building, and 'bistro' just fit, though it always looked squashed together. I got to have complete say over the food we served. Once I got over the shock and stopped panicking, I started to love the job. Every week Jen and I sat down together so I could tell her what I was planning. I didn't have to ask permission for my menu. My catering school friends were astonished when I told them that. Most of them were prep cooks, waking at 5 a.m. to chop mountains of onions, and there I was, designing my own menus.

Jen was thrilled and so was I. Finally, *finally*, I was an actual cook, just like I'd always planned. I don't want to paint it as the perfect job, because the hours were punishing and it was sweaty and nerve-racking. Still, it felt like my dream had come to life.

Within a few months we were gaining a good reputation around the town, and people had to book for dinner on weekends. And sometimes even for lunch. But no matter how packed the bistro got, my parents still weren't convinced. 'What do you want to do next?' Mum asked every single time I visited, like I was working behind a McDonald's counter instead of running my own restaurant.

'This *is* what I want to do,' I always answered. 'Why else would I have gone to catering college?'

'I still have no idea,' she'd say, 'when you could have gone to university. Though I suppose this could be a leg up the ladder, if you leverage it. But darling, you've got the brains to be on your way to the boardroom, not doing dishes in a kitchen.'

Maybe I shouldn't be bringing this up now that Mum's gone. After all, it's wrong to speak ill of the dead. But it was harsh, so there's no use pretending that she was a saint. You may as well know what she could be like.

Mum always followed up with her main objection to my career plans: I should be challenging myself to do more than even my parents had. They were entrepreneurs with a successful building firm, but Mum always saw corporate jobs as better than what they had. That's where you could really *get a leg up the ladder*. She and Dad did what they could without any education or family money. She wanted more for me.

The problem was that every time they told me I could be more, all I heard was that I was less. That's hard to accept at any age. I was still a teen. Meanwhile, my brother did everything they wanted. Maybe his aspirations really did align with theirs, or maybe he was brown-nosing. Whatever the case, he made them happy while, as long as I worked in a kitchen, I wasn't going to measure up to Mum and Dad's dreams for me. No matter what I was doing there, no matter how perfectly it matched what I wanted to do. Even after I'd been head chef for six years and built the bistro into a restaurant with a waiting list for reservations, and won awards for my cooking, they weren't as convinced about my success as I was.

The more they harped on about all the ways I could be doing better, the more I tried to ignore them. After all, I was happy with my progress. I was doing exactly what I'd set out to do. Their criticism couldn't hurt me. At least, that's what I thought.

Now I'm not so sure, because Mum's not here anymore, and still there's a nagging little voice in my head. It's not paying me many compliments.

'You're miles away,' June says, pushing my hand towards the glass of Pinot Noir she's just poured. 'Do I dare ask?'

'I'm just thinking about Mum.' We're sitting at a corner table in our local pub. We've been coming here ever since we got each other dodgy fake IDs for our sixteenth birthdays. We'd never have got away with that in such a small town if the man who took over the business hadn't been from outside the area. And short-sighted and desperate for business.

Even without the early memories, this is still my kind of pub: full of old wood panelling and mismatched tables and chairs, with soft lighting and no TVs showing football. Just lots of familiar faces and the happy buzz of conversations going on all around us.

I'm in my chef whites as usual, but June looks nice. She always wears smart trousers that suit her slender figure, and trendy tops – sometimes floaty and sometimes, like tonight, with cutaway shoulders, depending on what's hot in *Glamour* – and she wouldn't be caught dead in my clogs or with her hair scraped back in a ponytail. I probably embarrass her with my checked trousers and overuse of dry shampoo.

When June pulls her mouth into the sympathetic I'm-listening pout that she uses whenever one of the residents has a whinge, the guilt sweeps over me. She's mistaking my words for nice, normal, missing-Mum-now-that-she's-gone thoughts.

'It will get better,' June says. 'It has only been a few months.'

I take a deep breath. 'I wish it was that easy.' But when she reaches for my arm, I say, 'No, it's not what you think. I'm really *pissed off* with her.'

'For dying? That's normal. It's one of the stages of grief, remember the notes?'

She gave me a packet of papers after Mum died. June likes to be prepared for everything. With handouts. 'Yeah, but that's not why I'm angry. Which means it's not normal and I'm some kind of freak of a daughter.' Even though I hate admitting that, in a way it feels good to get it out. It feels so good that, once I start, I can't stop myself. Even though June knows all this, she's happy to listen.

I knew I wasn't cut out for university years before I breathed a word to my parents. I'm not like my brother, Will. By which I mean I'm not academically-minded or completely afraid to go against our parents. He was making plans for uni while he was still in primary school. But I'd discovered cooking by the time I was that age, and I loved every bit of it. Even the tedious prep work and the cleaning up. The idea of turning a bunch of ingredients into something completely different seemed like magic. It still does.

'Everyone's parents drive them bonkers, right, even though we love them?' June nods at my question. 'I mean, sometimes I couldn't stand Mum when she was being so judgmental. Especially after the bistro burned down.'

One minute I was running my own kitchen, feeling like all the hot and sweaty work, awful early hours and miserly pay cheques were worth it. More than worth it. I was on top of the world.

And the next minute it was all gone. I was no longer a chef.

The worst part was that it wasn't my fault. I hadn't poisoned any critics or sneakily served horsemeat burgers or even taken our success for granted. Every single dish that came out of the kitchen was made with the same love and commitment. Then one stupid wiring fault put half a dozen people out of work, ruined a business and my career for a while.

That's when I really needed the support, yet Mum acted like the fire was the best thing that could have happened to me. She thought her daughter might finally make her proud. Now I could get a proper job, she'd said. That place was holding me back, she'd said.

We argued, Mum and I. A lot. That *place* was where I'd built my chef career. That place was where I was happiest. So, when Jen decided that she wasn't going to bother to rebuild it, or find another building to reopen… well, you can imagine.

It was all well and good that she and her boyfriend were going to move to France. Hurrah for amour and all that. She'd been less interested in the restaurant since they'd started going out anyway, but what was I supposed to do now?

Mum and Dad thought they had the answer. I could buy out Jen and own the bistro myself. It might not be as good as being a banker like my brother, but it was a start. At least I'd be a businessperson instead of just a cook.

They wouldn't accept that I *love* being a cook. This is what I've always wanted to do. I've got no interest whatsoever in being a businessperson, even when that business is a restaurant. I'd watched Jen struggle with all the paperwork and worry about hiring and firing. The taxes and business rates and marketing. No, thank you. I just want to cook food that people love to eat. That's why I went to school, not to end up a business owner who also cooks.

I think that was the last straw for my parents.

'You never got a break,' June agrees. 'And it was unfair because of the way they treated Will, like he was the golden boy who could do no wrong. That would have pissed anyone off.'

'It still does,' I say. 'But what am I supposed to do about it now? I can't yell at her, can I? Or make her realise she was wrong, that I love what I do. I'm perfectly happy. I missed my chance to make her understand, and now I'm stuck with all this… *stuff*. Where's it all supposed to go?'

'Honestly, I don't know,' June says. 'Would it make you feel better to yell at her grave? I'd go with you, so at least we'd both look deranged.'

That's a true friend. We both laugh at the idea. It feels good.

She glances at her phone as it vibrates on the table. 'Please tell me you're seeing Callum soon,' I say. I can tell by her smile that it's his text. 'When are you going to stop torturing the poor bloke?'

She giggles. 'Believe me, this hurts me more than it hurts him. I'd jump on him every second of every day if I could.'

'You can,' I remind her. 'Speaking as someone who hasn't done any jumping in ages, why wouldn't you?'

It's a rhetorical question. We've been over June's entire strategy a million times, but I let her tell me anyway. 'Because the more I keep him at arm's-length, the keener he seems to be. I can't suddenly throw myself at him now. He'd run a mile.'

'But June, don't you want someone who throws himself back at you when you do that? If he's only interested because you're acting like you don't care, then that's not an honest relationship. Don't look at me like that,' I say at her hurt expression. 'I'm not saying that's why he likes you. I'm saying he'd probably be insanely nuts about you anyway so you don't have to pretend. Then again, I'm the last person who should be giving you relationship advice.'

'It does no good to keep beating yourself up, you know,' she says. 'You made one error in judgment. Nick's not holding a grudge, so you shouldn't, either.'

'I'm not.'

'I mean a grudge against yourself, and you are. Let it go. You're just as close as you ever were and I'm sure he doesn't even think about it now.'

I shake my head. 'I'm sure he does still think about it and it wasn't an error in judgment. It was a massive foul-up.'

MICHELE GORMAN

Chapter 6

'What about dinner, two courses only, in a public place,' Davey says. 'And since you're one of those feminists, I'll even let you pay.'

In Davey's mind, anyone who objects to sexual harassment is 'one of those feminists'. I close my eyes and take a few deep breaths. 'Sorry, no.'

'Okay, I'll pay, and we'll skip starters. Main course only and you can pick the restaurant.' He punctuates his proposal with a head-shimmy chest-rub combo.

His Morrison's green uniform doesn't look horrible on him, but he must know it's not his best look. I've got to give him credit for persevering with his seduction attempts every time he makes a delivery.

'No.'

Especially when he always gets the same answer.

'Drinks? One drink?'

'Davey, don't you have other deliveries to get on with?' I don't feel like humouring him today. I forgot to defrost the lamb last night and now I've got to come up with something else for lunch. We had quiche yesterday. The women went for second helpings, but I can't do it two days in a row.

'You're a tough one, Phoebes, but I love a challenge.'

That must be why he never gives up. June is right. The more a woman plays hard to get, the more the bloke tries hard to get.

And I hate when he calls me Phoebes. 'Davey, really. You're wasting energy on something you don't even really want.' I tuck a lock of hair back into my ponytail, catching a whiff of minty shampoo as I do. It makes a nice change from the usual piña colada scent of my dry shampoo. 'You should aim higher,' I tell him. 'There must be better options around.' Davey deserves someone who's actually interested in him.

'Not in my delivery area,' Davey says. 'Besides, I don't mind a fuller-figured woman,' he says. 'And you're not bad-looking, Phoebes. You might look hot if you made any effort.'

'Thanks, I think, but I'm happy with the effort I make.' I might not look like I've stepped from the pages of a magazine, unless that magazine is *Foodservice Equipment Monthly*. But I'm generally tidy and mostly clean. It's not my fault that beauty standards are over the top. Perhaps expectations should tone down instead of expecting us to step up. Not everyone wants false lashes and statement lipstick, or to be filled, plucked, tucked, straightened, glossed or buffed.

He stacks his plastic boxes to carry back to the truck. 'Same time on Thursday?'

'Yeah, thanks, Davey. See you later.'

I know. I'll do pizza. I was going to use the basil for a pesto pasta, but I can roast some vegetables and use it with the goat's cheese. Maybe toast some pine nuts. Though Sophie won't like the carbs in the base and she's already told me off twice this week. The butter in my home-made granola offended her and she hasn't had enough purple in her diet.

The aubergines take just a minute to slice and throw into a roasting tray filled with cold salty water. She'll probably kick off about that too, but it's what makes them taste so good when they're roasted. *There's your damn purple food*, Sophie.

I quickly knock up a dough and set it in the old boiler cabinet to prove.

I love it when I get a few minutes like this to relax and think about what I want to cook next. That used to be my favourite part of my job at the bistro. I usually designed my menus on Monday, when we were closed. Sitting at the table in the window with my notebooks and all the old menus, I got to let my imagination run loose. What was in season? Was the brown crab in yet at the fishmonger, or the pheasant at the butcher? Did the apricots look good at Peter Pepper's or were there English strawberries at the fruit stall? Sometimes I foraged in the countryside for wild herbs like sorrel for a sauce to use over mackerel, or mint or bay for home-made ice creams. There were always elderflowers in summer to make cordial, and velvety oyster mushrooms for my stir-fries.

I still forage when I've got time, but I'm a little more restricted now with the other ingredients. Everything has to come through Davey's supermarket deliveries and the budget is a lot tighter. Max would lose his mind if I blew the week's shopping budget on beautiful Brixham crabs in summer or the Gower salt marsh lamb in the autumn.

But I like that challenge too, to make the best dishes I can with what I've got.

June pops her head around the corner. 'Max wants to see us.'

'What, now?' It's 10 a.m. in the middle of the week. He's supposed to be at work.

The home is a side business for Max. He followed his father into accountancy, for some firm down in Ipswich. That's why he usually leaves us alone, except on Saturdays, when he likes to play Lord of the Manor in front of the residents' families. 'Did he ring first?'

June shakes her head.

That's never a good sign.

Nick and Max are already in the office when we get there. It has only two desks – one pushed up against the wall and heaving with three-ring binders – and two chairs, but none of us sits down. Nick leans beside me against the spare desk, careful not to knock over any piles. When he crosses his long legs at the ankle, I can see the muscles flex in his thighs beneath his jeans. Which just sends my imagination soaring, though I manage to stop myself before I get too carried away.

I really do need to accept that we're only friends. I say 'only', but that's pretty good, right? Friends can last a lifetime. It's proving harder than I thought, but I *can* get over Nick. Really, I can. I would have already if it weren't for his perfect smile. And the way it plays on those kissable lips, and his faintly tanned complexion and deep brown eyes that I could gaze into for hours.

Shite. I've been staring at him again.

I *have* had a strong word with myself about all this, but obviously I've not been persuasive enough.

June pulls down the hem on her top and smooths the front of her trousers. That's her I-mean-business adjustment. 'What's going on, Max?'

Max doesn't adjust anything. He always means business. He's wearing his usual suit trousers, shiny black shoes and a rumpled white shirt, with the buttons straining over his tummy. 'First, I've got some good news.' He flashes us a smile. He's got bad teeth. They all slant in, except for his canines, which stick out. That gives him a vampirish vibe, though he's much more of a Muppet Count von Count than he is the hot bloke from *Twilight*.

June and I glance at each other. If Max has a 'first' bit of good news, that means there's a 'second' bit that's bad.

'I've found a new waitress and she can start as soon as tomorrow. I told you we'd sort something out to replace Mary.'

And not a moment too soon, either. Nick has been helping with the lunch service and I'm handling dinner, slowly, but it's not really fair for us to work harder just because Max's father can't keep his hands to himself.

The worst part is that it was Mary who always brought Maggie – the madam – her meals upstairs. Maggie holds a grudge against Amber, the other waitress, for once being on the phone while she brought up the tray. She's banned Amber from the room ever since.

Now that I've got to do it, I dread climbing those stairs to the top of the house. I'd love to just drop her tray off and leave, but she makes me sit there while she tastes everything and gives me a full critique.

At least I won't have to deal with her now that there'll be a replacement for Mary. 'That's good,' I say to Max.

'No, it's not,' June objects. 'Max, all hiring is supposed to go through me. We agreed that, remember? Either I'm running your business or I'm not. Who is this person, anyway?'

'You're going to love her,' Max says. 'It's my daughter, Tamsyn. She's just come back from her year abroad and she's looking for work.'

Even Nick thinks that's preposterous, judging by the snort next to me.

'Max,' June says in her talking-someone-down-off-a-ledge voice, 'you can't just give jobs out to your family.'

Ooh, she's really pissed off now. She's practically whispering.

Max draws himself up to his full height, which is over six feet, though I sometimes forget because he seems like a much smaller man. 'June, I own this home, so I assure you, I *can* hire whomever I like. You need a waitress and I have someone who'll do the job for minimum wage. You didn't even have to interview her. That saved you time and effort. You don't need to put her on the payroll. That saves paperwork.'

That also saves Max having to pay her National Insurance. Now I see. Our new waitress will be working under the table.

June knows it's no use arguing with our boss. He only digs his heels in harder. 'What's your other news?' she asks.

I dread to think, if he calls foisting his daughter off on us good news.

Max looks happy to be moving on. 'You know my father isn't well.'

We all nod. It *had* come to our attention.

'We didn't want it to come to this,' Max says, 'but he can't keep living on his own in that house. It's not safe, and too much time alone is making him difficult.'

Nick snorts again. I dig him in the ribs. If Max wants to believe that his father is, deep down, a normal functioning human being, then we should let him.

'So, we've decided to move him for his own good.'

Max's pale eyes are glistening and red. Is he getting emotional? I didn't think he cared that much, but I suppose he must love his father, even if he doesn't like him.

I make a sympathetic face at his news, only because that's what you're supposed to do when someone tells you they're putting a parent in a home. Everyone here will be glad to get rid of Terence.

'I'm sorry,' June says. 'Have you told your dad?' When Max nods, she says, 'Did he take it well?'

'Oh, yes. He's looking forward to it.'

Well, that must be a relief for them. Nobody wants to see Terence, as unpleasant as he is, being dragged away.

Max fishes a Kleenex out of his trouser pocket to blow his nose. 'Damn allergies. It's the tree pollen. I need another tablet. Anyway,' he continues, 'he'd like his old room. My parents' room, the front corner one on the first floor. It shouldn't be too much hassle to move whoever's in there, with all the spare bedrooms.'

It takes a second for that to sink in.

'He's moving in here?!' June blurts out as my mouth falls open. Max is moving Terence into *our* home? Not some nice, faraway place where we'll never have to set eyes on his miserable face again? 'He can't move in here,' June goes on. 'You cannot move him here. Max, this is the Happy Home for *Ladies*. That's how your mother set it up. Men aren't allowed. It's for ladies.'

Terence is definitely no lady. 'Why can't you put him somewhere else?' I ask.

'Do you have any idea how expensive residential care is?' Max snaps. 'I mean somewhere normal. The rates are twice as high anywhere else as they are here. This place is barely staying afloat. I can't afford to pay fees for him. And why should I, when there are perfectly good bedrooms upstairs? I'm only being practical.' He holds his hands up in front of him, like that will protect him against June once she gets going. 'I don't expect an argument about this, June. It's my business, not yours. The incorporation papers say that it's set up for women, you're right. But there's nothing legally prohibiting men from living here too. I checked with a solicitor, so you don't need to worry about breaking any rules.'

That is *so* not what's worrying any of us.

'You're going to get an argument from the residents when you tell them, Max,' June says calmly.

'I'm not telling them,' he says. 'That's your job. You're the manager. Besides, you're all so friendly with them that I'm sure you'll find a way to tell them so they understand. The other option is that we increase their fees so I can afford to put Dad somewhere else.'

He knows most of the women couldn't pay more fees.

He looks at his phone. 'Now, I've got to go back to work. I'd like Dad moved in as soon as possible, please, and we can get that cottage up for sale.'

'He can't do this,' June says as soon as Max leaves.

Nick shrugs. 'He is doing it.'

'And it sounds like he can,' I add. 'Let's not tell anyone just yet. We'll think of the best way to do it.'

'We'll do it together,' Nick tells June. 'There's safety in numbers.'

Not that I won't pounce on any old excuse, but I could kiss him for being in this together with us when he doesn't have to be. He's too nice to leave June to break the news alone.

'June, try not to worry too much,' I tell her. 'We'll figure something out. If the worst comes to the worst, we'll quarantine him.'

'We could brick him into his room,' she says.

'Or make him wear a bell,' answers Nick. 'Our cat had one to warn the birds.'

Unfortunately, our birds can't fly away when they hear it. 'I've got to get back to the kitchen or lunch will be late. I'll come straight back after.'

The pizza dough will need knocking back soon. I can pound all my frustrations into it.

It doesn't take long for us to decide that the residents need to know about Terence sooner rather than later. It's only fair to let them have as much time as possible to get used to the idea. As if one could ever get used to an idea like Terence.

There's no good time to pull people away from the TV, though. Between *Loose Women*, *Judge Rinder*, *Escape to the Country*, *Antiques Road Trip* and *Come Dine With Me*, plus all the evening programming, someone is going to whinge. As it is, there's a running battle over whether to watch *Countdown* or *Judge Rinder*.

But this is important, so everyone is rounded up into the huge living room. If a stranger were to look at our residents, they'd probably see a relatively homogeneous group of seventy- and eighty-somethings – mostly grey and mostly wrinkled. So far, so mundane. But they couldn't be more wrong. These women are anything but boring.

You might mistake Dot, with her apple-green reading glasses on a delicate gold chain around her neck and her habit of wearing forties-style day dresses with sturdy shoes, for just a mild-mannered English literature teacher. They'd never think that she'd been with the protesters flour-bombing the Miss World contest in Royal Albert Hall or had chained herself to Downing Street's railings during the Vietnam protests. Beneath that genteel veneer of old lady sweetness beats the heart of a revolutionary.

Every single woman here has a story. Some are personal triumphs and battles. Others touch history. From Christine, who's been through about half a dozen different kinds of cancer and beat them all, to Judy, our reigning Scrabble champion, who took her driving test seventeen times. Not seven. Seventeen. She never did pass, but you've got to admire that kind of determination, and wonder why someone who can come up with seven-letter triple-word scores isn't able to parallel park.

There's Maureen, who's been to circus school, and sisters Ruth and Shirley, who married brothers and spent most of their lives in Uganda. Sue was a hospice nurse during the worst of the AIDS crisis in the eighties, and Ann-Marie is a qualified plumber, which comes in handy because our pipes aren't what they should be. And Rosemary had nine children. Nine! That should qualify her for some kind of medal for valour.

Most of these women aren't a big part of this story, but make no mistake: in real life, they're far from invisible old people. They're the people that surround me every day, and because of them, I can't imagine a better job.

I've even convinced Maggie to come downstairs. She's sulking off to the side in one of the wing-backed reading chairs. It's one of the grey ones, so aside from her aqua and black long silk cardigan, she blends almost perfectly into the furniture.

We keep all the chairs and love seats clustered in little groups around the antique coffee tables. That way, nobody has to sit on their own. But Maggie took one look at our thoughtful configuration and dragged her chair to the wall. She's sitting ramrod-straight in it, coolly appraising the other women.

Naturally, they're curious about her. Aside from these sporadic enforced meetings, sightings are as rare as those of Bigfoot. Clearly that's the way Maggie likes it.

But I'm not afraid of her.

All right, I'm a bit afraid of her, but June needs everyone to be as amenable as possible when we break the news, so I pull a chair up close to Maggie's. Her look of disdain nearly makes me back up. 'Isn't the sun lovely in here?' She can't object to a weather chat. It has been greasing the wheels of awkward social interaction since the dawn of time.

'I don't know how anyone can watch the TV with all that light,' she says, shooting a dirty look at the French doors that run all along one wall. 'Those curtains need to be drawn to see anything.'

'Well, the TV's not on now.'

'Yes, thank you, that's obvious.'

I will not run away. I will not. 'Do you have any programmes you like to watch?'

'No.'

'I like those mystery dramas, especially the foreign ones. Did you watch *The Killing*? No, no, you said you don't… I like Jamie Oliver's shows. And *Bake Off*, and I used to like *MasterChef*, but I've gone off it recently. The professional one is okay, I guess, if there's nothing else on.'

She's just looking at me. Possibly praying to make me stop rambling.

'I didn't know that you're a doctor,' I say. Now I'm grasping at straws.

'I'm not.'

'Oh. But I thought June said you were.'

Maggie narrows her eyes. Anxiously, I wonder if June has broken some patient confidentiality rule. 'I am not anymore.'

I can't control my gasp. 'Did you lose your *license*?' This is way more interesting than talking about the weather or what's on TV.

Now it's her turn to look appalled. 'Certainly not! Now, if you don't mind.'

How I'd love to shut people down like Maggie does. What a valuable life skill. Every time she does it, I feel like putting on a coat against the cold.

'Right, so,' June says, causing a few of the others to shush each other. Without naming names, let's just say a certain legwarmer-wearing resident likes to think she's boss, and others do follow her lead. 'We're going to have a new resident.'

But when polite cheers go up at this news, June shoots me a look. That was the wrong way to start. Now the women are only going to be doubly disappointed when they hear who their new housemate will be.

'It's always nice to have someone new joining us,' June soldiers bravely on. 'In this case, it's a person you already know.'

Nick nods encouragingly, but when she hesitates, he says, 'It's Terence. I'm sorry, but it is.'

I'm not surprised when a chorus of 'What?!' and 'It can't be' and 'Not *him*!' goes up across the room. In other words, exactly the reaction we had ourselves, and we're not even the ones who'll have to live with him.

Maggie rises from her chair like she's going to say something. This is so rare that everyone settles down. But then she turns towards the door. 'Maggie?' I say.

'Is that all the news, or is there more?' she says.

'Well, that's all the news. Don't you want to talk about it?'

'I don't see why. It sounds like a fait accompli, and I don't see how it will affect me anyway. I won't have to *mix* with him.'

She likes to use that word against us. It's punishment for daring to use it when we suggested that she might like to come down from her room occasionally to be social. You can imagine the reaction.

'Well, I want to talk about this,' Dot nearly shouts. That surprises everyone. 'I don't want him in this house!'

'You talk like he's a dog who's out in the rain,' Nick points out as Maggie leaves. That woman is impossible to reach.

'I'd rather have a wet dog in here,' she says. 'And I'm allergic to dogs. That's how much I don't want him here.'

'But why does he have to live here?' Sophie asks, her owly eyes going even wider. 'Why can't he stay in his cottage? That's bad enough. Tell them, Laney.'

Laney looks startled. 'Oh, yes, of course. Tell them what?'

'You've had more trouble with Terence than most,' Sophie prompts. 'Tell them you don't want him living here.'

'Well, he lives here already,' she says. When she sees our confusion she says, 'I mean he lives at the back.'

'But he's going to live in the house,' Dot says.

'Is he?'

Dot pats Laney's arm.

June explains that Terence needs full-time watching. Well, anyone can see that he shouldn't be left on his own to get up to no good. She deftly answers why he can't go somewhere else, which the women must understand. They're all on fixed incomes too. They know what a good deal this place is compared to other care homes.

But that's not to say they're happy to welcome Terence under their roof.

'What about the loos?' Dot puts her glasses on, which is just for effect because they're reading glasses. 'He can't use the loos down here. He'll have to go in his own room.'

'He never will!' Sophie says. 'Terence wees in the bushes. He might not even bother to go outside now. Has anyone been in his cottage? Does it smell of wee in there?'

Nick waves away her question. 'I've been in there and no, it doesn't. Really, ladies, I don't think he'll cause much trouble. We're on hand to make sure he doesn't, and the carers will be here too.'

Dot makes an aha point with her finger. 'Yes, well, what about them? They can barely keep up with everyone now. They're supposed to take him on as well?'

But Max has already thought about that. He's finally hiring the extra carer that June has been asking for. It's the least he can do after sticking us with Terence.

'Couldn't you just give him a chance?' Nick asks. 'He's got nowhere else to go, and maybe it won't be so bad. He's only one person. How much harm can he do?'

Dot whips off her glasses with tears in her eyes. 'I'll tell you how much harm. He can ruin a person's life. Ruin it! I will not have anything to do with that bastard.' With that she storms off towards her bedroom.

The others take the news pretty well compared to Dot, and there should be a few things we can do to pretend this whole thing isn't happening. He'll have his own table in the dining room so that nobody has to sit with him, unless they want to, and we'll try to restrict him to his own ensuite loo. We quickly finish the meeting so the women can catch the end of *Escape to the Country*. That should cheer them up a bit, at least.

'Maureen, could I have a quick word outside?' June says as the TV goes back on.

Of course. Maureen is in Terence's old room. I just hope she takes her move better than Dot is taking Terence's arrival. I can understand everyone's strong feelings about it, but this is really upsetting her. Dot is no man-hater. She's always been very friendly with Nick, and Davey, and even Max, who doesn't really deserve it. I wouldn't expect her to be so rude about Terence. Though he completely deserves it.

Later, June, Nick and I are in the office. It's the end of the day and I've got my clogs up on the spare desk that Nick is leaning against. June is chipping away at her email mountain with a cold cup of tea at her elbow.

This has been a long day, but next week will be even worse when Terence arrives.

'At least Maureen was okay about moving rooms,' June says.

'Well, she would be,' says Nick. 'She's used to juggling.' He waits for us to get it. 'She went to circus school? Juggling...? Sorry, I'll get my coat.' Then he says to June, 'I hope you didn't mind me jumping in, but I thought that if they were going to shoot the messenger then it might as well be me.'

June smiles her thanks. We all know he's the women's favourite. They'll even let him talk about their diet and fitness, which can be a sensitive subject at any age. He does it with such smiley friendliness that it hardly seems like criticism. If the women were going to spare anyone, it would be him. 'I think we all got hit with shrapnel, though,' June says. 'And what about Maggie? Talk about someone who can kill with a look. I wouldn't mind not having to deal with her anymore.'

'Do you know she denied being a doctor when I mentioned it?' I say. 'She definitely is though, right? You told me. Why would she say she wasn't?'

'She definitely is,' June confirms. 'She's a PhD. It says she's a doctor on all of her forms. Maybe she thought you meant a regular doctor who can write prescriptions and do exams. I can't see her doing that. She'd never willingly touch anyone.'

I don't mention that I accused Maggie of losing her license. 'Maybe. It's weird, though, don't you think? I'd be proud to be a doctor. I'd want everyone to know. In fact, I'd make you all call me Doctor.'

'Even me?' June asks.

'All the time.'

'Hmph.'

Chapter 7

Today is D-Day. Or maybe it's T-Day. Whatever you want to call it, it's the day that Terence comes to live with us. The mood in the house is jumpy and watchful, as if a thunderstorm is about to start outside.

But the storm won't be outside, and the women are preparing. They're curious, naturally. Everyone enjoys a little titillation, and Terence is sure to give us that. I just hope he doesn't completely alienate everyone the second he arrives.

Dot is still especially surly about her new housemate. And this is the woman who says things like 'Turn that frown upside down' every time one of us has a bad day. I don't get it. She spent decades teaching at an all-boys school. If anyone should be used to their nonsense and their clumsy social interactions and more-than-occasional pong, it's her. She's acting like Hitler is about to goosestep in with his suitcases.

I'm starting to think she knows something the rest of us don't. After all, she was Mrs Greene's best friend from childhood. And Mrs Greene was married to Terence and they probably all had dinner together, and maybe holidays. But Dot's not telling me anything. She hasn't even come out of her room yet today.

Nick went up to try to talk her out. I would have thought that bloke could have cajoled an agoraphobic to leave the house. But he can't budge Dot. 'She hates him for some reason,' he tells me as we lean against the stainless-steel worktop in the kitchen, sharing our usual morning tea. It's a habit we got into not long after he started. There's a kettle and teabags and instant coffee in the corner of the dining room for the residents, but Nick came into my kitchen for a cuppa that first week, and it has been his unofficial break room ever since.

Even though he does most of his work in the dining room right beside my kitchen, his schedule is pretty hectic during the day, so I don't see him much. Max gets his money's worth out of him, between his occupational therapy sessions for Dot and a few of the other women who either need rehab after an injury or, like Maureen, are struggling with arthritis.

He's got an entire programme to help keep our residents nimble. There's a kind of hand-held obstacle course on trestle tables running along one side of the dining room, with loads of jars on one end for the women to open and close, and different-coloured balloons filled with rice, flour and dried beans for squeezing. There's a big bucket full of rice to dig around in too, which does wonders for wrists and fingers. If I didn't already knead dozens of loaves every week, I'd use it too.

There are picture cards with designs for coloured blocks that they replicate as quickly as they can, and writing paper, pens and a few poetry books to copy out text if they want to keep their penmanship up to scratch. It all helps to keep their hands mobile.

While lots of older people can't open a bottle of ketchup, our residents could probably rock-climb if they wanted to.

Some of the women come into the kitchen too, if they're interested in helping. Many of them like to cook. Even if it's just mashing the potatoes or doing some of the chopping, they enjoy it and I'm always grateful for the prep cooks.

Same thing with the garden. Anyone who fancies it can give Nick a hand with the planting and weeding, which, aside from being good fun, improves their strength and flexibility.

It's not all about rehab and therapy around here, though. We used to have an activities person for all the crafty stuff, but Max cut her job not long after I arrived. Now the women themselves run all the activities.

The crafts cabinet is stuffed with a rainbow of yarn balls and threads, knitting needles, crochet hooks and needlepoint hoops. That's the home turf of our resident sisters, Ruth and Shirley. Those two could knit a cover for the Houses of Parliament, and they love showing everyone else how to do it.

Plus, there are the usual paints and sketching materials that mother-of-nine Rosemary hauls out to nurture her inner Monet in the garden. And I've already mentioned Judy's Scrabble title, so it'll be no surprise that she and Nick run all the games together.

'What are you making?' Nick asks me between sips of tea from his favourite mug. It's one of the case full that Max got from a baker who closed down, with a swirly motto that says 'Grab our soft buns'.

He's watching me pour milk into the poaching pans. 'Fish pies. I've got frozen salmon to use up.' Nick loves fish. Of course he does, being half Greek. I can imagine him hauling in the day's catch from the faded blue fishing boat bobbing on the sparkling sea, the sun beating down on his tanned torso – he never wears a shirt in my fantasies – and his glistening biceps straining against the fishing nets.

That's because in my dream he was raised on the set of *Mamma Mia*, when, in actual fact, he was brought up in a Bristol suburb. He got his fish from the supermarket, same as me.

Just stop it, Phoebe.

'When do we get fish and chips again?' Nick asks, though I've half forgotten what we were talking about, what with all the hauling and glistening. 'Hot and crispy with a little bit of vinegar. Mmm, it's heaven on a plate.'

'I can do it next week,' I answer. 'That was always one of our bestsellers at the bistro. I dabbled in a few fancy variations, but people don't like to stray too far from a classic like that.'

I stare into my pans, but I can feel Nick watching me. Finally, he says, 'You get a really wistful look when you talk about the bistro. You must have really loved working there.'

'I did.'

'Then why didn't you reopen it yourself? It might not be too late, you know. You could renovate it, fix the fire damage and reopen.'

I can tell he's excited by the idea. 'It's already reopened,' I tell him. 'Another restaurant moved in about a year ago.' When it happened, all the feelings I'd buried – encased in lead and paved over just to be sure – came rushing back to knock me nearly off my feet. It felt like having an ex that you're still in love with get married, and his bride looks, sounds and acts exactly like you. The restaurant was carrying on as normal. It probably didn't even miss me, the bastard.

It's not the same, I explain to Nick. 'My feelings about it are… complicated. I loved being there, yes, but I don't want to work there again. Sometimes I long for the feelings I had then, though. I know it's not possible to have them again because they came from having firsts in my career. Now I've got lots more experience. I won't ever feel the thrill of doing those things for the first time – my first solo menu, first newspaper mention, or award or fully booked service. I guess it's like childhood or, I don't know, maybe your university years. You can't really go back to another time in your life, because so much is different. *You're* different. I admit I'm nostalgic. I wish I could feel the same excitement over those things, but I can't. Going back wouldn't be the same.'

Nick's face has slipped into sadness as I've been talking. 'What's wrong?'

'Now I'm getting nostalgic!' he says with a laugh.

'Isn't that a good thing? Because it means we don't have to look backward to be happy. Our happiness lies ahead of us.'

'Phoebe Stockton, you have a way of making me see things differently. I love that about us.'

Us.

My heart starts to speed just as my phone vibrates across the worktop. 'Sorry, it's my dad,' I tell him. The man with the worst timing in the world. 'Hi, Dad.'

'Phoebe, this is your father.'

'Yep, hi.' He's never going to get the whole phone thing.

'Are you working?'

'Yes, but that's okay, I'm glad you rang. What's up?'

'I wondered when you're coming next,' he says. 'The flowers on Mum's grave are getting wilted.'

'Oh… I assumed you'd be changing them every week?' He only works ten minutes from the cemetery. The man runs a building company. Surely buying a few flowers isn't beyond his abilities.

Silence on the line.

Maybe it is beyond him.

Nick sips the last of his tea and jerks his thumb toward the dining room.

'I'll just be a sec,' I tell him, but he's already on his way out.

'You're here?' says Dad.

'No, I'm not there, Dad, I'm in Framlingham. I didn't mean— I was talking to my colleague.' I watch Nick go. 'Okay, I can come visit this weekend.' It's my Saturday off. 'Has Will been over to see you?' Or even to visit Mum's grave, I want to ask. He stayed for about two hours after the funeral before coming up with some bogus excuse to get back to London. Of course, Dad let him do it.

'Your brother is very busy,' says Dad.

'Too busy to visit his father? I'm busy too, you know, Dad.'

'Does that mean you're not coming?'

'No, no. I'll make the effort. Unlike Will. I can bring something for dinner, okay? You don't have to worry about cooking.'

'I wasn't,' says Dad. 'See you Friday.'

Nick had said 'us'. Us! But when I go into the dining room, he's not there.

If only Terence were the type of person we could sneak in quietly, then maybe the women would see that he wasn't any trouble before they even noticed him here. But Terence isn't a quiet bloke.

Nick drew the short straw and had to go get him. I'm not sure why I thought that would only involve a suitcase or two and maybe a lamp or a few photo frames.

Nick staggers through the door with what looks like a fridge box. 'Don't drop it!' Terence barks as Nick struggles to set it down without a crash.

'Have we got any small boxes?' he says to me with a grimace. 'I think I put my back out.'

'What's in there?' It says Frostbite Zero Degrees on the side. Surely Terence won't have a fridge in his bedroom.

'Books,' says Nick. 'All hardbacks.'

'That's because paperbacks are rubbish,' Terence says. 'They're cheap pulp not worth reading.'

At least Dot didn't hear that. Her love of literature doesn't discriminate between formats. She's just as happy reading on her Kindle as she is a signed first edition. The important thing is the story. As I'm sure she'll tell Terence the first chance she gets. If she ever speaks to him.

'Easy for him to say,' Nick grumbles. 'He didn't just carry them all up the lawn. We'll have to repack the rest into smaller boxes for the next trip. I could barely lift this one.'

Terence is standing with his hands on his hips, glaring around the hall. At least his hands aren't in his pockets and his fly is zipped. I'm grateful for small mercies. He doesn't look the tiniest bit grateful to be here, though.

'You've changed the walls,' he says. 'Why yellow?'

'They were that colour when I started,' I tell him. 'I guess they thought it looked cheery.'

'Hmph, cheering them up as they wait to die, eh? White was always good enough for us.' He perches his wire-rimmed glasses on the end of his nose and looks up through them.

Max must take after his mother's side because there's hardly any resemblance between Terence and his son. Terence's hair is full and wild, dark and peppered with grey. His eyes are grey too. Grey hair, grey eyes, beige wrinkled chinos that bag at the knees and a khaki shooting shirt. It's only his ruddy complexion that saves him looking washed out. I can see that he would have had a good face when he was younger, possibly even attractive, but now he's too miserable to be appealing.

'Where's Patricia?' he asks.

He means the painting of his wife, rather than the actual person.

'We've hung Mrs Greene in the living room,' Nick says. 'People are in there more than they are here, so we thought we'd move her.'

'She always loved being around people,' he says.

Unlike you, you ropey old fart.

June hurries towards us. 'Sorry, sorry, I got stuck on the phone. Welcome, Terence. Shall I show you to your room? We can bring your things up.'

'Why the hell would I need you to do that?' he bellows at my poor best friend, even though she's only trying to help. 'This is *my* house! I know where my own room is. For God's sake, don't be stupid.'

'Now, there's no need to be insulting,' Nick says. 'She was only trying to make you feel welcome.'

'In my own house,' he mutters. 'Don't you forget that, girly.' Then he notices the women standing in the hallway that leads to the living room. They're trying to look like they've got a reason to be there, perhaps inspecting the paintwork in the bare hall. 'Well, hello, ladies,' Terence says, with none of his usual venom. 'Don't be shy.' He beckons them over.

Sophie leads Laney and the others into the hall. You'd think they were approaching the gorilla cage.

Terence isn't shy about his appraisal of our very own Sporty Spice pensioner. 'Don't you look like a fit one!' he says to Sophie.

'Sophie loves Zumba!' Laney answers, oblivious to Terence's innuendo. 'She's fitter than all of us. Do you like Zumba?'

'I don't know who she is,' Terence says. 'Sounds foreign.'

That sends Sophie into a fit of giggles.

Terence does seem slightly tamer inside. Maybe he can be house-trained after all.

'Are you Ruth and Shirley's brother?' Laney asks. Then she looks confused. 'I mean husband. One of their husbands. No, that's not right, either…'

'Laney, this is Terence. Max's father,' June explains. 'Remember? He lived in the cottage out back?' She doesn't mention his other traits: pisser of bushes, groper of waitresses.

'Oh, I see.' Laney smiles, glad to have that mystery cleared up. 'Terence, yes of course. Who are you visiting, Terence?'

'He's going to be living here, Laney,' Nick says.

Her forehead wrinkles. 'Living here?' She turns to Sophie. 'But he's not a woman. You're not, are you? One has to ask these days, you know.'

'I'm a man,' says Terence. 'Come here and I'll show you, if you like.'

Luckily, he doesn't make a move for his zipper, but June shoots him a warning look anyway. 'Terence. You cannot speak to the residents like that.'

'I *cannot*? I've got news for you, girlie. I can do what I like and you've got no say about it.'

'Stop calling me girlie. You know my name is June.' Her voice is dangerously quiet.

'You seem like more of a girlie to me.' He glares, daring her to keep challenging him.

'Come on now, everyone please calm down,' Nick says.

'Everyone?' says June, shooting him a withering glance. 'No, not everyone, Nick. There's only one problem here. If you'll go get the rest of his things, we can get this over with as fast as possible. Terence, why don't you go to your room?' As she turns on her heel to leave she mutters, 'And stay there.'

'Do you want help with those boxes?' I offer.

I will feel no guilt about using the trauma of Terence's arrival to snatch a few extra minutes with Nick. There were weeks, after the supper club fiasco, when we avoided each other. Plus, Nick was angry. It's hard to imagine him angry, isn't it? He's normally so happy, so even-keeled. Well, believe me, he was.

Chapter 8

It's inevitable. Whenever I go to my parents' house, I travel back a hundred-odd miles and ten years. By the time I get through their front door, I'm a (less elastic) seventeen-year-old again. There must be a foldy bit in the parental space-time continuum.

'Hello?' I call down the long, wide corridor that leads to the kitchen. 'Anyone home?' My tummy clenches as I realise I don't need to say 'anyone'. It's only Dad in the house now. 'Dad?' Kicking off my shoes, I readjust the cool bag on one shoulder and my weekend tote on the other.

'In the great room,' he calls. I guess that name is going to stick, with or without Mum here to remind us.

She was always the enforcer in the family, in good ways too, not just pretentious ones. Take holidays, for instance. We never got away with anything mundane. Mum was the unerring cheerleader for an entire week off at the end of the year, packed with Christmas family fun. I did love it when I was little, until my teenage self would rather die than be seen with my parents. A little sullen animosity never put Mum off, though. She booked plays and museum visits and made us go on forested walks come rain or shine. Mostly rain. When the Christmas markets became a thing – crowded stalls full of gaudy knick-knacks and grown-ups desperately trying to pretend they were in Bavaria, not South Bank – we trudged around them while Mum and Dad got tipsy on overpriced mulled wines. At home we did the newspaper quizzes and crosswords and watched *Bad Santa*, where Mum and I mostly drowned out the dialogue arguing over whether Billy Bob Thornton was hot (Mum) or not (me).

I've grown to love mulled wine, even overpriced, and don't even mind a walk in the forest. Who's going to make sure we do that this Christmas? Who'll argue with me over Billy Bob?

Dad's sitting on the sofa with a plate balanced on his tummy. I say tummy. I mean his fairly-fit-for-fifties midsection. He's never been fat, though he's solid. I do think he's lost weight lately, though.

He's still in his usual white dress shirt and jeans from work. Mum always tried to get him into proper trousers or even a suit at the office, but in this one thing, she didn't get her way. Dad might come across as pliant, but the more he's bent, the faster the cement hardens in his head, till it takes a bulldozer to shift him. I learned this first-hand from age zero to sixteen.

His shoes are under the coffee table and a selection of jackets are piled on the reading chair that Mum had covered in raw silk and never let anyone sit in. 'You haven't ruined your appetite, have you?' I say, bending to kiss his cheek.

'Always room for more,' he says, handing me the plate littered with Babybel waxed casings.

'I could get you some good cheese, you know, Dad. The supermarket even sells it, right where you found these. They're the ones that look like they're for grown-ups.'

He smiles at my lame joke. Genetics might have been unfair about my brown eyes and squat legs, but at least I got Dad's big, toothy smile. 'Babybel is fine for me. What's for dinner?'

'Stuffed chicken breasts and mashed potatoes. It's stuffed with cheese,' I say, because I can see the question on his lips. 'Heart attack special.' Then I feel a jolt. It's still a bit early to joke about that in our family.

'That beats a takeaway,' he says. 'Makes for a nice change.'

I throw myself down into one of the chairs opposite the sofa. This was the year Mum wanted to change the upholstery again. It won't happen now. Somehow, I can't see Dad sifting through fabric swatches. 'You know it's never too late to learn to cook,' I say. 'You do have a daughter who does it for a living. I could show you a few things.'

But Dad shakes his head. 'I hate cooking as much as your mother did. We always joked that we needed a wife for that.'

Even overlooking the casual sexism, there's so much wrong with what he's just said. 'Mum didn't hate to cook. She loved it,' I say. Everyone knows that. She did it all the time, and she let me help her. I probably wasn't much actual help in the early years, but that's how I came to love it too. I had my very own stool in the kitchen to reach the worktop. They've still got it in there, even though I didn't need it by the time they moved to the new house. It's one of those retro chrome step chairs, with fold-out rubber-topped steps and an aqua seat.

When one of the local magazines featured the bistro for our five-year anniversary, the journalist did an interview with me about my *influences*. That's right. I had influences. She'd asked all kinds of questions, and I'd totally planned to mention the Michelin Star chefs that I idolised, but before I knew it I was walking down memory lane in Mum's kitchen. And that's what made it into the article: how she encouraged me not only to love food but to experiment with my own cooking. So, eat your heart out, Michel Roux Jr., my mum got the namecheck.

'I'm sorry to disappoint you but trust me when I say: she hated cooking,' says Dad, unpeeling another Babybel, cool as you like, as if he isn't shattering my entire childhood.

This can't be right, when I've got such vivid recollections of us together in the kitchen. They're good memories, some of my happiest when it comes to my mother. The kitchen was the one room where she usually left her criticism at the door.

'She called it lino prison.' Dad drives in another nail. 'We argued over it a lot. *Barb, babe*, I told her, *life's too short to slave over a hob*. But you know your Mum.'

Obviously I don't, not nearly as well as I'd thought, because what *I* remember is someone who was always volunteering to bring something for the neighbourhood picnics and barbeques. People raved about her food. That always made me so proud. I wanted to be just like my mum.

'She always had to be perfect,' he says to explain away Mum's delicious contributions. 'She didn't want people thinking you kids grew up on ready meals.'

We did sometimes eat them, but that's neither here nor there right now. 'But she used to say she loved it,' I murmur. She loved cooking as much as I did. We were miles apart on most things, but we had that in common. Dad can't take that from me, now that I've got no chance of finding any other way to feel close to Mum.

Dad shrugs. 'What can I tell you? She didn't love it. I can probably count on two hands the number of times she made meals after we moved. We get takeaway or go out.' He catches himself. 'We... did.'

'Hang on, Dad, no, that can't be right. I rang home loads of times when Mum was in the middle of cooking.' I couldn't have imagined that. I'd ring. Mum would be distracted, in the middle of getting dinner ready. 'And how do you explain that she used to send me recipes she'd made?'

He shrugs. 'She hated to cook. She didn't use recipes. Phoebe, does it really matter whether she did or not? There are lots of things she didn't like doing.'

That gets my attention. 'What else?' I ask, though I don't know if I can hear any more right now. I've got enough going on, what with the dismantling of my childhood memories and all.

'God, I don't know.' He scratches his temple. 'Socialising with our office. Killing spiders, cutting the grass. Riding horses. She was terrified of them. And the spiders.'

I knew all that. Still, I feel cheated. That's super, Mum, thanks very much. Lie about the one thing that always connected us. 'But you're not trying to deny that we did cook together, right? Because that's why I'm a chef now.'

'I'm not disputing that,' Dad says. 'I'm only saying she didn't like it and it doesn't matter. You ended up being a cook anyway.'

'It does matter! It matters because…'

Because why? Because this goes against what I knew about Mum. Not what I thought. What I knew. That's unsettling, to say the least. And it's not like I can get her in here to tell us the truth.

'Who says you get to be the authority on Mum now that she's gone?' I say, exactly as petulantly as I would have at seventeen. See what I mean about travelling back ten years? 'You don't own her, you know.'

Why can't my memories be the true ones? And if she did lie about something as fundamental as daily meals, what else did she lie about?

The weekend is starting off well.

We eat our dinner from trays balanced on our laps in front of the TV. It's clear no one has sat at the dining table since the funeral, though neither of us mentions this. We don't talk about Mum at all, and that feels like we're avoiding her. But I can understand why Dad would want to. He's got a huge network of business contacts to deal with every day – clients and suppliers, plus the company's accountants, bank managers and various official people. He's taken on all of Mum's jobs, so when people first get him on the phone instead of her, he's got to explain why and then listen to how sorry they are. Then he's got to make them feel better, even though it was his wife who has died. That would wear anyone out, and especially someone who is not a fan of emotion. Plus, most people mean well but, as I quickly saw at the funeral, sometimes condolences aren't just for the bereaved. Maybe I'm being too harsh, but I noticed it every time someone at the funeral insisted on telling me about how upset *they* were over someone they'd lost. Like I cared at the time. I wanted to shout *This isn't about you!* in their faces.

I hate to say it, but there were a few who could barely hide their excitement when they heard what happened. Granted, Mum's judgey perfectionist streak would have rubbed some people the wrong way – myself included – but cut us some slack. Don't ask for details on the day we bury her. Car crash ghouls.

How relieved I was once everyone around me finally knew. June told our mutual friends and everyone at the home, so that I didn't have to keep repeating the same story. She rang those closest to us and posted on Facebook for everyone else. Once again, she gets my nomination for Friend of the Century.

Dad gets up as usual at the crack of dawn on Saturday. It's a half-workday for him, and he doesn't need to ask what I want to do for breakfast. We always go out to the same caff when I'm home.

He's just paying the bill when he springs his question on me. 'Want to come to the office?'

'Your office?' Just to clarify. He's never asked me before.

'No, the Prime Minister's office. I thought you could advise the Cabinet about Middle East peace.' Then he softens. 'Your mum always worked with me on Saturday. There's nobody else there.'

I want to hug him, but he won't appreciate that here, in front of all the other caff regulars. 'Yeah, I'll come. I could help you with the filing or something. What did Mum do there on Saturdays?'

'Everything,' he says. 'She always did everything.'

I remember when they opened the office. Up till then they'd worked out of the utility room at the back of the house. It meant timing client calls between the washing machine's spin cycles and there were always building samples everywhere. That drove Mum mad, and unhappy Mum meant an unhappy Dad, so everyone was relieved when they moved to official premises where household chores didn't interrupt business and Dad could have all the samples he wanted.

Of course, Mum being Mum, they couldn't just move in quietly like most people would have. There were balloons, colour-coordinated with the smart new shirts they got for everyone, and about a square metre of cake that spelled out 'Congratulations' in ornate icing hammers, saws, ladders, tape measures and screwdrivers. She even got the newspaper to do a feature about how they started from nothing and now look at them, one of the most successful building firms in the area with more than fifty employees.

'I appreciate the company, Phoebe,' Dad says as we pull up out front of the office. It looks nearly the same as usual. The company vans are parked in the fenced lock-up at the side and the low brick building is neat and functional. But the company sign is starting to peel. Dad will need to have it redone. I wonder if he'll keep 'Simon and Barb Stockton, Proprietors' underneath. Since they're not a plural now.

'You probably have better things to do than hang around with the old man,' Dad goes on. Then he hesitates. 'Your mum was the one who always kept tabs on how you are, you know, with work and personally and all that. It's not my area of expertise, but I hope you're doing okay? I mean, you're happy with your job and… everything else?'

He looks like I'm going to slap him. Or worse, tell him something icky and personal. This must be *killing* him. To put him out of his misery I say, 'I'm fine, Dad. Happy. Thanks.'

And it's true. I love my job. It's the… everything else that probably needs some attention.

If only I hadn't messed things up with Nick. If Dad's this uncomfortable just asking about it, imagine how *I'd* feel having to tell anyone about it. I will tell you, even though it's mortifying, because otherwise you might agree with June when she says that things aren't hopeless with me and Nick. Then hopefully we can all forget this whole stupid crush and I'll live out my days as a spinster in the Happy Home for Ladies. It probably won't be so bad.

Chapter 9

It only took a few weeks after he started for Nick and I to get flirty. It wasn't obvious to others, I don't think, but I noticed. And Nick must have too, because one afternoon he came into the kitchen while I was preparing lunch.

I went tingly at the sight of him. He was still new to me, and although I was a keen student, I hadn't learned every gesture, dimple and perfectly formed muscle of him yet. There was still so much to discover.

'I have a proposal,' he said. 'I know how you love to eat.' He noticed my quizzical expression. What was this, an intervention? 'I mean that you love trying food. I've got an extra ticket to the Mad Hatter's Supper Club. Have you heard of it?'

Who hadn't? It was the hottest reservation within a hundred miles. 'But those tickets are impossible to get!' June and I had been trying for almost a year.

Nick was delighted by my reaction. 'You can thank my friend Seth yourself. He got us a table and we've got an extra ticket. I thought you might like to take it?'

The Mad Hatter's meals were talked about in the same reverent tones as some of the hottest chefs in Paris, New York and London. I wouldn't pass up the chance to actually taste one, and only a short drive away in little old Ipswich. The fact that Nick was asking me was the buttercream on the cake.

Was it a date? Was it? It sounded close enough for me to hope so.

'We'll share a big taxi there and back so that we can drink,' he said. 'Seth and a few others are meeting us, since they're local. Sorry for the short notice. It's Thursday. That's still all right?'

Oh, no. Any day but Thursday. 'This Thursday?'

'Yeah, sorry. You can come, though?'

I smiled. 'Of course, Thursday is fine. There's literally nothing that would get in the way of going!'

Not even an endoscopy.

My GP had ordered it just to make sure I didn't have anything scarier than an ulcer, which was pretty scary in itself. By then, antacids had become a major food group in my diet, so I knew I needed to find out once and for all. I just wished it didn't have to be on the same day as my first date with Nick.

June would need to go with me to the appointment, on account of the sedative they were using. I should have had just enough time to get back to Framlingham to change, let June do my hair and make-up and be gorgeous for when Nick picked me up.

It shouldn't be a problem, though I couldn't risk telling him about the hospital appointment. Nick was just the type of thoughtful person who'd want to cancel rather than cause me any more stress. And then I might never get the chance again.

At least the prospect of our date helped take my mind off the procedure itself. Until June and I walked into the hospital.

'I don't want to do this,' I told her. 'I really don't.'

She grabbed my hand. 'It'll be fine. They won't find anything wrong.'

'It's not that so much as having them rooting around in me.'

'I know,' she said, 'but you won't feel anything with the sedatives. You've got to go through it and then you'll know for sure that everything is okay.'

'Except that something is still causing the trouble.' I gave my name to the hospital receptionist and she sent us to the second floor. Her look of sympathy didn't help matters.

Briskly, June said, 'Yes, well, we'll just deal with that later. And look on the bright side. With all the worry, you probably dropped a few pounds. You'll look great tonight for your date.'

'June, really?'

'Sorry.'

The procedure itself wasn't as bad as I'd feared. The sedative worked a treat. I felt *fine*. Nice and relaxed. That should have been my first clue that keeping the date was a bad idea.

It took longer than I'd thought, though. They don't just let you leave straightaway, so we were a little behind schedule getting back to my flat to get ready.

But that was okay with me, because I felt *fine*. Did I mention that?

The last words I remember June saying were 'Are you sure this is a good idea?' as the doorbell went.

'That's my ride!' Mad Hatter's Supper Club, here I come.

Nick looked gorgeous, and I mean gor-geous. I was used to seeing him in jeans and tee shirts or tracksuits, so I'm sure my mouth hung open when I opened the front door and got a look at him. He had on a smart jacket with super dark jeans, and a crisp button-down shirt with little blue flowers on it. He'd put something in his hair to make the waves even more wild than usual, and as he held the minibus door open for me, I got a whiff of a delicious citrus fragrance. It was going to be the best night of my life!

Nick's friends were already inside the minibus: a couple in the far back seat and two girls in the middle row. The door was high off the ground and I assumed my jeans were too tight because it wasn't easy stretching my leg to step up into it.

Nick introduced me around, but I guess I wasn't paying enough attention. I didn't remember any of their names.

The ride was jolly and I could feel Nick staring at me. No wonder. June had curled the ends of my hair so it bounced around my shoulders, and I even had on make-up. I'd opted for nice jeans and a floaty top in the end because I didn't want to look too prissy in a dress.

The supper club was hidden in an old wharf building on the river. It looked so derelict from the outside that the taxi driver double-checked the address and even then, said he wouldn't be responsible for dropping us off.

'This is properly mysterious,' one of the girls said as we made our way to an open door.

'I'm really glad you're here,' Nick said. At first, I thought he was talking to the girl. But then he caught my eye. He meant me!

The industrial lift creaked to the top floor and tipped us out into the shabbiest shabby chic space imaginable. The paint was blistering off all the ironwork and the wooden floor was bashed, dented and gouged from decades of deliveries from the ships. Long scaffolding board tables and mismatched chairs dotted the cavernous room, lit with dozens of dripping candles. All manner of industrial equipment filled the warehouse: winches mounted on chains in the ceiling, exposed pipes running along the walls and huge metal sorting bins pushed into the corners. The sleek open-plan kitchen was set up at the far end, where steam and smoke billowed up into the rafters high above. How fun would it be to snoop around that kitchen.

Maybe later, though, since everyone was frantically getting service ready. I hated when people came into the kitchen when I was trying to get food on to plates.

Three blokes were already sitting at our table. One of them shared out the last of a bottle of wine between the other glasses. 'Seth, this is Phoebe,' Nick introduced me to the wine topper-upper.

Seth and Nick could have been differently coloured twins. Equally tall and muscly-shouldered, Seth's hair was a pale blond, but as thick, wavy and moppish as Nick's, and his eyes were the deepest blue. He had the same strong nose, though his eyebrows were more under control. Or at least pale enough not to look so caterpillary.

'Are you brothers?' I asked Nick.

'No, but people usually think we are.' Nick put an affectionate arm around his friend. 'We're like brothers, though. I love this guy.'

'I'm really happy to meet you, Phoebe,' Seth said, pulling me to him for a double-cheek kiss and knocking me a little off balance in his enthusiasm. 'Please, come and sit down.' He pulled the chair out beside him. 'I'm not nearly as big a food expert as Nick says you are, but I've been dying to come here for months.'

'Me too!' Gratefully I took the seat he offered. That felt better. All the worry, and then the procedure, had really wiped me out. Just as well that this was a sit-down dinner. Seth and I smiled happily at each other.

Over the laughter ringing out around the table, Seth asked Nick and me about the home. As we told stories about our residents, talking over each other and finishing each other's sentences, it felt very coupley. I was sideways in my chair, facing Seth, and I could feel Nick sitting just behind me, giving off a sexy gravitational pull. If I leaned back, I could probably have rested my head on his chest. But I was a bit dizzy, so I didn't, in case I missed.

Blimey, Seth could not be a nicer bloke. It was easy to see why Nick loved him. *I* was starting to love him and we'd only just met. I loved everybody at the table.

'Red or white?' Nick asked, reaching around me for my wine glass. I definitely could have leaned into his chest. Or at least have latched on to his arm.

I wasn't supposed to drink after the sedative. Or drive, operate heavy machinery or sign any legally binding documents, according to the leaflet from the hospital.

But it was only a drink, not a legally-binding contract or a forklift, so when Nick filled my glass with the musky red, I took a tiny sip. Just to taste it. Mmm.

An amuse-bouche arrived for the table: marrow bones stuffed with pine-nutty deliciousness. 'Oh my god, that's good!' I said, licking my fingers with delight as Nick laughed.

'I've never met anyone who loves food as much as you do,' he said.

'I love a woman with a good appetite,' Seth added. 'Heroin-chic never did anything for me.'

'That was *so* amazing!' came a voice from across the table. We all looked over at their friend, one of the girls who took the taxi with us. 'I could eat another ten.'

'You're such a glutton, Veronica,' laughed Seth.

Veronica's face fell just before she turned back to her friend. The poor thing. She was obviously crushing on Seth. Nobody could eat ten marrow bones, for one thing. For another, her face had flamed bright red. I knew how she felt. I'd spent the past month around Nick looking like I'd had my head in a hot oven.

By the time our starters arrived I was feeling fuzzier at the edges, but having such a good time listening to the conversation bouncing around the table. To be honest, I couldn't follow it very closely. I was too busy trying to concentrate on what Nick and Seth were saying. I wasn't completely sure what they were laughing at. It didn't matter. Because I was having a *fine* time.

I lifted my wine glass, but it was empty.

Nick watched me sipping on air.

I've replayed that night so many times, and always come to the same conclusion. I should have realised that I wasn't thinking straight. There's a reason the hospital prints those leaflets.

So, when Seth told me how lovely I was, I lavishly returned the compliment. 'I think you're lovely too. Very, very lovely,' I said. 'In fact, you might be the loveliest person here.' Then, just to show I didn't really mean that, I said to the table, 'No offence, everyone!'

'Are you okay, Phoebe?' Nick asked. When I reached for my glass, he put his hand on my arm.

Normally that would have been oh so nice, but I knew what he was doing. He was trying to stop me from drinking the lovely wine. So that made it not nice. Not oh so nice at all. 'You're not my father, Nick.' I didn't go for more wine, though. 'I was just telling Seth how lovely he is. And he was telling me how lovely I am.'

If I'd wanted to make Nick jealous, it was working, though I was too whacked on sedatives and Shiraz to pay attention to the cold edge that crept into his voice. 'Yeah, I heard you,' he said. 'You and Seth are the loveliest people here. Congratulations. I'm happy for you.'

'Thank you very much,' I said. I still cringe when I think of what an idiot I must have seemed.

Dessert was served, and I know I had some of the chocolate mousse, because I found it all down my top the next day. But I'm jumping ahead. You wanted the whole story, minute by humiliating minute.

By then we could have bowled with all the empty wine bottles on the table, even though I didn't think I'd drunk much myself.

The next thing I remembered was being shaken awake at the table. 'Mnuh?' I jerked my head up with a snort.

'You had a little nap, Phoebe,' said Seth. Everyone else was carrying on like I hadn't just been snoring in the middle of a restaurant.

'I'm so sorry,' I slurred. 'Must have been all the food.' I looked around for Nick, but he was sitting at the other end of the table. He glanced over, but he didn't move from his chair.

'Everyone's going on for a drink.' Seth considered me with his gorgeous blue eyes. 'I'm guessing you're not up for that?'

I couldn't think of anything I'd rather do less. But I was sharing a taxi with the others. I took a deep breath. 'They're my ride.'

'I could drive you back if you like. I haven't had anything to drink. My car's not far.'

'Would you really?' I wasn't even pretending to care about putting him out of his way. I was *so* tired. 'I'd love that, thanks.'

'You would?'

I nodded. Did I guess then what was going to happen? I was definitely flattered by Seth's attention and, let's be honest, I wasn't doing anything to put him off. Well, aside from accidentally falling asleep in my dessert, but he didn't seem to mind that.

Seth called down the table. 'I'm just going to drive Phoebe home. I can meet you at the bar in an hour.'

'Is that okay, Nick?' I asked. At least I had the presence of mind to ask that.

'You don't have to ask my permission. I'm not your father.'

I looked for the smile that would tell me he was joking, but his expression was tense. 'I don't need anyone's permission, Nick,' I said. 'I asked because I came with you.'

'And you're going home with Seth.'

'I'm not going *home* with him.'

He shook his head. 'That's not what I meant. Go home and get some sleep. Text me when you get there, okay, so I know you got home safely. See you later, Seth.' He turned back to his conversation with Veronica who, I noticed, was looking at him the way she'd looked at Seth earlier. Worse, Nick seemed to be enjoying it.

Well, I thought, that's put me in my place. Though I wasn't sure what I expected from him when I was the one bailing on the night. I also realised later that I forgot to thank him for the invitation, and I didn't even say goodbye to the rest of the table. He must have been mortified that he'd introduced me to his friends.

Seth and I walked together to his car. I felt pretty wobbly, but concentrating on staying on my feet kept me from thinking more about Nick. Obviously, he was miffed that I wasn't going on with them later, but how could I? I could barely keep my eyes open.

The first wave of sickness washed over me just as Seth pulled away from his parking spot. We hadn't gone a mile before I started to worry that I was going to be sick.

'Seth, I don't feel well.'

'Uh-oh.' He slammed on the brakes, which rocketed my queasiness to the front of the queue. 'Just let me pull over.'

'Sorry… it's the car.' I took big gulps of fresh air at my window. 'I'll be okay. Just give me a minute.'

'Would you feel better walking?'

'It's more than thirty miles!'

He laughed. 'I didn't mean you walking home! Crikey, what kind of a bloke do you think I am? I only meant having a walk outside. There's a little park. Hang on, stay there.'

He went around to my side to open the door. What chivalry! Or else self-preservation to get the sick woman off his upholstery.

I was glad, as we walked slowly along the park path under the tall old-fashioned lamps, that Seth did the talking. He told me about when he and Nick first became friends, rooming together at uni, and a little about his job working as a sports physio. He had a nice Midlands accent that washed easily over me.

'Feeling better?' he wondered.

'I think so.' But I dreaded getting into that shaky-shaky car again.

As if reading my thoughts, he said, 'My flat's not far, if you'd rather not risk travelling home tonight. I've got room.'

I looked at him then, with the light glinting off his blond hair, which had only gone madder over the course of dinner. Something passed between us. I understood that he was offering two things: the safe option, and the not safe one. I didn't make my choice right then, but I did make my decision to have a choice.

'If that's okay, yes,' I told Seth.

Why would I want to do that, given how I felt about Nick? It's not an easy answer to get my head around either, but I can't completely blame the sedatives or wine. Hurt played a big part too. Nick sounded pretty willing to believe I'd jump into bed with his friend, so what must he think of me? I was stung by the unfairness. I'd never given him any reason for doubt, but if he was indicting me anyway, then why not give myself the option?

Talk about cutting off my nose to spite my face.

There was some spite as well. I wanted to punish him for thinking that of me.

That's so unflattering, but there is no use sugar-coating it.

Seth didn't quicken his pace as we made our way back to the car. I must have, though, because I got there ahead of him.

It was only a few minutes to his flat.

'I'm sorry it's a mess,' Seth said as he let us into the Victorian flat. The bare floorboards creaked as we stepped inside. It was a bit untidy – a few tea mugs on the glass-and-chrome coffee table and some clothes in one corner of the brown leather sofa – but it wasn't nearly as bad as it could have been. My brother was the only bloke I knew who kept a perfectly neat flat, but then he would because he's so uptight. 'Cup of tea? I've got regular and green.'

'I won't, if that's okay,' I said. 'In case it doesn't agree with me.'

'Fine with me,' he said, gesturing to the sofa. When I sat, the cushion farted.

'That wasn't me!'

'I'm so sorry. I should have warned you that it does that. Rude sofa. But what's a little couch parping between friends?'

The way he was looking at me, he wasn't thinking about furniture noises. Neither was I. The (reach-acrossable) space between us crackled with electricity. Had we been like this all evening? I was having trouble remembering the dinner clearly. We'd definitely had the banter down pat, and laughed a lot, but someone would have thrown a drink over us if sparks like this had flown over the table. So, I was pretty sure that the tension only ramped up when we were alone in the car.

I stifled a huge yawn, but Seth caught it. 'I should get you to bed,' he said. A smirk played across his lips.

Again, we locked eyes, as I smiled back at him. Was it an invitation? That's the moment I've replayed about a million times, that split second between *Nothing to see here* and *Please look away now*.

I know I leaned towards him. I know this because I remember thinking that I'd face-plant into his lap if he didn't meet me in the middle.

He did meet me in the middle. His lips were full and soft, his kiss so deliciously slow. He puckered first to break the kiss, then pressed his lips to mine more urgently, again slowly, again breaking off before moving in more deeply. Those were proper last-scene-in-a-film kisses and I was light-headed with the sexiness of it all.

It seemed to go on for hours but despite the urgency, Seth didn't hurry to take things any further. Which was fine with me. Kissing without expectations is way underrated. Not that I speak with much authority, but with everyone live-streaming porn every second of the day, I think a good old-fashioned snogging session has fallen out of favour.

Seth definitely appreciated the finer points of a good snog.

'I could do this all night,' he said, 'but I'm guessing you're tired?'

I had to nod, though it might mean an end to that fabulous kissing.

'Should we go upstairs?' he asked.

'We?' Maybe it didn't mean an end to the kissing.

'So I can show you where everything is?' He took my hand to help me up from the sofa.

What followed was a disappointingly chaste tour of Seth's upstairs.

'Well, it's pretty straightforward,' he said, switching on the lamp beside his bed. 'Sorry, the bed's not made. Here, turn around for a sec.'

I did and heard him flapping the duvet over the mattress. 'Okay, that's a little better.' He took me by the shoulders and turned me back into the room.

But he didn't let go. 'So, you're welcome to sleep here.' He was giving me *that* look again. I knew what question he wanted me to ask.

I played my part. 'Where will you sleep?'

'I can take the sofa, or…'

'I feel bad kicking you out of your own bed. We're adults. We could share.'

'We could,' he said. 'I'm good at sharing.'

I'd bet he was good at a lot of things. 'You get a gold star,' I said drowsily as I flopped on the bed. Full of poise, that's me. 'God, this feels good.' I meant lying down, with the fluffy pillows under my head. I was already starting to nod off.

The last thing I remember was Seth crawling in beside me. 'G'night,' he said, softly kissing my lips. Oh, those lips. I'd have snogged his face off if I wasn't so delirious with tiredness.

When I woke up, I was on the opposite side of the bed to the door. I must have crept in the night. Poor Seth probably had to climb over me at some point to get a clear spot in the bed.

He snored softly beside me with one arm thrown over his eyes against the early morning light coming through the flimsy curtains.

Moving slowly so as not to wake him, or jostle my splitting headache, I lifted my head to look for my jeans. Because I couldn't help but notice that they weren't on my legs.

I spotted them folded neatly on the black swivel office chair next to Seth's desk. I did have a vague memory of taking them off when I got too hot under the heavy duvet. So at least I'd undressed myself.

The other thing I spotted on Seth's desk was the framed photo. Either that was his girlfriend, or he was very close to his sister.

'Um, Seth?' I shook him. 'I'm really sorry to do this to you, but I've got to go to work. In Framlingham.'

He took a deep breath with his eyes still closed. 'You're killing me, Phoebe.'

'I'm sorry, but I didn't plan on the diversion to our journey last night.' I swung my legs over the side of the bed and scooted, half crouched out of view, towards my jeans. 'I could try to take a bus or something, but I don't know where I am.'

Then he opened his eyes and smiled, reaching out for me. 'Of course you're not taking a bus. I'll drive you. Can you give me five minutes to have a shower?'

But I didn't feel like flopping back into bed with him. Especially not with his girlfriend right there looking on. 'Okay, I just need to be back by about nine-thirty. We've got time.' Everything sounded like an innuendo, and that was the last thing I wanted.

What had I done? 'This is bad, Seth.'

Seth sat straight up. 'Why?'

'Well, because of Nick, for one thing. I mean, I went to the supper club with him last night, and I ended up with you.' At least I had the sense to realise that in the cold light of day. Even if it was too late.

'But you're not— I mean, Nick isn't… I'm sorry, Phoebe, but Nick never mentioned you in that way. He told me you were a cool colleague who loved food. If he'd even hinted about liking you, then I'd never have brought you back here. You might not believe me, but I do have some morals.'

Which didn't seem to extend to being faithful to his girlfriend. 'We're not… I mean, Nick isn't my boyfriend or anything.' And now, thanks to me, he never would be.

'Just to check,' Seth said, looking really worried. 'I didn't misread the situation, did I, or do anything you didn't want me to? Because I'd— That would be…'

'No, no, not at all. I'm not blaming you for anything, really I'm not. This was me not thinking.' Mum's words were ringing in my head. *You're not thinking of your future.* She always did have terrible timing, but, in this case, I had to agree. My future was the last thing I'd been thinking about last night.

As Seth went into the bathroom, I had to stifle my panic. I'd ruined everything with Nick and I couldn't even blame anyone but my own stupid self. Sure, drinking wine while on sedatives was the definition of unclever, but I hadn't done anything I didn't want to. Seth was *hot*, and nice, attentive and obviously – based on the photo on his desk – good boyfriend material. If it wasn't for Nick, then I'd probably be strategically hiding my purse or my keys down the back of his sofa just to make sure I had an excuse to see him again.

Oh, you so would too.

But I couldn't do that because Nick *was* in the picture, at least as far as my feelings went, and I wasn't going to see Seth again. Even though I'd ruined everything with Nick and probably had no chance with him, either.

Dear NHS: you should have included 'Don't kiss crush's best friend' on your warning list.

Plus, there was the not-very-small matter of Seth's girlfriend. Oh, the guilt, the guilt! If I'd known about her, then even in my sedative-addled state, I wouldn't have done anything. I owed more respect to the sisterhood. So not only did I let myself down. I let down my whole gender. I'm sorry.

I didn't even wait for Seth to put his pants on. 'I didn't know you had a girlfriend,' I said as he came back with a bath towel wrapped around his waist. 'That's not cool.'

He followed my eyes to the desk. 'She's not really my girlfriend. We see each other sometimes.'

I scrutinised their beachy faces. Those were the smiles of people on a romantic break together. Ones who definitely weren't sleeping in separate beds. 'You see each other sometimes? When, on holiday?'

Seth shrugged. 'Is that a problem? Last night was just a bit of fun, Phoebe. Nothing really happened. And, honestly, she's not my girlfriend. I wouldn't do that.' He pulled boxers on under his towel and shrugged into a tee shirt. 'I wouldn't play away on someone I really liked.' On went his jeans. 'I'm not that kind of person.'

But, clearly, I was. And none of last night was even the slightest bit against my will. It was my will. At one point a little voice had whispered, *This isn't a good idea.* But then another voice said, *Are you kidding? Look at this guy!*

'Sorry, I didn't mean to accuse you of anything. You did nothing wrong. Could I use some of your toothpaste? Then I'm ready to go.'

We didn't talk much on the ride back to Framlingham. I was too busy trying to come to terms with just how badly I'd screwed everything up. By the time I reached work, I'd come up with a plan. I hadn't technically done anything wrong, I reminded myself about a million times. Yes, okay, it wasn't clever to snog my crush's best friend, but Nick didn't know I'd done it. Maybe I wouldn't have to tell him the details.

But I did have to tell him about staying over at Seth's. Nick might have doubted my moral code, and that still hurt, but I wasn't about to lie to him outright.

'Hi, sorry I didn't text when I got home,' I said when I got into the kitchen to find Nick leaned against the worktop sipping his tea. 'I didn't feel well in the car, so Seth let me stay at his flat.' There. Straight and to the point. A perfectly grown-up, unguilty explanation. That didn't sound so bad.

'I know.' He took another sip and rooted around in the biscuit pack. 'I talked to him.'

A chill ran down my spine. 'You did? When?'

'It was late. I hadn't heard from you and you weren't picking up. So I rang Seth to make sure you got home okay.'

'But… I was with Seth. I'd have heard his phone. What did he say?'

Nick shook his head. 'You were upstairs when I rang.'

Oh, the judgment in that one word: upstairs. *In Seth's bed*, he meant. And I couldn't deny it. Instead of staying with nice thoughtful Nick who'd invited me out in the first place, I'd gone off and snogged his fit friend.

'I misjudged you, Phoebe,' he said. 'Last night wasn't cool. I think you know that.'

'I do, Nick, I'm so sorry!' I could blame the sedatives or the wine or the full moon or PMT or whatever excuse I wanted. I'd done it and Nick had every right to be angry.

Nick's eyes didn't leave mine. 'Sorry because you did it, or sorry because I know you spent the night with my friend? Tell the truth.'

'Both,' I said. 'But nothing happened!'

'Nothing?' His voice dared me to lie.

He flinched when I said, 'Nothing... much. I'm sorry, Nick.'

Then he shrugged. 'You're an adult. You're free to do what you like.'

'I won't see him again, you know.'

'That's none of my business, Phoebe, and I'd rather not hear about it, okay? I'll see you later.' He emptied the rest of his tea down the sink and put the cup into the dishwasher.

Unfortunately, even knowing how conclusively I've wrecked everything hasn't stopped my feelings from getting stronger as we've worked together. And now you know why those feelings are hopeless. We've never mentioned that night or Seth again, and I haven't seen or talked to Seth, either. Nick is perfectly friendly and acts like nothing happened, which is probably more than I deserve. But I'm afraid the spark he felt – that I'm sure I didn't imagine – has been snuffed out, thanks to me.

MICHELE GORMAN

Chapter 10

'It's nice to see someone's love life going well,' I tell June as I watch her apply lipstick in front of the loo mirror. She's found the perfect berry colour to offset her blondeness. On me it looked like I'd bruised my lip. It's no wonder I don't bother.

She knows that's not me talking sour grapes. My grapes are as sweet as a treacle tart. What happened with Nick was months ago now. Yes, it was a monster of a mistake, as humiliating as anything I've ever been through. And that's coming from someone whose mother raised public shaming to an Olympic sport. Like I said, Nick hasn't mentioned it again, and neither have I.

I'm getting over it.

At most, it's only a niggling bother that I forget about for days at a time. Sort of like a toothache. You may know you've had it, and you may even remember which side it was on, but it's nearly impossible to reconjure the actual pain.

At worst, it's a dull ache that you vaguely recall when you bite down wrong on something hard. No more than a sharp reminder that it was once excruciating (and, thank goodness, isn't it better now?).

Mind you, there is a kind of stabbing pain every so often. It's not all the time. Say, only when you eat ice cream, though then it's enough to make you howl. But nobody eats ice cream *all the time*, do they, so it's bearable. Or it would be, if you didn't also have cold drinks, and hot ones and have to eat three meals a day and then you find you're remembering that pain in forensic detail *all the time*.

All right, maybe I'm not over it quite yet. But I am happy for June and Callum. 'When's he due?' I ask her.

They're going to a country pub that serves amazing food. It's in a gorgeous village that was in the Domesday Book. Callum has done well this time. He shouldn't get too cocky, though, because I don't think he's in the clear yet. This is no time to pop the champagne, but June's battle plan seems to be moving into a new phase. She's even been returning his calls.

'He's probably here already,' she says, slipping her make-up bag back into her tote. She can't keep the smile off her face. 'The table is for seven, but he wants to have a drink in the garden first.' Her expression turns bashful. 'I'm starting to think this is a real thing. I mean, it has potential now, right?' She takes a deep breath. 'That scares the shite out of me.'

'You can't let it, June! You're going to sabotage things if you do. Take it from someone who knows about that. Callum is a great bloke, and you're nuts about him, right?'

She nods. 'But I don't want to say it out loud in case I tempt fate.'

'Fate's got other things to worry about,' I tell her. 'I really think it's okay. Callum likes you and you like him. We don't usually get both, so enjoy it when it happens.'

'I'll try,' she says. 'Yes, I'll try.'

'So, you promise you won't freeze him out again after dinner?'

Her look turns to pure filth. 'There's no frost in tonight's forecast,' she says, just as her phone buzzes. 'That's him!'

As we leave the loo, I spot the new 'Ladies' sign Nick screwed to the door. It's meant to keep Terence out of the communal loo. Everyone does try to use the private ones in their rooms, but their bladders aren't what they use to be and, for some of the residents, neither are their legs. And while we should be grateful that Terence isn't relieving himself in the rhododendrons, nobody wants to hear him whizzing like a racehorse beside her. We've repurposed the smaller one off the dining room as the new men's room.

'You can come in, Callum,' I say when I see June's boyfriend waiting at the side door.

'I didn't want to disturb June before she's ready,' he says, giving my best friend a devastating smile.

Callum is hot, and I don't usually think that about someone with a man-bun. I've never seen his hair down, but I can imagine. He's as blond as June, though his locks – shoulder-length at a guess – are wavy rather than curly, and his skin is about six shades darker than hers. That's because, she told me, he goes on a tanning bed. He's not orange, though, and if June hadn't told me I'd have assumed it was from working outside.

'I'm ready,' June says. 'Sorry again about Tamsyn,' she tells me. Max's daughter turned up for her first day of work today. 'I hate when he goes over my head like this. You'll be okay?'

I shrug. 'Don't worry about me, we'll be fine. You have fun. I want a full report.'

'That's a little personal, don't you think?' Callum says.

'I meant the food! Dirty mind.' But I smile. For June's sake, I hope his mind *is* dirty.

'We'll take pictures,' June says.

'Of the food,' we say together.

'June's gone?' Nick asks as I get back to the dining room where he's packing away the art supplies. There are a dozen or so small canvases set up on the trestle table. Rosemary's art group has been painting a vase full of worse-for-wear sunflowers for about the last two weeks. They're in their Van Gogh period. Last winter it was Rembrandt with a bowl of fruit. I had to keep replacing the spotty bananas and making cake with them. We had fruit flies throughout spring.

'On her way to The Cricketer's,' I tell him.

He makes a face. 'I can't believe I missed him again. You saw him, though, so he does exist?'

'With my very own eyes. I promise he's real.'

He nods happily. 'Well done to the lad. Their plans sound romantic.'

'She's having fun, that's for sure,' I say. 'I get the feeling you'll meet him eventually. Things seem to be going well.'

'Is he as dreamy as everyone says?' He puts his chin into his hands and bats his long eyelashes. 'Ah, to be crazy for someone like that. It's the best feeling in the world.' Our eyes snap to each other's faces.

'It is,' I venture.

His gaze holds mine while our silence hovers between us. But what am I supposed to say now? I can't apologise again, when I want him to forget about what happened with Seth. I have to let the moment pass, though with the way he continues to look at me, it doesn't feel completely wasted.

'Why didn't Rosemary clean up before she left?' I ask him.

'I don't mind doing it,' Nick says. He covers for the residents a lot. I know he's trying to help, but he really shouldn't. This place works because everyone pitches in.

I scan the tables, which are exactly the way I left them. 'Where's Tamsyn gone now?'

'On her phone, I think,' he says. 'She seemed to be having some problem over text earlier.'

'She shouldn't even be on her phone while she's working.'

It's Tamsyn's first day and already I can tell that she's useless. She's worse than useless. At least Amber, who can barely bring the women their meals at the best of times, does try. Tamsyn is entitled and spoiled. But I'm her boss, which makes that an unprofessional thing to say, and you should probably ignore it. 'She was supposed to set the tables,' I tell Nick.

'I can do it if you need to get on with the meal,' he offers.

But I'm not about to let her off that easily. 'No, thanks, Tamsyn needs to do it herself. That's what she's paid to do.'

'I'll go get her,' he says, leaving me to wonder why he knows where she is.

She's been here less than eight hours and she's already acting like she owns the place. She's not even pretending to be grateful that we're giving her a job. No ingratiating smiles or anything. You'd think she's doing us the favour. I don't know what's wrong with Max's family that makes them so horrible.

Oh, she did smile, though, when she got a look at Nick, like he was her long-lost best friend. Or even worse, the next bloke in her bedroom plans.

But that's not (the total reason) why I don't want her here. It really is also because she's a waste of space.

When she and Nick return, I tell her that we need the tables set.

Her eyes challenge mine. She's got false lashes on that are about an inch long, and her eyeliner flicks up at the ends. That's the only reason her eyes are so startling to look at. Without all the make-up they'd be a very average green. Possibly even hazel. She's really pushing the Isla Fisher references, just because there's a passing resemblance thanks to her long red hair and size zero frame. It's obviously something she's used to hearing because she didn't bat a falsie when Sophie mentioned it this morning.

'I've been thinking,' Tamsyn says. 'Why do you bother setting up all the cutlery and napkins at every meal? Why not just have them at the side and let people take them as they want? It would save you a lot of clearing and washing up.'

'Because this isn't a McDonald's, Tamsyn, and the residents don't want to have to serve themselves.' Now's not the time to mention that we do have buffets sometimes.

'Have you asked them?'

'We don't need to ask them.' I don't bother keeping the sneer out of my voice. 'We know our residents. Please set up the tables.'

She throws a scornful glance at Nick.

To my surprise, instead of eye-rolling me, he says, 'I can help if you want.'

She smiles her not-quite-Isla smile, hands him the cutlery bucket and pulls out her ringing phone. 'Hi, yeah, no I can talk,' she says to the caller.

The next day, screeching in the hall sends me running from the kitchen. I just hope nobody's fallen out the window this time. Unless it's Terence. Or Tamsyn.

It is Tamsyn, but she hasn't fallen. Although *something* has happened. 'What is wrong?' I say.

Tamsyn's hair is plastered to her head. There are pieces of corn, potato and chopped leek still dribbling in creamy rivulets through the waves, even though it must have taken her a minute or two to come down from Maggie's room. Which means that's the entire bowl over her head.

'Look what that witch did to me!' she wails.

What Maggie did is obvious.

The question is why she did it. This ought to be good. 'You've given Maggie her lunch, I see. It looks like she gave it back to you.' I can barely keep the joy from my voice. I know this is a serious situation. There's been an assault, of sorts, anyway. Although I don't know if leek and potato soup counts as a dangerous weapon.

'You go up there,' Tamsyn says, 'and throw her out. She can't do this to me!'

'I agree she shouldn't have,' I say. I've got to be professional about this. Tamsyn is my employee. 'Was there a misunderstanding?'

'That was no misunderstanding. She lured me in and threw it over my head.'

That doesn't sound like Maggie. It's too, well, obvious, for one thing. 'Tell me what happened.'

Finally, she starts to calm down a little, though as soon as she sees Dot and Sophie staring at her from the corridor, her voice rises again. 'I've never met anyone so rude,' she says, clearly enjoying her new audience. 'She commanded me to set out her lunch. Commanded, which I did, and then she dismissed me like I was a servant, without even a thank you. I'm not going to let anyone treat me like that, and I told her so.'

I can just imagine how that went over. Well, I can see. It went all over Tamsyn. 'What did she do then?'

Dot and Sophie have crept closer so they don't miss anything.

'She said, "Come here, girl." And when I did, she threw the soup over me! If you don't get rid of her, I'll tell Daddy and he'll do it!'

Fat chance of that. Maggie's the only resident paying decent monthly fees around here. A little humiliation is worth a lot to Max.

Which means it's going to fall to me to smooth things over. 'Let me go talk to her,' I say. 'You should stay here.'

'As if I'd go back,' says Tamsyn. 'You'd better bring a raincoat.'

My knock at Maggie's door is tentative at first. But then I think, *Man up, Phoebe*, and knock as if I mean to come in.

Maggie doesn't answer. I know she's not sleeping. It has only been five minutes since Tamsyn came down and, anyway, heaving a bowl of soup isn't exactly tiring.

When I push open the door, Maggie doesn't even look up from the book in her lap.

'That wasn't nice what you did to Tamsyn. She was only giving you your meal.'

Maggie gazes at me over her reading glasses. 'She's an insolent girl.'

'I know she is, Maggie. She's a nightmare, but you can't go throwing soup over her.'

'I won't be throwing anything over her, because she's not to come in here again,' Maggie says. 'You can bring my meals as usual.'

'Or you could come downstairs. Maggie, don't you think that would be good for you, even if it was just the occasional meal? It's not healthy to spend so much time on your own.'

She actually seems to think about it, which spurs me on. 'We've got so many things you might like to get involved in too. I've noticed the paintings,' I say, looking again at the little oils hanging over Maggie's bed. They're not destined for any museum, but they're not bad.

'Oh, those. They're just… nothing.' Her hand drifts to her brooch. 'Just fooling around.'

'Well, we've got all the supplies in the crafts cabinet if you wanted to start painting again. There are groups—' I catch her expression. 'Or you can be on your own, of course. And Dot runs our book club. You'd probably love that, what with all these… books…' My voice trails off because the temperature in the room feels like it has dropped by about twenty degrees. 'Or not.'

'No, thank you, Cook. That will be all.'

Damnit, she knows my name! I'm about to leave when something occurs to me. 'You're not always going to get your own way, you know, Maggie, by being difficult.'

Her eyes meet mine over her glasses again. 'It has worked fine so far.'

I think I catch the tiniest smile on her lips as she goes back to her book.

Well, at least that solves that issue. Although it means I'm back to bringing Maggie all her meals.

I'll tell Tamsyn how sorry Maggie is that she tripped and spilled soup on her. Maggie is an old woman, after all. She's not as steady on her feet as she once was. That's why she needs her meals brought up.

She's not unsteady, but that's the story I'm sticking to. I don't want to deal with assault charges on top of everything else.

Chapter 11

Max is at the home again and no one is happy to see him. Every time he turns up, bad news follows. 'What is it this time?' I ask June, slipping into her office. She's arranging a gorgeous bouquet of pink and orange flowers. 'From Callum, I'm guessing?' I reach for the card, but she snatches it away. 'What's the matter, did he describe the sexy times in writing? Did you bring him to the heights of ecstasy?' I'm cringing even teasing her about it. I only do it because I know it's even more cringey for her.

'Yes, they're from Callum. No, he did not,' she adds primly, 'and absolutely none of your business.'

She let Callum have a sleepover after their dinner at The Cricketer's. I know they weren't eating popcorn and doing each other's hair. 'You've thanked him?' I sound just like my mother.

'I will,' she says.

'Oh, June. You're never going to learn.'

'I said I will, Phoebe. I do know what I'm doing.' With that, she looks at her phone again. Waiting for his text.

'He's only going to text you because he thinks the flowers got lost. And then it's rude not to have thanked him sooner.'

That does it. She rings him. 'Hi. I did. Thank you so much, you didn't have to. Aw.' She hunches a bit, as if hugging herself, curling the phone closer to her mouth. 'Yeah, I love them. Course I do. I know you remembered.' Then she straightens up. 'Sorry, Callum, I've gotta go. My boss just turned up. Okay, 'bye.'

'Happy?'

'Much better,' I say, and we go to see what Max wants.

This time he's got Tamsyn in the meeting too, even though she's been here all of about a minute and probably couldn't name even one of the residents. She and Nick are leaning against one of the dining tables. They could be in a shampoo advert together, all shiny and fit. Even in her apron, Tamsyn looks good – she's a jeans and tee shirt person, with ridiculous taste in shoes. They're platforms. Nice platforms, if I was being unbiased about it.

But still. I feel like a frump sitting awkwardly next to her in my chef whites and clogs. Who'll get the last laugh, though, twenty years from now when Miss Trendy will have sore bunions, I tell myself weakly.

Clothes have never really interested me. Mum wouldn't believe that, but it's true. So being a chef is perfect. I could also happily have been a bus driver or a postman, uniform-wise.

I do have some presentable things, and even shoes that aren't clogs, all thanks to June, who makes me go shopping with her at least every leap year. She also gives me her hand-me-downs, although I think she sometimes buys things and just takes the tags off before passing them over.

My point is that I'd never be able to compete with a woman like Tamsyn, who probably has colour-coordinated closets and looks perfect all the time.

Why am I thinking about competing with Tamsyn anyway?

'This is a quick one,' Max says. 'Now that my dad is settled and doing well—'

My snort stops him. 'Sorry. Sneeze.'

'Now that he's here, I think there are some other ways we can look to increase revenues.'

I hate when he starts talking all accountant-y. He does it when he's worried about us. Or not *us*, exactly, but the bottom line, as he calls it. He's always worst in January after he's balanced his books. Then we become assets in business-speak – instead of employees – who leverage our services for our customers, when we're really just running a nice home for nice people.

'Charge admission for visitors?' June proposes. 'A fiver for the buffet on Saturdays?' Then she sees that he's thinking about it. 'Max, I'm only joking.'

'Right,' Max says. 'It wouldn't be enough revenue anyway. You're thinking along the right lines, though. We need to get more residents.'

Well, duh. We've all known that for years. Max's mother wasn't overly worried about *her* bottom line when she opened. She practically gave the rooms away to the first residents. Many of them, like Dot, were her friends. The cut-rate pricing carried on for everyone since.

'Your father was a good start,' Nick says.

June rolls her eyes at me. I roll mine back. He's got to be kidding. What a kiss-arse he is sometimes.

'Nick, don't be stupid,' Max says. 'My father's not paying anything.'

But Nick isn't put off by our boss's insult. I guess he hears them too often. 'By the way, I've offered to work with him, one-on-one, to get his fitness back. Just some daily calisthenics, gentle stretches and a walk to town. I thought that might help.'

It would have to be one-on-one, since no one else can stand him. I stare at Nick, but his eyes are trained on Max.

This is a side of him that, if I'm honest, I'm not crazy about. Ever since he arrived he's had his lips firmly puckered. Everyone likes to be good at their job, and it's natural to want to get ahead, but Nick goes overboard. That only makes Max think he can get him to do anything, which is why Nick's informal job description is the length of Magna Carta.

But Max barely acknowledges Nick. 'So, from now on,' Max says, 'we'll be accepting applications from all over sixty-fives, not just women. I want to fill the empty rooms by the end of the year.'

'That's a great idea, Daddy!' says Tamsyn, looking up from her phone for the first time since the meeting started. 'This place needs some men. The women are old, but they're not dead yet!' She looks at me, June and Nick as if she expects praise for her witty comment. Only Nick smiles.

'It is not a great idea,' June says quietly. 'We've talked about this already, Max. We're the Happy Home *for Ladies.*'

'Not anymore,' Max says, looking smug. 'My father is here, so it's already co-ed.'

So Max had this planned all along. Terer
thin edge of the wedge.

'Why didn't you just tell us before,' June asks, 'when
you made us accept Terence? Then we could have told the
residents all the bad news at once.'

'It was better to ease everyone into the idea,' says
Max.

'With your father?!' I nearly shout. 'I wouldn't call
that *easing*.'

'We're not here to discuss how to run my business,'
Max says. 'I'm here to tell you to let the residents know that
there'll be some changes going forward. I've started
advertising in Ipswich, so hopefully we'll get more
applications soon. And I want to run open houses.
Prospective residents and their families will need to see
what we're all about. Starting next week, if possible.'

'What if the women refuse?' June asks.

I hold my breath as Max stares at her. 'Then they can
find somewhere else to live.'

For the second time in a month, we have to call an all-
residents meeting. They're going to start catching on that
bad things happen when we get them all together in the
living room.

The only person we didn't include was Terence. It
shouldn't make a blind bit of difference to him that men
will be living here. It's the women who're going to go
ballistic.

Although Nick doesn't think so. He's backing
Tamsyn's assumption that the women, after years or
decades living perfectly happily amongst their own, are
secretly dying to have a man around.

Honestly, I sometimes despair for the future of feminism if this is how our young women think.

We're about to find out who's right.

Even Maggie has come downstairs without much fuss. It helped that Laney asked her. As the oldest and the youngest residents, one stiff as a plank and the other as warm and lively as you like, you'd never think the two would be friends. But, for some reason, Maggie tolerates Laney and Laney actually seems to like Maggie. 'She never makes me feel dim,' Laney explained when I asked her. 'Not that the rest of you do. I know I can be daft as a brush, so I don't need to be told, really.' I promised myself not to call attention to Laney's oddities next time and mentioned it to June and Nick. I hate the idea that we might have made her feel bad.

There's a different atmosphere in the room this time. The women are warier, so June, who's always attuned to these things, comes right out with it. 'Max is accepting applications from men.'

I don't get any satisfaction knowing that I was right and Tamsyn and Nick were wrong. The women haven't been harbouring any secret desire to live with men again. It's pandemonium.

That's why none of us notices when Terence slips in. Until he says, 'Oh, stop your cackling. You sound like a bunch of old hens. You should be grateful that anyone wants to come here. We could use some men. I'm practically growing tits with all the female hormones swirling around this house.'

'You're a disgusting arse!' Dot shouts at him. That's sweet, gentle, not-normally-sweary Dot.

The women back up their friend with more jibes for Terence.

He's loving it. 'My bollocks are shrinking, that's no word of a lie,' he says with a smirk. He'll stir them up all day long if he can.

'Oh, well,' Laney says with concern on her face, 'that sounds like you should see a doctor. HRT has done wonders for me. Though I haven't got bollocks… so maybe it's not the same thing.' She turns to Sophie. 'Do they have HRT for men?'

'It's called BRT,' she answers. 'Bollock Replacement Therapy.'

I could kiss Laney for lightening the mood. Not that she's realised she's done it.

But when Maggie says, 'Well, that is unacceptable,' her cut-glass voice carries over the din and the laughter in the room falls silent. 'This is a home for women. Not women and men. Terence, if you're growing breasts, then perhaps eventually the transformation will be complete and we can all go back to living here the way we want to. What we cannot do is accept any more of *you*.'

Nick stands up. 'May I say something, ladies? Please don't judge all men by what you see here.' He gestures to Terence. 'We're not all like him.'

'Ta very much, my boy,' says Terence.

Nick goes on. 'The owner is already accepting applications, so let's work around this to make it as pleasant as possible for everyone. Wouldn't it be a better use of everyone's energy to be constructive?'

Only because Nick is Nick do the women consider his plea.

Meanwhile, I'm thinking about a few constructive ideas for Max's open house. If he wants us to roll out the red carpet, then the least we can do is show them what it's really like to live with women.

Just as everyone starts calming down, Tamsyn pops her head around the corner. 'Nick, I need a ride home from work tonight. Can you give me one?'

I know for a fact that she lives at home with her parents, at least half an hour's drive away. But instead of objecting, or ignoring her, like I would have done, Nick smiles. 'No problem,' he says.

He doesn't sound like someone who's surprised by her request. And she hardly waited for an answer. Which means she didn't expect a refusal.

Have I missed something? The last I knew, Tamsyn was fawning all over Nick and he was being his usual kind self back and I disliked her mostly because she's pretty and under the same roof as Nick. I'm big enough to admit that it has been my default since she turned up here with her skinny jeans and her glossy hair. I wouldn't have been nearly as touchy about him paying her attention if she was ugly, would I?

Do you mean to tell me that I *should* be jealous?

But before I can dwell too much on it (there'll be plenty of time for obsessing later), Nick's expression clouds over. 'Actually, that's rotten timing, Phoebe,' he says, 'because I wanted to see if you're free for a drink or something after work tonight. Sorry, I meant to ask you earlier, but then Max turned up and now I've said I'll give Tamsyn a ride. Could we maybe do it another time, though?'

Is that Nick asking me out? I can't ask in front of all the women, but it sounds like it might be, doesn't it? Doesn't it?! After months, he must finally really be over what happened with Seth.

And *right now* is when Tamsyn wants a ride?

'I'd love that. Any time.' That is, any time that he's not too busy doing what Tamsyn wants.

Chapter 12

It has been days since Nick's offer and I can't stop thinking about it. We've both been run off our feet getting ready for the open house, and he hasn't mentioned a drink again. Maybe that's because he's never free after work. As I feared, he's been too busy driving Tamsyn around every night. I don't know why she can't just wait for Max to pick her up on his way home from Ipswich, when he has to drive right by anyway. I'm afraid she's digging her claws into Nick. He's not exactly fending her off, is he? So maybe I misinterpreted his question. Or maybe I didn't, but a better offer has come along.

It's finally the open house today, and it's probably too much to hope that the slanting rain will keep people away. Not after June got a look at the adverts that Max has put out. He's been crying poverty for years, yet here he is offering a thirty per cent discount on his advertised rates. Granted, the advertised rates are still about twice what the women are paying, but it doesn't send a good message, does it? Cut-rate prices for sodden, cut-rate people. And he wasn't kidding when he said he wanted us to move quickly. It didn't leave much time for plotting... I mean, for planning a successful day that will draw in lots of lovely new residents. Of course that's what I mean.

'Are you sure we shouldn't let Nick in on it?' June asks when I hand her a cup of tea. Coming into the kitchen is a new thing for her. Usually she just uses the kettle in her office. That's how I know she's really worried.

Then she lowers her voice, looking around. 'He's not here, is he?'

'Of course not. You don't see Tamsyn, do you?' She obviously thinks he's her pet, playmate, driver and who knows what else. He doesn't seem too upset by any of that, either. Even if I could get him alone, I'm not sure he'd be on board with June and me. He's too busy cosying up to three generations of the Greene family.

He doesn't owe Terence or Tamsyn anything, but I suppose that keeping them sweet scores him points with Max. And that's clearly what he's after.

'It's best to keep him in the dark,' I tell June. 'He's too close to Max and Tamsyn, don't you think?'

'And Terence,' she adds. 'Which is the real mystery.'

I'm glad that June has noticed it too.

'Max is his boss,' she goes on, 'so you can see why he'd want to be... let's call it accommodating.'

'Let's call it a kiss-arse,' I say.

'Right. And Tamsyn's pretty. Sorry, hon, but she is. And Nick *is* a guy, so naturally he's going to be flattered by her attention. But even being civil to Terence goes above and beyond, if you ask me.' She checks the doorway. 'Something's been bothering me. About Nick.'

My skin prickles. Do I want to hear this? I'm still stinging from June admitting that Tamsyn is hot. Pretty. Hot. Whatever.

'Do you know how much Nick makes?' She checks the door again. 'I am *not* supposed to be telling you this, obviously, but it's not a lot. Like, well below the market for his position. Especially since he's got a first.'

'Maybe he doesn't realise he's underpaid?'

'Or maybe he's working here for another reason.'

'Like what?'

She shrugs. 'That's what I've been trying to figure out, especially when Max has him doing all the other menial work on top of his job. And he never complains, does he? It's like he can't do enough for Max.'

'Weird. Especially since Max is such an arse to him.'

'Yeah, weird,' she says. 'Don't tell a soul that I've said anything, okay? It's completely unprofessional of me to talk about another employee's salary.'

As if I ever would.

Later, back in the dining room, Nick won't stop glancing towards the door. That's exactly the same look our dog used to give us whenever we went near her treats cabinet. 'Don't bother, Nick,' I say. 'Tamsyn's too busy to actually come in here and help.'

'What do you mean?'

What does he think I mean, when it's so obvious he's practically salivating? But I don't say that. Let him think he's being subtle. 'I'm just saying that you'd have to look hard to find someone more self-centred and useless. There's no way June would have hired her if she wasn't Max's daughter.'

He doesn't say anything. That just encourages me. I can't stand her anyway and he may as well know what I think. 'We shouldn't be surprised, really. Look at her father.'

His glance is sharp, most unlike him.

'Obviously, there's some kind of deficiency there,' I go on. Seeing as I'm on a roll. 'Like father, like daughter. And even if you didn't think Max was a complete arse, when he's proving that pretty conclusively, just look at her grandfather. And she's got both their genes.'

He doesn't answer my yikes face, though. 'I think you're being harsh on her,' he finally says. 'Nobody can help which family they're born into. Your mum didn't sound very pleasant. Should you be judged because of that?'

Ouch. 'I cannot *believe* you just brought my dead mum into it.' I'm half kidding though, really, he shouldn't have.

He looks horrified. 'Oh my god, Phoebe, I'm so sorry! Jesus, what an arsehole I am. Maybe you're right.'

I shouldn't have goaded him into lashing out. It's fine for normal people like me and June, but Nick is too nice. Now he'll probably feel bad about it for years.

'Today's the day?' Davey asks as he unloads our delivery. I'll be ready for lunch, as soon as I put the finishing touches on the dessert. Three courses today. Talk about pushing the boat out for our special guests.

He wanders over to the hob to lift one of the giant pot lids. 'Are you laying it on thick for the punters?'

'Stay out of there,' I tell him. 'It's not for you.'

But it's too late. The whiff he's caught makes him reel back. 'Are you boiling dirty socks or something?'

I'm surprised he had to stick his head into the pot to notice. The whole kitchen reeks. 'I'm trying a new recipe for today. Trippa alla Romana.'

'English, please?'

'Tripe in tomato sauce.'

He repeats his question.

'It's cow's stomach lining. Mmm, mmm, doesn't that make your mouth water?' Actually, I've had delicious tripe, and I wouldn't make anything that tastes horrible, even for a good cause. It just looks and sounds revolting. Which is the point today.

'You fancy people and your stomach linings,' he says. 'It's all offal, offal, offal with you. What?' He smirks. 'You didn't think I knew what offal was, did you? You may also be surprised to know that I've taken cooking courses. I'm not only a pretty face, you know.'

It takes me a minute to square this information with my version of Davey. 'What kind of courses?' I half expect him to say Pot Noodles.

'Butchery. Vietnamese, Thai, Indian. Oh, and pasta in Florence.'

'You're kidding.'

He shakes his head. 'Phoebe, I've been telling you for months that I'm your perfect man and you won't believe me. I know. You see the uniform and think I'm all about the power.'

I stifle a snort as I take in his matching green golf shirt and trousers.

'I know what you're thinking.' He circles his face with his finger. 'And you're right. This face was meant for the big screen, but who wants to deal with the casting couch?'

How did I never realise that Davey is funny?

'What are you staring at?' he says.

'I just never knew you had such… depth.' Maybe I've been too busy obsessing over Nick to notice.

He nods. 'I can cook.' He's ticking off his fingers. 'I can also make cocktails, and have fascinating conversations, *and* I can shag you senseless. How does that sound for a perfect night out?'

It sounds like he's waded back into the shallow end of the pool, where he's most comfortable.

'Hellllo!' he says.

'Yes, I see you, hello,' I say back.

'Not you.'

That's when I glance at the doorway, where Tamsyn is standing.

'An angel must have fallen from heaven,' Davey says.

Instead of blanking him, like she usually does the rest of us, Tamsyn simpers.

'DaveyTamsynTamsynDavey.' Fastest introduction ever.

When she flashes her mega-smile, *I* nearly fall for her. The girl knows how to be charming. 'That's so kind,' she says, like Davey hasn't just wheeled out the tritest chat-up line on Planet Earth. 'I'm not always an angel, though.' With a flick of her bouncy hair, she turns on her heel. Making sure he gets a good long look at her backside, of course.

'Did you want something, Tamsyn?' I call after her.

'Just Nick,' she answers.

I'll just bet she does.

Davey shakes his hand, like he's been burned, or we're in an episode of *Happy Days*. If he says hubba hubba, I swear I'll put his head in the tripe pot. 'Don't get too used to her,' I tell him, 'because I doubt she'll be here long.' Angrily, I swipe away a lock of hair that's fallen out of the band. 'She does hardly any work and if she wasn't Max's daughter, I'd have had her sacked already.'

'Meow,' Davey says as he stacks up his delivery boxes. 'All right, tiger, retract those claws. Nobody's threatening your territory.'

'That's not what I—' But it is. There's no use denying it. Everyone wants Tamsyn and it's peeving me off. With a sigh, I say, 'See you later.'

I'm glad when Davey's gone because he's right. I'm pretty unattractive *deep down in my soul* right now.

'More are coming!' Dot whispers, peeking through the crack in the door. She's been hiding here in the kitchen for the past hour, reporting back on everyone wandering through for the open house. I can't look myself. I've got lunch to finish up.

The others are hiding out too, but they're in their rooms. All except for Terence. Nobody told him the plan, so he's sitting with a few of the men who've come. He's probably putting them off even without knowing our plan.

Max wants us to show off the home. Well, we're showing off the home: all the common rooms and the gardens and some really quite nice furniture. The only thing missing are the residents. 'We're not his trained monkeys,' Sophie had complained when we broke the news to everyone about the upcoming visit. 'Can he let strangers in here? Is that legal? It *is* our home.'

'So far it's ours,' Maggie murmured. 'But for how long?'

'Maybe they won't like what they see,' Laney had said.

Wishful thinking… but it gave everyone the same idea.

I stifle another giggle when I look over at Dot. Sophie has teased her hair up all on end and flattened one side as if Dot's slept on it for about a week. 'God, I keep giving myself a fright,' she says, wincing at her reflection in the old-fashioned medicine cabinet that's mounted beside the sink.

She looks strange without her usual rosiness. 'I wanted that forty-a-day pallor,' she says. 'It's just a little grey eye shadow mixed into powder. Effective, isn't it? I used to do all the make-up for our school plays.' When she smiles at the memory, not even her make-up can disguise her pleasure. 'You know, I still miss school every day,' she says. 'I thought those feelings would wear off by now. It didn't take nearly this long to get over my no-account husband after he left.' She laughs at that. 'That says something about where my priorities are.'

'Did you not ever… was there anyone special after your husband left?'

She makes a sound in her throat that tells me how she feels about that. 'Where would I have fit him in? Between working and trying to raise my boys, I was too busy to know what day it was, let alone deal with all that bother. I had my first love. That was enough.'

'That was your husband?'

'God no, Phoebe! But my first was special.'

I smile. I love finding out more about the women. Like I said, they might not think their lives have been anything special, but I could listen to them all day long. 'What was his name?'

A frown skitters across her expression. 'It doesn't matter. Let me bring out the buns, will you?'

'Sure, go ahead,' says Tamsyn, who's just wandered into the kitchen. She doesn't even look up from her phone to notice Dot's make-up.

I glare at her. 'Don't tax yourself, Tamsyn.' She disappeared for nearly an hour this morning. She must hide in one of the empty upstairs rooms.

'I won't,' she says as I follow Dot from the kitchen.

The few dozen guests watch Dot with concern as she carries the large platter towards them. I don't blame them. She's positively emphysemic in that make-up.

The men have come with their children, mostly their daughters or daughters-in-law, but a few sons have made an effort too. None of the older guests look happy to be here. The younger women and men, on the other hand, have the forced cheer of relatives searching for something to talk about with a difficult auntie.

'Here's a treat to whet your appetites,' I tell them as Dot puts the tray down on the closest table. 'I hope you'll enjoy them.'

Looks dart around the table as everyone gets a good look at the buns. I'm quite proud of them. They're perfectly round and smooth and the icing is the palest, shiniest pink. And the cherry on the cake is, literally, a cherry.

Everyone has leaned forward for a look, but nobody is going near them.

'Those look like…' says one woman. She frowns at the tray.

A few of the others are nodding. That is definitely what they look like.

'They're tits!' Terence shouts, grabbing for one.

Terence, language please!' I say. 'I'm sorry, everyone.' Then I pretend to notice the buns, as if for the first time. 'I guess there could be some resemblance, *if you're inclined that way.*' I make this sound like only total pervs would think so.

They're still not touching the buns.

'I like mine bigger,' says Terence. 'More than a mouthful.'

'Terence, really.'

He freezes me with a look. 'The buns,' he says. 'Though I guess you'd misunderstand, if you're *that way inclined.*' He nips off his cherry with enthusiasm.

Suddenly an air horn blasts through the home. A few guests gasp or grab their chests. I hadn't thought of that. If we can't scare them off, maybe we can kill them off.

'Some of our residents are hard of hearing,' I cheerfully explain. 'We blow the horn so they don't miss meals.'

The women stream into the dining room, looking like extras in the zombie apocalypse.

Most have gone for the neglected pensioner look: layers of clothes and bird's-nest hair. And not mismatchy clashing patterns that combine into a delightfully quirky ensemble, either. More like they've forgotten they've already dressed. A few times. Their well-applied make-up is gone too. It's jarring to see them this way, because usually they're all so nicely turned out. I can see the hilarious side, of course, and wish I could snap a few photos. But there's also a fragility to them that's making me a little sad. It reminds me of when Dot fell out the window. They are elderly, at the end of the day. I don't usually see that because they're my friends, and so full of life. This is a sobering reminder. I'll be glad when the men go and we can get back to normal.

I didn't tell the women about the buns beforehand, but they all seem to know exactly what to do. Even Laney catches on quickly. 'Mmm, my favourite!' she says, biting into one.

Sophie licks off a nipple with a perfectly straight face.

All the women are making appreciative noises over the sugary knockers, as if only a cretin would see them as anything other than an iced bun.

A few of the men start eating them, but they look like they're in pain. So far so good.

When Rosemary, mother of nine, heaves a photo album onto the table from the canvas cart she's wheeled in, I could kiss her. 'Would you like to see my children?' she asks the nearest prospective resident.

'Uh, sure,' he says politely, as she flips open the tome to the first page.

'This is Mark, he's my eldest, aged two weeks.' She points to one of the small photos on the page. 'And here he is at three weeks. Oh, and look, he's smiling there. And holding my hand in this one. He came out with that full head of hair, can you imagine? All my others were bald as a billiard ball.' She notices his head. 'No offence.'

'How many did you have?'

'Nine!' When the man glances at his watch, Rosemary pats his arm. 'Don't worry, we've got time before lunch. And after.' She pulls out four more giant albums. 'We won't run out of pictures.' She addresses the whole table. 'I like to go through them every day.'

'We love seeing your photos!' Dot gushes at Rosemary. 'Won't it be nice that now more people can enjoy them with you?'

A few of the guests nod politely. They're mostly the men's children, who won't have to sit through Rosemary's family photos for the rest of their lives.

While she reminisces over every holiday, sporting match and school play from age nought to thirty, Judy, our reigning Scrabble champion, nabs another visitor. 'Do you like Scrabble?' she asks him. 'We play every night.'

This was a risky strategy since a lot of people do love the game, but we decided to take the chance.

'No, sorry, I'm not a fan of board games,' he says, as barely concealed looks of dread bounce between the other men. B-O-R-I-N-G. That looks like a double-word score for Judy. Well done.

The men are losing the will to live by the time we serve lunch. A few are staring into space while others play with their phones. And the poor soul flipping through Rosemary's photo albums – probably only on about child number three – has his head cradled into one hand. Meanwhile, the women and men who've come with them seem to be having nice chats with the residents.

Amber staggers through the kitchen door under the weight of the enormous soup tureen. She's carrying it awkwardly, though, trying to keep her nostrils out of range. She sets it on the buffet table with a loud clatter. 'Cabbage soup.'

'Like the diet,' I hear one of the daughters say. 'Pardon me? Is it dietary? I mean for weight loss purposes?'

'Is it??' Sophie says, as if cabbage soup could be anything other than a decadent treat. 'We just love it. We have it at least three times a week. This or borscht. Beetroot is a superfood, you know.'

'Well, it sounds like everyone eats healthily,' the woman says as her father shoots her a dirty look. She's probably dying to find someplace for him to live. But I can tell he wouldn't eat beetroot without a fight.

I do feel for our guests. Nobody wants to put a parent in a home, and it mostly happens only after things get desperate. Which means they haven't got a lot of time to make decisions or wait for the perfect place. We're not making it easier for them, but we've got our own residents to think about.

'Trippa alla Romana!' I announce when Tamsyn carries in the main course. It's the least she can do after shirking all morning. To give her credit, she hardly pulls a face. 'Enjoy. There's also a vegetarian option, in case you don't eat meat.'

Rosemary's family photo captive is the first to spring from his chair. He probably thinks he's saved, but she's got her orders. Those albums will be waiting for him after lunch.

'That's an unusual pasta,' one of the men's sons says.

'Oh, that's not pasta, though with the holes it does look like it. It's tripe. Cow's stomach.' That stops him, mid-scoop. He nearly drops the spoon.

'You could have the seitan instead,' I tell him, smooth as you like.

'Satan?'

'It's a kind of wheat gluten. I barbequed it.' Tamsyn's just brought it in. This is probably the only work I'll get out of her today. 'It's quite tasty.' It was either tofu or boiled veggie hot dogs, but I didn't want to overplay the sexual innuendos.

The way the residents rush to scoop up the tripe, you'd think it was their all-time favourite meal. They're tucking in with gusto, oohing and aahing praise all over it.

'You've done it again, Phoebe,' Dot says. 'Delicious!' At that, all the women clap.

'Phoebe is so good about making sure our meals are nutritionally balanced,' says Sophie. 'Tripe's got lots of vitamins and minerals.'

'Not to mention it gives you a nice shiny coat,' I hear Dot murmur. 'Hair, I mean.'

Unfortunately, though, and to the disappointment of the residents, a few of the men like it too. 'This is very nice,' says one. Another recalls it as one of his favourite dishes from childhood during the war years. Sometimes I forget that our generation didn't invent nose-to-tail dining.

Even though we wanted everyone to be repulsed by lunch, a little part of me craves this praise. It's nice to hear that I can make even stomach lining appetising.

That was one thing that did always impress my mum. Not that she'd touch tripe, but I could make just about anything *normal* – her words – taste good. Even random bits that wouldn't usually go into a dish. I got such a buzz out of opening their fridge and putting together a meal that'd have Mum salivating. Those were the times when I felt closest to her. Maybe because she was the one who taught me to cook in the first place. Not even Dad's claim that she hated doing it can take away the fact that Mum was the person who made me want to be a chef. I can complain all I like about her criticism (and, as you know, I do) but she gave me that.

Her praise was so addictive that I didn't usually go out to restaurants with them when I visited. That and because Mum never got through her starter before telling me how I should be the one who owned the bistro, instead of just being a cook.

As I'm wrestling with this thorny memory – they sabotage me at the oddest times – I hear one of the visitors ask Laney something. She's so earnest and concerned that my heart goes out to her. It's absolutely what I'd want to know if I ever have to put Dad in a home. 'Tell me, are you treated well here?'

'Oh, yes,' says Laney. Then she catches my eye. 'That is… as long as we don't get out of line.' She makes an eek face.

Uh-oh. As much as I admire Laney's initiative, we don't want to be closed down over rumours of resident abuse. But I can't exactly correct her, can I? It'd just make me look heavy-handed and prove her point to the visitor. She'll be on the phone to social services before her cabbage soup digests.

Luckily, though, Sophie has heard Laney too. 'I can't imagine a place I'd rather live,' she says, 'and the staff are likc family. I can honestly say that I love them.'

I'm touched, but best of all, Laney takes the hint. 'They are!' she says. 'And I was only joking before. You should have seen your face!' Her laugh is so infectious that soon everyone at the table is smiling. 'Speaking of family, it's Nick. Hi, Nick.'

A chorus of 'Hi, Nick's floats across the dining room.

Self-consciously, he raises his hand. 'Hi, everyone. Enjoying lunch?' He strides to the buffet table. What is it?'

'Tripe. There's plenty left,' I tell him sweetly. 'Want some?'

He stops short. 'That looks… delicious, but no, thank you. I've just eaten. What a shame.'

'Nick is our occupational therapist,' I tell the visitors. 'He also runs the Zumba and other sporty things for us. Are you sure you don't want some food? Weren't you just saying you were dying to try this recipe?'

'Mmm, yeah, but I'm too full right now. Thanks, though.'

Cheeky, he mouths at me when he turns his back on the room.

That makes me smile. Until I remember that he's falling for Tamsyn.

Chapter 13

I thought for sure the tripe would put them off. Or at least that Rosemary's photo albums would make them think twice. But Max's adverts and ridiculous cut-rate discount pulled in the punters for every open house we've had. The women should be nominated for Oscars in the Battiest Actress category and, frankly, I'm sick to death of tripe and cabbage. But June's been swamped by new resident applications, and she can't turn them all away. Even if Max wasn't popping up in the office nearly every day asking how many have applied, those families are pretty desperate. They'd have to be, wouldn't they, to sign their loved ones up for meals of offal and holiday-snap marathons.

Men are coming to live in the Happy Home for Ladies, whether we like it or not. Though we'll have to drop the 'happy', because the ladies definitely aren't. I guess we'll have to drop the 'ladies' too. Now we're just The Home, like everywhere else.

'Are you ready?' Nick asks Laney. They're doing her memory exercises at one of the dining tables. Tamsyn got an urgent call before she'd cleared half the plates, so I've been cleaning up after her, as usual. You can imagine how happy that makes me. I'm so tired of being the childminder for Max's bring-your-daughter-to-work experiment.

'Telephone, tulip, tuppence, tarantula, erm, taramasalata,' says Nick.

'That's cruel.' Laney tries looking cross, but she hasn't got the face for it. Her wide brown eyes are sparkling too much. 'What if I didn't know what taramasalata was? Tar-a-ma-sa-lata,' she spells out as she writes.

That raises a laugh from Nick, who's timing her on his phone. 'But I know you're a woman of the world, Laney. You probably speak half a dozen languages too, you dark horse.'

'Done.' Laney slides the list over. 'I'm doing well today.'

He grasps her hand across the dining table and I can't help but chuckle at his enthusiasm. There's no doubt that he loves what he does. 'You're doing really well. One more or should we stop?'

Laney stretches her arms above her head. 'Let's stop, if you don't mind. I'm getting stiff from sitting here.' Then she reaches for the toes of her blue Converse.

Nick stands up to do some kind of complicated swami yoga leg stretch. Show-off. He's always contorting like this and then I have to try not to imagine him limbering up in only his boxers.

'We won't have many more nights like this,' Laney sighs. 'Peaceful, I mean. Without the men underfoot. I don't mean you, Nick. You're lovely.'

She and the others were so disappointed that their performances didn't work, and I completely sympathise with them. Imagine being comfortable and secure in your home – where you've been for years – only to have strangers suddenly imposed on you.

'Most did seem nice enough,' Nick says. 'They've got to be better than Terence, at least.'

Laney laughs at his tortured expression, but it only earns a dirty look from me. 'Oh, you poor baby,' I say. He can complain all he likes, but he's bringing Terence's abuse on himself. He's the one who fawns all over the man. No wonder Terence is grumpy. I would be too, if I had someone wedged so far up there.

It's hard to tell if Nick notices how tetchy I've been around him lately. If he does then he's not letting on. Though he spends every spare second pandering to Tamsyn, so he doesn't have time to notice much else. No wonder I'm tetchy.

He's sucking up to Terence too, delivering meals to his room now, like we're running flippin' room service around here. Though with Maggie still refusing to eat with the others, I can't quash it outright, so Nick trots upstairs with food three times a day. I'm surprised he doesn't trip, what with all the bowing and scraping he does.

I can see why he'd bend over backwards for Max. He is his boss. But he's wasting his energy on Terence. Max's father gets no say in Nick's career. He only owns this building and the land, not the business. Yet Nick is kowtowing all over the place just to get a leg up the ladder.

Oh, that gives me a shudder. *A leg up the ladder.* One of Mum's favourite motivational sticks. She was a big fan of climbing ladders. I hated how she wanted my whole life to be about getting ahead. But getting ahead of what, exactly? I never figured that out.

No surprise that I'm sensitive about Nick doing the same thing.

Just as Tamsyn comes in from wherever she's taken her latest phone calls, Laney bolts upright. 'It's eight. Are you ready?' she says to me. 'You asked me to let you know.' She double checks the tiny gold watch she wears. 'Phew, I nearly forgot to look. Yes, eight exactly.'

'Ready for what?' Tamsyn asks.

'Oh. Yes, what was it,' says Laney. 'Something Phoebe is doing…' Her lost expression makes Nick grasp her hand again. 'What was it now?'

'Thanks a million, Laney,' I say quickly. I can't bear that uncertain look on her face. 'You're a star. I'd have forgotten all about the book club!'

My bonhomie brightens her up again.

'That's right!' Laney digs around in her bag to find her book. 'I read this in school but I've forgotten a lot. Well, obviously, being me! Not about Mr Darcy, though. I remember *him*.'

'I know that one,' Tamsyn says, peering at the paperback. 'It was good.'

I wish she'd keep her nose out of our business.

'Then come with us!' Nick says. 'It's always a good laugh.'

It's not bad enough that I have to deal with her on work time. Now she's crashing my social life too.

But I smile my fake smile because I can't very well ban her just for canoodling with Nick (or, at least, trying to).

We all go into the living room for book club.

Dot's already in her usual wingback chair, presiding over the group. These meetings bring out the teacher in her. She almost makes me wish I'd gone on with school. But that would have been a disaster. I was awful at testing. No matter how hard I tried to study, the questions made no sense when I had to take the exams. There always seemed to be more than one way to answer. I usually picked the wrong one. No wonder I was sure I was thick. Then I got to catering school and found the practical exams so much easier.

I resisted joining the book club when June first started pestering me about it. I didn't want to be the dimwit that everyone had to be nice to. But if the women think that about me, they never let on. Sometimes I even feel clever. We don't always do Jane Austen books. That's probably how Mrs Greene would have wanted it, but we'd get tired of talking about the same ones all the time.

'June sends her regrets,' I tell everyone. 'She's out with Callum.'

'He's her Mr Bingley!' Laney says with a sigh. She's definitely the most romantic one here.

'They're hot and heavy now,' Sophie says. 'Good for her. I wouldn't mind a little of that.'

'Sophie!' says Laney.

'What? I might be seventy-eight, but there's still some life in me. Have you *seen* him? Besides, Laney, you're younger than me. You might be in with a chance there.'

'As if!' Laney laughs.

There's a core group of six of us: me, June, Nick, Dot, Laney and Sophie. But everyone is welcome and others do come and go, depending on what we're reading. It was standing-room only when we did *Fifty Shades of Grey*. If you want to be mortified, try talking erotica with women old enough to be your nan.

'Now we're all here,' Dot says, 'and welcome to Tamsyn. Let's make a start.' She perches her reading glasses on the end of her nose and opens her book. She doesn't read from it, though. It's all in her head. '"It is a truth universally acknowledged, that a single man in possession of a good fortune, must be in want of a wife."'

'Ha, show me one,' Tamsyn says. That gets a laugh from the others, but I see the little gold digger for what she is. Not that Nick is minted. Far from it, judging by what June says he makes.

It's her grandfather she's got the shovel out for. Every time she sees him, she acts like she's his best friend. It's disgusting. Terence is horrid, but I have to give him credit in one respect. He doesn't suffer fools. And he thinks Tamsyn is a fool. I could almost like him for that.

'Does that mean the story's not as relevant today?' Dot asks.

'It's very relevant,' I say, thinking of Mum. She wasn't silly or weak like Mrs Bennett, but the social climbing? Lizzy's mum was an amateur by comparison. 'Loads of people still think that way. Maybe they're not as obvious about it, but it's still there. Look at *Millionaire Matchmaker*, or *The Bachelor*. They're always about super successful, rich men who women have to compete for. It's depressing.'

'Twas ever thus,' comes the voice from the doorway. We all look over to see Maggie standing there. 'I'm sorry I'm late.'

Laney goes pale. 'Oh, my. Oh. I'm so sorry. I forgot. I asked Maggie to come.' She rushes over to push another chair into the circle. 'Here, Maggie, come sit by me.'

We're all trying not to stare at her. Nothing odd to see here, except that she's lived with us for two years and never willingly come downstairs before. How did Laney do that?

She's sitting straight up on the edge of her chair, not slouching like the rest of us. Her long silk cardigan has a gold diamond pattern on it and it flows over her wide-legged trousers to her knees. She's not got the brightest outfit in the room, though. Sophie holds that title tonight, in her pink and red skirt with purple legwarmers. But there's no doubt that Maggie's is the most commanding presence.

It's not until I remember the soup incident that I look over to see Tamsyn giving her the evil eye. Maggie catches her gaze and holds it till Tamsyn looks away. Ha.

Dot leads the questions. This is the part I like most. I always come away from book club buzzing with thoughts. 'Lizzy shows herself to be against these ideas early on. What do we think of her?'

'Which one is Lizzy?' Tamsyn asks.

'She's the main character,' I say. For God's sake. Why is she even here? But I know the answer. He's sitting right beside me.

'Oh, right, her. I love her! She's such a kick-arse, isn't she?'

I have to bite down my sigh. I assumed she'd spout some total nonsense for me to wholeheartedly disagree with. 'Just think how ahead of her time Jane Austen was,' I concede. 'She was going against society two hundred years ago to say that women had a raw deal.'

Tamsyn is nodding. 'She's great. She does those aristocratic characters so well. Like Anna Karenina.'

There's an embarrassed silence.

'Anna Karenina!' splutters Maggie.

'That wasn't Jane Austen,' Dot says gently. 'Leo Tolstoy wrote it.'

'Who cares who wrote it?' Tamsyn says. 'Keira was amazing.'

It takes me a second to catch on. 'Are you talking about the film?'

Maggie's mouth drops open as she reaches for her flower brooch.

But Tamsyn's not reading the room very well. 'Film, book, it's the same thing, really. It's the story that matters, right?'

'Well, no, not really!' I say. 'That's why this is a book club, Tamsyn, not a film club, or a podcast club or a whatever-you-want club!'

'Don't have a stroke, Phoebe. I know it's a book club. All I'm saying is that the medium's not as important as the story. Films bring them to millions more people than the book ever did. And to people who'd never read the book, so wouldn't know the story otherwise. Isn't that a good thing?'

Nick is nodding.

Yes, fine, she might be right. I could still punch him for agreeing with her.

Tamsyn settles down after that. Maggie doesn't say another word, even when the debate gets heated over whether Darcy is meant to be wholly unlikeable from the start. Personally, he appeals to me even at the beginning, but clearly my taste in blokes is questionable.

'Nick?' Tamsyn asks as we finish the meeting. I can tell what's coming from her wheedling tone. 'Could I have a ride home again? Please? I'll make it worth your while.' It's all I can do not to mimic her. *Meh-meh-meh-meh-meh-meh.*

'Sure, no problem,' says Nick. He can hardly keep the excitement out of his voice as she smiles her Isla Fisher smile. That smile has completely ruined *Wedding Crashers* for me.

I can tell myself a million times that this is nothing more than him being a calculating career climber, sucking up to Tamsyn because of who her father is. I *have* told myself that every day since she started here. He probably is a sucking-up calculating career climber, and that's bad enough. Though it's no secret. He told me when he first started that he'd do anything to prove himself in his job. He wasn't joking. That's not an attractive trait, but there you go. It's easy enough to overlook when he's got so much else that I love. Loved.

This isn't only about trying to get ahead at work, though, and the sooner I accept that, the better off I'll be. How many more ways do I need to be smacked in the face with the obvious? Must they actually have sex in front of me?

When the new residents start arriving later in the week, it's fair to say that their families look a lot happier about it than the men do. Aside from feeling as welcome as a cold sore here, they're having to give up whatever independence they had. They're now officially in care. That's got to sting.

Max wouldn't miss the chance to pretend he's Lord Muck. He's been in the office annoying June since before she even had her tea this morning. We've got three arrivals today, two more tomorrow and the rest over the weekend.

Max is a great one for swooping in when there's any whiff of glory to snatch. Even though it has been June who's done all the work, reviewing the applications, answering a million questions to put the families' minds at ease and sorting out the rooms.

If anything goes wrong, Max'll disappear just as fast. Which is why Nick and I are waiting with June for the first man to arrive. She needs the support.

'We missed you at book club,' Nick tells June. 'But it sounds like you had more exciting plans. When do I get to meet your Mr Bingley?'

I answer her confused look. 'We christened Callum Mr Bingley at book club.'

'He was the nice one, right?' she says. Then she smiles. 'That's all right, then. I'll see what I can arrange. Why, Nick, do you want to inspect him?'

Nick laughs. 'Of course, why else? I want to make sure his intentions are honourable.'

'I'm more of a fan of his dishonourable intentions,' she says. That makes Nick squirm.

'What's up with Sophie?' I murmur to June as the first new resident's car pulls up in the drive. Dot and Laney are talking quietly together, while Sophie stands a bit apart from them. I can't help noticing that she's not in her usual exercise top and legwarmers. She looks like she's dressed to meet the Queen later for tea. Plus, her face looks different. She's well-powdered as usual. For a second, I think it's because her deep brown eyes are fringed with mascara, but it's because she's not wearing her glasses.

'That's what we all want to know,' June whispers back. 'I've got my suspicions.'

So do I. Sophie looks like she's taken a leaf out of the *Pride and Prejudice* playbook on how to catch a husband.

The man who sat through Rosemary's photo collection appears at the door. His daughter has a grin plastered to her face, and he manages a fleeting smile before his expression settles back into one of worry. Maybe he's wondering where Rosemary is. He's safe for the moment. She's running the art group in the garden. The flowers in the borders are looking a little worse for wear now that it's the end of the summer, but she still finds enough to paint.

'Nick!' Max snaps. 'Don't let them stand there with their bags. Help them. June, will you please show Mr Campbell to his room?'

Max's order propels Nick towards the Campbells to take the suitcases.

'We've also got a few small pieces of furniture, and some books, in the car,' the woman says. 'You did say that's all right?'

'Yes, of course,' June says. 'Absolutely. We want all our residents to feel like their room is their home. It *is* their home. With the bonus of having friends under the same roof and three meals a day that they don't have to cook.' When she smiles at Mr Campbell, his smile back is real, and grateful.

'I'll be happy to help you move in,' Nick tells Mr Campbell. 'Just let me know and I can move the furniture, help you unpack, whatever you want.'

So Nick's now the manservant around here too.

But Max isn't pleased with Nick's offer. 'This is a private family moment,' Max says. 'Leave them to it. I'm sorry,' he says to the Campbells, as if Nick's not standing right there. 'He shouldn't be overstepping like that.'

'Oh… okay,' says Nick. 'I was just trying to help.' He looks like a lost little boy.

Mr Campbell picks up the smaller case.

'Nick! Help the man with his case!'

'But you said not to move them in.'

'Bring their cases up, Nick. Don't barge in on private family things.'

My heart goes out to him as he wrestles Mr Campbell's suitcases into the tiny lift and June takes them to his new room.

'See? That wasn't so bad,' I say to Laney, Dot and Sophie when Max has gone back to the office. 'I'm sure Mr Campbell will fit in well once he gets used to being here.'

Dot freezes me with her look. 'Phoebe. If we wanted to live with men, we wouldn't be here.'

Laney nods but, I can't help noticing, Sophie keeps still.

Chapter 14

We always knew this would be a hard weekend for Dad. There's the double whammy of Dad's and Mum's birthdays three days apart. That used to seem like a nice, easy stroke of luck. One weekend visit, one party and, if I asked Mum what she wanted for the house, one present for them both. She always did the planning for their party, and Dad always claimed it was over the top and unnecessary. Though I suspect he loved it because it made Mum so happy to stun and amaze their friends.

I'm not saying they didn't have fun. Only that that wasn't the point. As Ms Austen said: 'For what do we live, but to make sport for our neighbours, and laugh at them in our turn?' Although Mum never tolerated being the sport. She only liked to do the laughing.

Dad definitely doesn't want anything social this year. That might be because he'd be sad to have a party without Mum, or maybe it doesn't seem that long since she died (though it has been nearly six months). It's probably a little of both.

Will is already in the great room when I arrive. Miracle of miracles, my brother has found time to spare in his diary of ultra-important other things to do. 'Hi,' I say, giving him a quick hug. He's still in his suit, but he's undone his tie.

He's reading something on his phone. 'Hi yourself. Did you get Dad a present?'

'You can sign the card. Give me twenty-five quid. It's that beer-brewing kit he's wanted, by the way.'

He hands me £30. I'm not giving him change. Finder's fee. I take the card out of my bag. Otherwise he'll forget to sign it. Not that Dad'll think it's really from both of us. He knows Will as well as I do. 'Sign it before dinner. Did you ring him?'

'When?'

I turn on the oven and unload the cool bag. All the ingredients to cook Dad's favourite meal: chicken parmesan with Hasselback potatoes and mac and cheese. It's a cheesy carb overload, but he loves it.

'Today?' I say. 'For his birthday?'

'I'm here today,' he says. 'You did, of course, being perfect.'

'That's Ms Perfect to you.' He ignores me. 'Where is he?'

'Garden,' Will says, not looking up. What is it with people and their phones? I may as well be talking to Tamsyn. Except I know he's reading work emails. It's what he does every waking second that he's not actually at work. When Tamsyn ignores me she's probably snapchatting and putting big-eyed filters on her selfies.

The long end-of-summer days mean we can eat outside on the patio furniture. It was Mum's birthday present to Dad last year, so it's fitting.

I know Dad appreciates having us here. Otherwise he'd have to find friends to go out with, or stay home where he might get gloomy. Not that he'd ever admit anything emotional like that.

He scoops up the last bit of mac and cheese from his plate. 'That was delicious, Phoebe, thank you.' Then he stares out across the garden, scanning the borders and the grass and the pool. His expression is full of regret.

Of course, he must be sad, even with us here to distract him. Children aren't a substitute for an absent spouse. And Mum was larger than life. She'll have made a big hole to fill. Maybe he's wishing he'd had more time with her, or said some things he never got the chance to say. He probably misses the mundane nothings that we take for granted in a relationship, and even the stuff that drove him mad. I miss those things too, and I didn't live with Mum full-time. Sometimes the longing to see her again hits me randomly and has nothing to do with whatever I'm doing. Like when I'm brushing my teeth.

I reach over the table to squeeze his arm. 'What is it, Dad?'

He sighs. 'I'll need to close the bloody pool soon.'

That's what he's thinking? That draining the swimming pool is a real bugger of a job? He's not pining for the way he felt this time last year when he and Mum shared their birthday party, or wistful over how she had wrapped the ten-seater table and chair set in about a dozen rolls of birthday paper, with a giant yellow ribbon like they put on cars that get raffled off, and got so excited for him to see his gift. He's not even thinking how nice it is to have his children with him.

'Do you ever swim in it?' Will asks. They're cut from the same stiff, scratchy cloth, my brother and Dad.

'No,' Dad says, 'but your mother did. Valerie comes over sometimes to use it now. How's work?' He directs his question at Will. I tell myself that it's because Will doesn't talk to Dad as often as I do. Not that he's more interested in Will's answer than mine.

As Will tells Dad all about his latest *win* – yes, he does talk like a wanker – I'm suddenly hit by such a wave of sadness that it takes my breath away. Mum should be here. She was only fifty-eight. Everyone at the home is older than that and they've all managed to stay alive. It's not fair. Someone like Barb Stockton shouldn't be dead. She had too much to do. People relied on her. She was too important.

Let it be someone else's mum.

'Help me clear up the dishes,' I say to Will. 'We'll be back in a minute, Dad.' His birthday cake's inside. 'Will can make us tea.'

He follows me back into the house. 'I'm worried about Dad,' I say when he closes the French door. 'I can't tell how happy or unhappy he is. Can you?'

Will shrugs. 'He's just Dad. I'm sure he's okay.' He rinses the plates for the dishwasher while I get the cake out. 'Mum was the one with the feelings, not Dad. If there was something really wrong, you'd know. You talk to him all the time.'

'You should ring him more,' I say. It's a touchy subject, but when am I going to get him face-to-face again? Maybe Christmas. 'I'm not saying you should be ringing him every day, but more than now.' Then I play my trump card. 'You know Mum would want you to.'

'Oh, sod your guilt trip, Phoebe,' he says. I sometimes forget that he's no amateur in this. He grew up with Mum too. 'I don't have all the free time that you do. You should try working fourteen-hour days and then see how much you feel like chatting on the phone.'

'You're working too hard, then,' I say. 'The world won't stop spinning if you take five minutes to ring your father.'

Will shakes his head. That's when I notice he needs a haircut. I can't remember the last time he didn't have it shorn every few weeks. He's very particular about looking professional in his office. Luckily, I don't have an office. June trims my ends about every six months with the kitchen scissors. 'I'm not working hard enough, Phoebes.' His jaw clenches as he says this. 'Things aren't great at work.'

'But what about all your wins?'

'They're more of a draw, at best. It'll probably be fine. We just need one or two things to come in by the end of the year. But it means everyone's working like mad, so I'm not going to take my foot off the pedal now. Don't say anything to Dad.'

'I won't. Let me know if you need anything, okay?' Though I'm not sure that knowing how to make the perfect white sauce is as useful in banking as you might think.

He lights Dad's candles. 'Ready? I'll open the door.'

Neither of us mentions his work again. He leaves on Saturday to go straight to the office. And now, knowing why, I can't even give him a hard time about it, like I normally would. That puts me in a bad mood. On top of worrying about what Nick and Tamsyn might be up to.

I ring June. She always talks sense into me. 'Are you in the office?' I ask when she picks up.

'No, I'm in an echoey part of the flat.'

'There are no echoey parts in your flat,' I remind her. 'June, you promised.' I'm surrounded by workaholics.

'Don't have a go at me. I only came in for a few minutes to make sure the new residents are okay. The women have put "Reserved" signs on the dining tables, you know. They've hung them all over the living rooms too. The free chairs are miles away from the TVs.'

'I saw Rosemary making the signs in art club,' I admit.

'Isolating the men isn't going to help,' she goes on. 'Look at Terence. He needs to be around people more, not less. He's a menace when he's bored.'

The man actually took a sledgehammer to his bedroom wall yesterday. We thought the house was coming down. By the time Nick and June got up there, he'd broken through the plaster into the next room. He said he'd always meant to turn his bedroom into a suite. It was a good thing there wasn't anyone living next door to him.

Now June's had to move him into another room until the builders can figure out what to do about it. I think Max is crackers to let him get away with that. I'd brick up that wall and make Terence pay for it. Unfortunately, as Terence keeps reminding everyone, it's his wall, in his house, so he really can do whatever he likes. Max panics every time he threatens to cut him out of the will.

'I'm glad you rang,' she says.

'Even though I'm bollocking you for being in the office?'

'Even so. Would you like to go out with me and Callum for dinner?'

I'm sure she can hear the smile in my voice when I ask when.

'Tomorrow night. Nick is coming too. And don't say no, or that you want more notice or anything ridiculous like that. If I give you too long to get worked up about going out with Nick, you'll only be a basket case when the time comes.'

'I won't.' I would. 'There's nothing between me and Nick,' I remind her for the thousandth time. She wants me and Callum to get to know each other, and she thinks she's doing me a favour by having Nick there. Why would she let a little thing like his girlfriend – or as good as – get in the way of my love life?

'If there's nothing between you then there's no reason to be nervous,' she says. 'Nick's looking forward to it.'

'You've asked him already?'

'Uh-huh.'

'You know you're a scheming cow,' I say.

'And you love me for it. I'm so excited, Phoebe, honestly this feels like a real relationship now.'

'June, you've been seeing Callum for months. It has gone way beyond a casual hook-up. As much as you tried to make him think it was.'

She laughs. 'I mean it feels like he's really here. With me. He wants to be with me. Like a real relationship. I'm so excited for tomorrow!' she says again.

Actually, so am I. Only it's not because I'll finally get to know Callum better.

Chapter 15

My tummy could be on Great Britain's Olympic gymnastics team. Its double backflip is a gold medal winner, for sure. I'm still on the motorway when my phone rings. Nick's name lights up as it vibrates across the passenger seat. Tempting, but I'd hate for my obituary to read: Sadly, it was the first time she'd ever used her phone while driving.

'Any chance you want to meet early for a drink?' he says when I ring him back from the parking spot in front of my flat. I haven't even unbuckled my seatbelt.

My heart soars. Yes yes yes yes yes. Then I yank it back down to earth with a thump. Get over yourself, Phoebe. This is a friendly invitation, not a romantic one. 'If you want. I'm just back from my dad's.' It's nearly six already, and we're meeting June at seven-thirty.

'Do you need to go home first or…?'

No need to mention that I am home. I should go inside, throw in a load of laundry so I don't have to wear my swimsuit bottoms to work, and calmly meet him at the restaurant as planned. Or at the very least, unpack from the weekend. Dad sent me home with about half a dozen half-eaten cheeses. They should go into the fridge, not stink up my car while I go drinking with my hopeless crush. Even if it weren't for the cheeses or the swimsuit bottoms, I shouldn't drop everything just because he's asked me. I could probably learn something from June. Cool is definitely better.

'Nope, I can meet now,' I say, digging around in my bag for my hairbrush. I might have an ancient eyeliner in there too. What else are rear-view mirrors for? I'll worry later about sounding like a desperate Sally no-mates. 'I just need to ring my brother quickly. See you soon.'

My brother oozes his typical warmth and kindness when he answers my call. 'What is it?'

'Just checking in to see that you're all right.'

'I'm busy, Phoebes. We're in the middle of something.'

'You're in the office?' I'm surprised he picked up.

'I told you it's crazy right now.'

'Right, well, just making sure you're all right.'

'Thanks, Mum,' he says.

He means to be sarcastic, but that makes me smile. 'Play nice with the other boys,' I say, then hang up on him.

The pub where June and I usually go isn't far from the restaurant, though it's not till I'm walking towards the door to meet Nick that I wonder whether suggesting it was a good idea. Someone I know might start talking to me, and then I'll have to introduce Nick and there'll be three of us in the conversation when I really *really* want Nick to myself. Or the local friendly train spotter could be there. What if he gets his logbook out to show me? It does happen, and I'd be happy to talk to him any other time. Just not tonight.

'You look nice!' Nick says, jumping up from one of the barstools when he sees me.

I wouldn't normally have fancy clothes with me when I go to Dad's, but being his birthday and all, Mum was in my head as I packed. *Do try to make an effort, Phoebe! It's an occasion.* As it happened, Dad and I slobbed out all weekend without leaving the house.

The car's gearstick didn't make it easy to get my tights on, and I couldn't zip my dress till I got out, but Mum would be happy seeing me make the unusual effort tonight. She wouldn't like my ponytail, though. I did try taking it down, but having it up in a hair tie the entire weekend meant my hair had a ridge along the back that gave it a very White Cliffs of Dover effect.

'I don't usually get to see you without your chef clothes on,' he says. His eyes catch mine.

How does he want me to take that? He's still watching me. I have to say something. 'Play your cards right.' I murmur this. If he didn't mean anything, then I will absolutely pretend I didn't say it.

'I'm hoping for a lucky hand,' he practically whispers.

I'm not imagining things. Nick *is* flirting with me! He could have just laughed it off or changed the subject or pretended he's deaf in one ear. My breath hitches in my throat as I grin at him. We are, finally, truly back to the way things were before the secret supper club.

When we get our drinks and move to one of the small tables, our chat is as relaxed as it ever was. I tell him about my weekend at Dad's, and how hard it is to be sure he's really all right. I've got this gnawing fear that he's sadder than he lets on, that I'm not doing enough for him.

Nick is nodding. 'I thought Mum was a rock when my dad passed away,' he says. 'But she was broken inside. She was just too worried about me to show it. We didn't talk about that until years later.'

'That doesn't make me feel any better, you know, but thanks.'

'Sorry. I'm sure it's different with your dad. You're older than I was. Plus, he's not responsible for you. What I mean is, I was still a child. Mum wanted to keep everything normal at home. My dad passed away the week before my fourteenth birthday. Poor Mum went ahead with a party for me and my friends, even though it was in the middle of her having to make funeral arrangements too.'

'That sucks,' I say. When I reach out to squeeze his hand, it feels like the most natural thing in the world to do.

Nick turns his palm to mine and grips my fingers. At first, I'm sure my feelings can't possibly measure up to all that I've imagined for so long about this moment. But then I realise that they do. I never want to let go of his hand. I can always learn to feed myself with the other one, and trade in my car for an automatic.

'It does suck,' he says. 'But at least it wasn't a heart attack. Sorry. I mean that it wasn't sudden with Dad. He got cancer, so we had time to say goodbye. On the other hand, we had to watch him go. So, it still sucked.' He sips his pint.

'My mum seemed perfectly fine the last time I saw her. I mean, she was in hospital and had monitors on… reluctantly, but she was just as—' I almost say difficult. 'Just as strong as ever. It was hard to believe she died. It still is sometimes. I forget, you know? I'll see or hear something and forget that I can't tell Mum.'

And then there's the small matter of her still talking to me in my head.

He understands exactly what I mean, and while I'm sad that he's lost a parent, because I'd never wish that on a friend, I'm comforted that he's lost one too. Chances are his dad didn't criticise him at every turn, though, so I'm keeping further thoughts about Mum to myself.

Our fingers have unwound by the time we finish our drinks, but I don't mind now that I know Nick feels the same way I do. 'What did you get up to this weekend?' I ask him when we're nearly ready to go meet June and Callum.

I thought a lot about that question later. Did I want to be hit with a reality check? Because I must have known, or at least suspected, the answer. I should have been braced for it, boarded up and waiting for Hurricane Tamsyn to make landfall.

His eyes slide away from mine. That's most unlike him. 'Just some errands and stuff, nothing much,' he mumbles. 'It was a quiet one.'

He was with her.

June is already at the table when we arrive, but Callum is late. She looks nervy. 'He's just making a big entrance,' I tell her.

She laughs, but the worry is still there underneath. I hadn't thought about Callum not showing up tonight. He'd better not be playing games with her. It has taken long enough for her to trust that he won't do a runner. If he dares break her heart now, I will kill him.

Besides, I've had enough game-playing tonight. I glance again at Nick. The worst part might be the disappointment in him. I really, *really* didn't think he was a player. Yet he couldn't even look at me while he evaded my question. In all the months we've been friends, he's never been dishonest. At least I don't think he has.

I push those thoughts aside. It's about June now.

'Are you worried?' I murmur to her as Nick gives the waiter his drink order.

'Uh-huh.' She bouffs up her curls. She's smiling, though, so she doesn't want to bring up any concerns in front of Nick.

He leans into the table. 'All right, June, before he gets here, let's dish on Callum.'

'Dish?' I say. 'While it's just us girls, you mean?'

He doesn't have to be so damn amusing.

As June goes into forensic detail about their relationship so far, I watch Nick absorb it all. If he's not fascinated, then he's doing an excellent acting job. His face is alive as June talks. His dark eyes dance, his smile is quick and warm and even his too-thick eyebrows are cute when they bounce up and down. Which just makes me feel worse.

'He sounds like the perfect man.' Nick raises his beer bottle. 'Seriously, June, he does, and he sounds perfect for you too. I haven't known you that long, but I feel like I do know you a bit.' He straightens up. 'He'd better turn up soon or he'll have to answer to me.'

June and I both snort at the thought of Nick fighting. He's more likely to hug a person to death. 'Luckily he's off the hook. See for yourself,' she says, looking over our shoulders. Her grin couldn't get any bigger. 'Here he is.'

'I'm so sorry I'm late,' says Callum, hauling June from her chair. Then he envelops her in his arms and they kiss with swoon-making passion. Oh my. To be kissed like that.

His hair is down tonight, and I was right, it falls in shiny waves just to his shoulders. With the tan, he looks even more like a surfer than he does when it's up in a bun. 'Phoebe, hi!' He pulls me into a bear hug. 'It's great to see you. And you're Nick? I've heard a lot about you. The man of many talents.' He sticks out his hand. 'June says the home wouldn't run without you.'

Nick shrugs. 'It'd just be weedier, that's all.'

June can't keep her eyes off Callum as he talks to us. She practically shoots off sparks every time he touches her. But she's not saying much, which isn't like her. Normally I can barely shut her up. Nerves, maybe, about him being with us.

She's practically mute all the way through dinner. And June's not really June if she's not wading in with her opinions. She might be measured at work, but out in the wild she usually likes to let loose.

'Where'd you study?' Callum asks Nick when he explains his job.

'Brunel.' He's talking into his beer bottle.

When Nick doesn't elaborate, Callum shakes his head. 'Where's that?'

183

'In London. Near London. Uxbridge. What about you? Where'd you go?'

'Warwick,' says Callum. 'The coursework was intense but aside from that, I loved being there. It's so much better than the real world, isn't it?'

He's looking at me. 'I didn't go to uni, so I'll take your word for it.'

'You went to catering college, though,' June says. 'It's kind of the same thing. Callum, Phoebe is the most amazing chef.'

She doesn't want me to feel left out. No matter how many times I've told her I wasn't interested in university – about a million – she never quite believes me. I guess it's hard not to judge someone else by what you want for yourself.

It's really true, though. Even Mum at her judgey worst couldn't make me wish I'd gone. I don't feel like I've missed out. I would have missed out on the bistro if I'd gone to uni.

But that's a serious answer for a friendly Sunday night meal, so instead I say, 'Except I didn't have to spend three years in classes and the library, and I was already making a living while you were searching down the back of the sofa cushions for beer money.'

June raises her wine glass to mine. 'You always were the smart one.'

Nick smiles at me too. 'Cheers to the road less travelled.'

It's tempting to be excited by this small attention. Everything inside me craves it. But I know it's not real. Yes, at this very moment I'm having a great time, and Nick might even be thinking the same thing. But as soon as he goes home tonight, he'll be back in the real world where he's seeing Tamsyn. And I'll be… what? Tragically lusting after him. I wish hearts were as easy to change as minds are.

Nick's mood weirdly shifts when June announces, 'Callum owns a yurt company!'

'… Yurts?' Nick says.

'You know, tents,' June says.

'Thanks, I know what a yurt is.'

Callum takes a last swig of his beer. 'Yeah, we set them up for festivals and weddings, any event really. And it's my parents' business, not mine,' he gently chides June. 'I'm the day-to-day manager. I usually get to swing tickets to the festivals. It's important to be on-site, you know.' He laughs.

But Nick's not laughing. Maybe he hates glamping. He gets up and feels his jeans pocket, where I can see the outline of his phone. ''Scuse me. Just need the… I'll be right back.'

Callum gets up too. 'Relax,' he says, laughing at Nick's surprised look, 'I'm not going in with you.' He takes his vape from his pocket. 'I swapped one bad habit for another. Do you mind?' he asks June. 'I'll be quick.'

'No, go ahead, and take your time. Phoebe and I want to talk about you anyway.'

He gives her a devastating smile.

'Is he not amazing?' she whispers when he's barely left the table. 'This is it, Phoebe, the real thing. I can't even start to explain how it feels.' She lets out a huge sigh.

'He's really nice,' I say carefully. 'Though is everything okay? You do seem a lot quieter than usual tonight.'

'Of course everything is okay. It's perfect.'

'Are you just nervous? It seems like you're holding back or something.'

'Not at all.' There's an edge to her voice now.

But she definitely is. Maybe this isn't the right time to say anything, but I've started. 'I've never seen you so demure.'

'Demure? You've been reading too much Jane Austen.' She laughs.

'Yeah, probably. As long as you're being completely yourself with him.'

'What do you mean by that? Who else would I be?'

'You tell me. You're acting different. It's noticeable. I wouldn't want you not to be yourself, that's all. He will like you for you.' Even though I'm not a hundred per cent sure this is true. She's fought every instinct to be herself since they started going out. What if he only likes the false June?

'So, I've tricked him into liking me.' She crosses her arms. 'That's what you're saying.'

This is going downhill. 'I've only said what you already know: you've been playing games so far, but you don't need to.'

'Stop it, Phoebe. Just stop. I'm happy, that's all. If I'm letting Callum talk more than me, it's because you already know *me*. You've heard all my nonsense.'

'Too many times to count.' When I smile, to my relief, she returns it. I think we're okay.

Then I notice Nick and Callum. 'Look, they're chatting by the door,' I tell June. 'That's good. I'm sorry, I didn't mean to upset you. Callum is really nice.'

We get the bill when they return. That's when June suggests the pub for one more.

Nick and I are nodding, but Callum says, 'Ah, sorry, you go ahead. I'll need to be up stupidly early tomorrow for work. I'm sorry, June, is that okay?'

'Of course it is!' she says with false cheer. 'You get your beauty sleep. Talk to you tomorrow?'

'Definitely.'

He gives her another scorcher of a kiss and sends the three of us off to our local to talk about him. I really do feel bad for what I said before. That's probably why I spend the whole time saying how perfect they are together, until the barman calls last orders.

MICHELE GORMAN

Chapter 16

There's been a vague weirdness between June and I ever since dinner last week. She claims we're fine, that she's just extra busy getting the new residents settled in. But I know freezer burn when I feel it. Also, we've fallen out before, as lifelong friends will. The symptoms are familiar.

She has to talk to you some time, Mum would advise. *So, pester her until she does. Eventually she'll get tired of putting you off.* That was always her approach. Barb Stockton never met a hurdle she couldn't leap over, climb under or bash through. This was the woman who started her own building company. She wasn't even a builder herself. Dad was involved too, but he would have kept working for himself if it wasn't for Mum. It was very much her business, and she was a master at wearing a person down. That's why Dad usually gave in. It's why we all did. Mum is right again.

But I'm too much of a coward to bring it up with June. I had to go and open my mouth about her not being herself. That wasn't the time, right in the middle of her telling me how much in love she was. How would I have felt in her shoes, if I'd just handed her that precious, amazing, wondrous fact and she'd told me I'd lured my boyfriend under false pretences? Poor show, Phoebe, poor show. And after she'd gone out of her way to invite Nick too. She'd done that just for me.

I can't believe I'm saying this, but it's a relief when June leaves for the day. I'm not quite tiptoeing around her, but I haven't gone looking for her, either. Her office hours are regular, where mine are early till late, with long breaks between meals. It means around nine hours of actual work for me, though I don't always go home on my time off. Especially for the lull between breakfast and lunch. It hardly seems worth the bother when I'll only have to come back in a few hours.

Plus, the women need me right now. Complaining about the new residents to June probably feels too official, so I'm the unofficial peacekeeper. I wear my blue hat reluctantly, but I can't leave my friends to fend for themselves. It's a big disruption to suddenly have all these men underfoot. They're not coping brilliantly so far.

'I thought we left all this behind in school,' I murmur to Nick as we watch Sophie, Dot and Laney lead the other women into the dining room. Those three have always been close, but since the men arrived, they've moved into thick-as-thieves territory. They're up to something.

'Cliques are cliques,' Nick says. 'Everyone wants to belong. I get that. Weren't you in a clique?'

'It was always just me and June. I don't think that counts as a clique.' As I say this, a little jab of guilt gets me right in the chest. 'What were your friends like?'

'Well, you met them,' he says quietly. His usually gorgeous lips thin into a tight line.

He's thinking about me 'meeting' Seth. Well done for reminding him.

Then I remember that I'm not the only one at fault around here. 'Maybe neither of us should be judged by the company we keep.'

He looks like he's about to say something but stops himself.

As the women go to their usual tables, the penny starts to drop around the room. Dot marches towards us. 'What's happening here?' She points at the 'Reserved' signs I've laid out in front of a chair at each table.

As it happens, they're the signs they made to keep the men segregated at mealtimes. 'Feel free to spread yourselves around the tables tonight. Just leave the reserved seats free.'

'For *whom* are they reserved?' she asks. She's not about to let a little anger ruin her grammar. 'We have teams already.'

I laugh at that. 'Since when have you ever played Scrabble in teams?! Just leave the reserved places free, please.'

She goes back to report to the others. They must know what's coming. Or *whom*.

The men arrive right on time, with Terence at the lead and Tamsyn hanging off his arm. I can barely get her to set foot in the dining room to work, yet here she is strutting in with her grandfather like she's going down the red carpet. 'Where do you want to sit, Grandad? Here's a nice chair, right here.'

'And what makes it so nice, hmm?' he snaps. 'Does it compliment me on my arse when I sit down?'

Tamsyn titters with laughter. 'Oh, Grandad, you are funny!'

'God hates a bootlicker,' he tells her. 'So just leave off, will you? You're worse than your father. I've got a good mind to leave everything to the cat's home when I go, so don't push me.'

Tamsyn blanches.

Believe it or not, Terence actually seems to be lightening up. At least when he's around the new residents rather than his family. We've got six men altogether now, but June could only convince three of them to come to Scrabble night. One of them is Mr Campbell, the one who sat through all of Rosemary's photos.

'Oh, good, come in, gents,' I say. 'Welcome. Please find any reserved seat you like.'

'Not this table,' Dot tells Terence as he goes to sit between Laney and Sophie. Judy is their usual fourth, but replacing the reigning Scrabble champion isn't what's got Dot so cross. She might be tiny compared to Terence's tall frame, but she looks like she'd bite his head off if she could reach.

'Oh, come on, don't be such a spoilsport, Dot. Afraid I'll beat you?'

'I am not.' Dot sits in the chair opposite and glares at him. 'You may frighten the others, but I'm not intimidated by you, Terence Greene. Far from it.'

I'm afraid that Dot's show of resistance could whip up everyone else. 'Hey, Dot?' I call over. 'Can I ask your advice about something in the kitchen? I think the elderflower cordial might be too watery. Come see?'

As soon as the kitchen door swings shut behind us I say, 'What is wrong with you, Dot? It's like you hate Terence or something.'

She crosses her arms. 'I do hate him.'

'But why? Was it something to do with Mrs Greene?' I know how I'd react if someone hurt June. 'Did he cheat on her, or treat her badly?'

Dot sighs. 'I'd rather not talk about that if you don't mind.'

That's her schoolteacher tone. 'I do mind, though, Dot, because I don't want you to be upset. Isn't there anything I can do?'

'Are you able to rewind time by sixty years? No? I didn't think so. Then there's nothing anyone can do. Thank you.' She takes a swig of the cordial. 'That tastes fine.'

Back in the dining room, Laney and Sophie are taking the table reassignments better than Dot. Maybe a little too well, in Sophie's case. She's been to the hairdresser's, and her dramatic dark eye make-up is especially startling in her pale, powdered face. She reminds me of something – not an owl this time – between her pallor and the black dress that's hugging her stout frame.

That's it! Mum once got a mime for Will's birthday party. A plain old clown wasn't sophisticated enough, she thought. He'd made some of the kids cry with fright.

Sophie could be stuck in a glass box, silently trying to get out.

Dot notices. 'What are you all dressed up for?'

'Can't a person want to look nice?' Sophie gives Terence a shy smile.

'Not bad,' he says.

You'd think he'd crowned her Miss Universe with the way she's beaming.

Meanwhile, Laney's been staring at Sophie. 'I think you look nicer when you're normal.'

Come to think of it, aside from Zumba class, I haven't seen Sophie in legwarmers since the new residents got here. She must disappear upstairs straight after exercise to change.

'Where are your glasses?' Laney asks, watching Sophie squint as she pulls the board as close to herself as she can.

'Oh, I don't really need them.' Even the powder can't keep her blush from showing.

Her nose is nearly touching her tiles.

'This is too painful to watch,' Dot murmurs as she lifts the golden chain over her head. 'For God's sake, just use my glasses.'

Things settle down as the games get going. Normally I'd play too, but with the new additions, all the tables are full this week. Which is why it's absurd that Tamsyn has her chair jammed up next to Nick's. As if Scrabble is meant to be some kind of spectator sport.

'Phones aren't allowed, Tamsyn,' I tell her.

'But I'm not playing,' she says. Proving my point that she's got no business sitting there.

'No phones at the table. That's the rule.'

'Fine.' She makes a big show of putting it away. 'Actually, this is boring. I'm off anyway.' She starts for the door. 'Nick? Don't forget tomorrow.'

'What's tomorrow?' I ask him as he studies his tiles. I probably shouldn't, when knowing the truth only makes me feel bad. Sad. Mad.

'I don't know, Thursday?'

He can see that I'm not about to be put off that easily. 'She needs a ride to work, that's all,' he finally admits.

The rest of the table is watching Nick now too. 'You're blushing,' says Shirley.

'She fancies him,' her sister adds.

'That's because he's irresistible!'

Nick laughs. 'What can I say?' Then he shakes his head. 'Nah, really, it's not like that.' He stares at me. 'It's not.'

What is it like, then, Nick? I want to ask him. I know what it looks like from here.

It's not bad enough that he's giving her rides home at night. Now he's going to get her in the morning too? Why can't she just get a ride from her father, when he's got to leave for work anyway?

Because maybe she's not at her parents' in the morning, and that means Nick isn't going anywhere to get her. Maybe they're leaving from the same place.

No. I cannot let myself jump to conclusions like this. I'm liable to drive myself mad.

'Well done, Dot!' Laney cries. The games go on as if I'm not in the midst of a crisis of confidence. 'And a double word!'

Dot is pleased with herself as I read her word. 'Zinc. Well done.'

'Thank you. That's thirty.' She glares at Terence.

He studies his tiles. 'Thanks, Dot, I'll take that.' He lays i-t-e at the end of her word. 'Eighteen for me. Still beating you, I believe.'

'Only by three points.'

At least she's speaking to him.

But when it comes around to his turn again, I wish she wasn't.

'What's pen-il-ee?' Laney pronounces a long 'e' at the end.

'You are a vile man!' Dot cries. 'Leave it to you to lower the tone.' She looks like she's about to flip the board. That's never happened in the history of games night, and things can get heated here when they start going for the triple-word spaces.

'It's penile,' Sophie murmurs to Laney.

Terence feigns surprise. 'I don't know why you're getting so upset. It's not "bollocks" or "fucker". Not that I have a "k", anyway. Dot, you're not usually such a prude.'

'How do you know what I am?! Don't pretend to know me, Terence.'

He shrugs. 'Do you see another one I could make with those letters?'

She glances at the board. 'What's wrong with senile, right there?'

'Nothing, except that it's a lower score. I'm fine with my word, thanks.'

'You're vile,' she says again.

'Maybe so, but I'm still ahead of you.' When Terence smiles, Dot turns away.

It's after nine when I ring my brother. Hopefully he's not still in his office. I'm one to talk. I'm just coming home from work myself, and I'm not even getting paid for it. Sometimes I wonder if I'm doing my twenties right. Other people we know have big groups of friends that they're out with all the time. I never had time when I was at the bistro. Chefs work nutty hours. I didn't miss it, either, with June always there. Now I do question whether it's completely healthy that the vast majority of my friends are old enough to ride the buses for free.

I'm not really expecting Will to pick up. He claims he doesn't screen calls, but I've seen him do it. It's stupid that I feel honoured when he answers. It's just my pillocky brother, not Prince Harry.

'I'm just checking in,' I tell him.

'You mean checking up. Worried about me?' But he laughs. 'Well, you should be. I've lost my job.'

'Oh, no, Will, I'm sorry!' He may be a pillock, but nobody deserves that awful feeling. 'Is there anything I can do?'

'Will you go to the office and break my boss's nose?'

'I'll bring my rolling pin if you want,' I say.

'You're deadly with that thing.' It has been almost twenty years but he still hasn't forgiven me for sending him to A&E at Christmas. Mum and Dad gave me my very first rolling pin when I was eight or so. It was acid green with my name in big purply letters along the roller. I'd never loved anything as much as I did that rolling pin. I didn't let it out of my sight. I even slept with it. The only time I had to leave it behind was when I used the bathroom. That's when Will took it. As I was wrestling him to get it back, I *might* have swung it at his face.

'Phoebes, I need you,' he says.

Finally, he admits it. My heart goes out to him. Once the shock of being out of a job wears off, the Why Mes are going to get him. Those are the worst.

'I need you to smooth things over with Dad,' he goes on. 'He didn't take it well when I told him.'

'But you're the one who got sacked, not him.'

'Thanks for that. He doesn't understand that it's nothing I did wrong. And I wasn't sacked, I was made redundant. It's different. It's just a numbers game in banking. I wasn't the only one. It's LIFO.'

'What-o?'

'Last in, first out. I knew I shouldn't have switched jobs last year. But I wanted to trade up. No risk, no reward.' A little of my sympathy dies with every word he utters. He's better off out of banking if it makes him talk like that all the time.

'Make him understand, will you?' Will asks. 'I don't need him judging me on top of everything else.'

'Oh, poor baby. I'm sorry Dad is judging you, probably for the first time in your life. Try being me.'

'Great, you'll talk to him, then?' My sarcasm is completely lost on him.

Of course, I'll help smooth things over with Dad. I know how it feels.

Chapter 17

June isn't crying yet, but I can tell she's thinking about it. And at work too. This is really serious. 'I'm so sorry,' I tell her again. I don't know what else to say. We've been over the details with a focus that would make a murder enquiry look haphazard.

It started first thing this morning when I burst into her office to blurt out how sorry I was about what I'd said at dinner the other night.

Actually, no, technically it started last night with Dad's phone call.

'Phoebe, this is your father ringing.'

'Hi, Dad, I was going to ring you. You've heard about Will's job?'

'He told me. Bloody stupid.'

'You don't mean Will, right? Because this doesn't sound like it's his fault. He said it's LIFO. Go easy on him, Dad, can't you? You don't know what it's like to lose your job. Believe me, it's the worst. When the bistro closed down it really knocked me.' I do feel for Will. I didn't tell my parents about the restaurant fire until I'd found another job. I couldn't face them – especially Mum – using it as another excuse to get me to *do something with my life*.

'It's hardly the same thing,' Dad said. 'He's not a lunch lady. Jobs like his aren't easy to find.'

'As it happens, Dad, I'm not a lunch lady either.' That's what Mum used to call me sometimes. She claimed it was to motivate me to do better. You can imagine how well that worked. 'That's mean, by the way. Really, Dad, you know I ran the whole restaurant. Like I run it now at the home. Have a little respect.'

'I'm not being mean, darling. I just mean that he's a specialist in complex financial instruments, not lasagne.'

'Oh, right, as long as you're not being mean. Why don't you say what you really think about my career, Dad?' He's no better than Max, thinking that I just heat up ready meals.

'I thought we were talking about your brother, Phoebe, not you?' Dad said.

'Well, seeing as you've belittled my job, again, we're talking about both.'

Dad did apologise, but I was still stinging from the call when I rang June. The conversation with my father had been the perfect eye-opener of how I'd probably made her feel at dinner. It was time to say sorry.

But she didn't answer. I hoped she was out with Callum, being in love and not ignoring me.

'Where were you when I rang last night?' I'd asked when I got into work this morning. I assumed I'd hear good news.

'I was screening,' she admitted. 'Not just you. I didn't want to talk to anyone. Except Callum, and he wasn't ringing.'

That's why we've been huddled in the office for the last half-hour. Callum's not returning June's calls.

'He didn't ring the day after dinner, but he did say he'd have loads of work on, so I didn't think anything of it. He sent me a text that night. But then I didn't hear from him for a few days after that, so I rang him. I only meant to do it once, but then I wondered if he was out of phone reception. You know how dodgy phones can be at festivals with everyone clogging up the signals. I thought he might be out in a field somewhere not even knowing that I'd rung.'

'How many calls, June?'

She wouldn't meet my eyes. Then she sighed. 'Oh, five or six. The first day.'

'No, June.'

'More after that, plus messages. Every time he'd ring me back I ended up phoning multiple times before he rang me again. I got crazy. I was just so relieved every time he rang.' She puts her head into her hands. 'He thinks I'm a stalker. Now he's not even picking up.'

There were tears in her eyes. 'You were right. He didn't like who I really am.'

'No, June!' God how I wished I'd never said anything. Now she's blaming herself. 'You did what any normal person would. It's not unusual to want to talk to your boyfriend. There shouldn't be rules about how many times you talk to each other or who calls who. If he's being weird about that, then he's got the problem, not you. He should be ringing you back! In fact, I'd be furious with him if I were you.'

Our conversation carried on like this, with me saying what every good friend would. It's not you, it's him, the wanker.

I'll completely backpedal on everything if he turns up here tomorrow with flowers saying he's been in hospital or his phone was nicked.

'You didn't imagine anything, June. He definitely did like you.'

'Maybe in the past tense,' she said. 'Then what happened?'

'I have no idea. I'm so sorry.'

She went to the office door, closed and locked it. Then she fell into my arms and sobbed her eyes out.

I'd like to kill that bloke for making her so miserable. How dare he, after chasing her for months and months and acting so loved up. One little stalker episode and he runs away? The spineless worm.

'Art class!' Rosemary knocks on the office door just as June's touching up her make-up. She should be able to get away with saying she's got allergies. September is known for it around here.

'Are you okay to go?' I ask her. 'I've got to get the pies in, but I could get Terence started if you like.'

She shakes her head. 'Keeping busy is good. Will you stay with us, though, just at the start? I might need backup.'

I push up the sleeves of my chef's whites. 'I'm right behind you.'

It's safe to say that the women aren't welcoming Terence into their home with open arms. In Dot's case, it's more like a closed fist. And she's in art class today too.

Nick carries all the easels and chairs to the garden. The leaves aren't turning yet, though the borders are looking pretty bare. 'What are you working on today?' he asks Rosemary.

'I thought we'd try trees,' she says. 'I had an idea about capturing them in all seasons. Maybe the same tree throughout the year on the same canvas, like a time-lapse.' She turns to Nick. 'You're not planning to cut any of them down, right? Because it'd be a shame if someone's subject disappears halfway through the study.'

Nick promises not to make any drastic changes to the scenery.

Terence is ambling across the lawn towards us. 'Where do you want me for this?'

'How about Wales?' Dot mumbles. She's got her own paint box, a present from her son last Christmas. He also gave her a beret, but she doesn't wear that.

'Anywhere you like, Terence,' Rosemary says. 'The idea is to choose a single tree.'

There are only five in the class today. Sophie claims she's not got an artistic bone in her body, so she never comes. And Laney only turns up if someone happens to see her just before. Sisters Ruth and Shirley are here, though. They might prefer to work in yarn, but they like to keep their hand in with most arts and crafts.

Everyone starts off to find their subject, as Rosemary calls it. Ruth and Shirley pick the same white birch, but they sit on opposite sides of it. They like to have different perspectives, but not *too* different. That's probably why they married brothers.

Rosemary heads straight for the cedar trees on the border with Terence's cottage.

And Terence follows Dot. 'Find your own tree!' she shouts at him.

'I am finding my own.'

'I mean away from me.'

'I'm not *near* you.' He continues to trot after her. He should get *some* credit. He is trying to be friendly. He's just picked the wrong person to try it on.

'Thanks, Phoebe, I'm okay now,' June tells me when I start to follow her back to her office. 'I need to get some work done.'

'All right, but I'm going to check in on you in a bit. Fair warning, you're going to get sick of the sight of me.'

She smiles a wobbly smile. 'That's what friends are for.'

Tears prick my eyes as I go back to my kitchen. My heart is breaking for June. To see that disappointment in her face. I know how she's feeling. It's so hard to get over the realisation that you've so completely messed everything up, and all the blame that goes with it. How do you forgive yourself for making such a stupid mistake? Why are we all so good at carrying this guilt around with us?

Nick wanders in. 'Want a tea?' he asks, reaching around me for the kettle. His citrusy cologne smells better to me than any baking cake ever could. 'I can't wake up today.'

'I didn't sleep well, either,' I tell him. I wonder what kept him up. Never mind. Don't want to know.

My heart leaps into my throat when he grabs my hands. 'We need some exercise to get the blood moving. Come on. Jumping jacks.' He starts flailing his arms and his legs as if they aren't attached to the same body.

False alarm, I tell my hope. He's not being romantic. He's just being silly Nick. 'I am not exercising with you. Especially not like that. Do you need me to ring 999?'

He laughs. 'Zumba, then. Come on, feel the rhythm.' He starts blasting some hoo-hoo-hoo drummy noise from his phone. 'If you won't come to the Zumba—' and I never do '—then the Zumba will come to you.' His arms swing about as he marches in place. 'You can do it.' He starts wriggling his hips and chest-pumping to the beat of the drum.

'I beg you, please stop doing that in my kitchen.'

'Turning you on?' He laughs.

'I can hardly control myself…'

His strutting falters as he catches my eye.

I blush. 'Maybe we'll just have a tea instead,' he says, turning off the music. 'Hey, Phoebe?'

Something about the way he says my name gets my attention.

'Do you want to get another drink with me some time?'

My heart doesn't seem able to accept what my brain knows. Or else it wouldn't be pounding right now at the thought of a date with Nick. Who is *not* in a position to date, I remind myself. He might not think it's a big deal to be with two women at once, but I do have some pride. Why should I have to share while he gets everything he wants?

I'm saved from having to go into that, though, because just then, Tamsyn appears in the kitchen.

'Nick, here.' She hands him his sweatshirt. It's the black one that makes his eyes go dark as wet coal. 'You left it at the house.'

I don't know how much more of this roller coaster I can take. If I were at Alton Towers, I'd have already been sick.

Nick looks embarrassed. As he should. He's been at Tamsyn's house. Taking his sweatshirt off. Amongst other things, probably. Now I feel as if I've just done a thousand jumping jacks.

'Thanks,' he mumbles.

'I'm leaving now, Phoebe,' she says. I could say no, but we both know I'm not really her boss. Besides, I want her and her Nick-stripping ways out of my sight.

'You and Tamsyn are close,' I say to Nick when she's left. I mean for it to come out exactly as accusatory as it sounds. 'If you're leaving clothes at her house.' I couldn't feel any more awful. We may as well get everything out in the open and make it official.

'I'm not leaving clothes at her house,' he says.

'Nick, come on. You left your sweatshirt. That's why she's just handed it back to you.' He can't honestly try to deny that. 'Why don't you admit that you're together?' I almost say that it makes no difference to me, but those words stick in my throat.

'Phoebe, it's a little complicated, but please believe me when I say that we're not. Do you think that we're sleeping together? Because we are not.' His eyes are begging me to drop it. I'd love to, if it meant I could stop imagining them together.

'Fine,' I tell him. 'It's none of my business anyway. You can do what you want.'

'I'm not, though.'

'You're not what?'

'Doing what I want,' he says. 'I want to have a drink with you.'

And I want Tamsyn not to be bringing Nick's cast-off-in-a-moment-of-passion clothes to work. We may as well both be disappointed. 'I'm sure you could find plenty of people to have drinks with you,' I say. Miniscule as it is, I do have some pride left. I'm sure that'll make me feel better about taking the high road. Maybe once this searing sadness wears off. 'There's always Tamsyn.'

'I thought you knew me better than this, Phoebe.'

'I think I do, Nick.'

He leaves without making his tea.

Let's say, for the sake of argument, that I do believe Nick and Tamsyn aren't boyfriend and girlfriend, and that they're not actually sleeping together (since that's the technicality that Nick seems to be claiming). Now imagine that I do go out with him. We'll have an amazing time. I know that much. Which will just make me like him more, and I'll want to see him again, and again, until it feels like we're a couple. Only we won't be a couple, because all the while that I delude myself into thinking that he's mine, Tamsyn will be there too, maybe thinking the same thing.

I might be happy in the short term but, ultimately, I'm going to get hurt. I need to keep telling myself that, because right now my head is no match for my heart.

I've just put the pies in to bake for lunch when I hear the women's raised voices in the dining room. 'You did it on purpose!' Dot is shouting when I kick open the kitchen door to see what's happening. 'We're not stupid.'

The women are all lined up against Terence, holding their canvases in front of them like shields.

'I can't help it if you've got an overactive imagination,' Terence says. 'It's a tree.'

'It's *not* a tree. It's a… phallus. Phoebe, isn't it?'

Leave it to Terence to offend the women with a painted willy. I suppose on the plus side, at least it's not the real thing. 'Let me see.'

Well, even though it's green and leafy, there is definitely a resemblance.

'You women have dirty minds,' he says. 'That's not my problem.' Then he smiles wickedly. 'I'll look forward to painting my tree through the seasons, especially when it gets its growth surge in spring.'

'Disgusting,' Dot announces. That's starting to sound like Terence's new nickname.

I guess you could say that, given the iced buns we served at the open house, this is really just tit for todger.

Maggie is at book club again this week. It's going to take us all some time to get used to seeing her. She's as stoic as usual, though she doesn't blank Sophie when she dares to smile at her. Laney is the only one who doesn't seem to notice that Maggie is scary. You'd think they were best mates, which is so odd because of all the people you wouldn't expect Maggie to tolerate, Laney has to be near the top of the list. Not because there's anything wrong with Laney. She's warm and friendly, light-hearted and funny and, well, that's the opposite of Maggie.

June's come too, although I'm not so sure that's a good idea after Dot called Callum Mr Bingley last time. If they tease her about him tonight, she might crumble. As it is, she has had to claim week-long allergies to explain her red puffy eyes. 'You both get them?' Nick asks us.

'Why, are my eyes red?' I look at June, who shakes her head.

'In the spring,' he says. 'You suffered terribly, don't you remember?'

'Oh, yeah…' I say. I did claim pollen attacks after messing things up with Nick over Seth. 'Yes, same thing.'

I'm grateful to see the tiny smile that raises in June. I've gone back and forth all day about whether I should just ring Callum myself. He wouldn't recognise my number and might pick up. I could even ring his business. Then he'd definitely get on the phone and I could explain that June's not really crazy. My head says it can't do any harm at this point. He's not talking to her anyway. Though my gut tells me there's still the tiniest chance that he'll eventually come around on his own if I don't meddle.

I want to do something, but it has got to be the right thing. I feel so helpless watching her suffer like this.

'I'd like to raise a point before we start, please,' Sophie says. 'What about letting men into book club?'

All the women say no at once.

'Don't bite my head off, I was only asking,' she says. 'I can't believe you're so against the men being here. It's like you *want* to live in a nunnery.'

Max doesn't seem to understand the women's feelings any more than Sophie does. He's got even more adverts out around Ipswich.

Dot glares at Sophie over her glasses. 'We're here because we want to be in a women's home. What's so strange about that? There are plenty of mixed options for people who want to live with men.'

I hope Dot's not suggesting that option to Sophie. They may argue over Sophie's meal dictates, but they've never seriously fallen out before.

'We don't want to live with men, Sophie,' Dot goes on. 'That means we don't want them in our book club, either.'

'We have let Nick in,' Laney says.

'He's different,' says Dot.

'You mean I'm not really a man,' he adds. 'No, it's okay. I don't mind at all.'

Dot smiles. 'We like you, Nick. Unlike the male residents who've been foisted upon us. Sophie, it would get too disruptive if we open up the group. Besides, the books we read are more for women.' She glances again at Nick.

'No offence taken,' he says.

'Who wants to allow men in?' Sophie asks. Predictably, she's the only one who raises her hand.

'You're overruled,' says Dot. 'No men. Except Nick.'

'Who's not really a man,' Nick adds.

It's a relief when we start talking about the book. We're up to the part where Mr Collins, the boot-licking clergyman who's looking for a fitting wife, visits the Bennetts. Then, to Lizzy's dismay, her best friend, poor Charlotte, accepts his proposal.

Dot reads aloud from her tattered copy: '"I am not romantic, you know; I never was. I ask only a comfortable home; and considering Mr. Collins's character, connections, and situation in life, I am convinced that my chance of happiness with him is as fair as most people can boast on entering the marriage state."'

'I don't think I could have done it,' I say. 'I hate that she's sold out for money. She's not in love.'

'You can understand it, though,' says Nick. 'She can't survive on her principles. Charlotte needs money to live and stay respectable. I'd probably do the same thing in her shoes.'

June and I trade glances – because isn't that what he's doing anyway? Between going out with Tamsyn and the way he kisses up to Terence and Max, he's setting himself up pretty well.

'But what if they fall in love later?' Laney asks. 'Then it won't matter how they got together in the first place. Love can grow with time, can't it? I think it can.'

'Esteem can grow,' Maggie says, startling us. It's as if the armchair has just spoken. 'A kind of love can grow. But not romantic love.'

'Why do you say that?' Laney asks. 'People can fall in love after the fact. Sometimes friends do.'

But Maggie seems definite on the subject. 'You mean the feeling of being in love? That's only lust. "Love looks not with the eyes, but with the mind; And therefore is winged Cupid painted blind."'

'Who said that?' June asks.

'Shakespeare,' answers Dot. '"Who ever loved that loved not at first sight?"'

'Shakespeare again?' I say.

Maggie nods.

'I don't think Jane Austen wanted the reader to think that Charlotte would be truly happy with Mr Collins, either,' says Dot. 'She had quite a lot to say about it. "Nothing can compare to the misery of being bound *without* Love, bound to one, & preferring another. *That* is a Punishment which you do *not* deserve."'

Maggie's eyes appraise Dot. 'From her letters. You're a scholar,' she says. 'She had a lot of advice about marrying for love, didn't she? "I am perfectly convinced that your present feelings, supposing you were to marry *now*, would be sufficient for his happiness; but when I think how very, very far from them you are..." excuse me, I mean "how very far it is from *Now*, & take... and take everything that *may be*... what may be..." No... "everything that *may be*, into consideration, I dare say... I dare *not* say 'determine to accept him.' The risk... the risk..."'

She looks around the room, horrified. 'Excuse me. I'm sorry.'

'Where are you going?' Laney asks.

'I'm sorry,' she says again as she rushes for the door.

'What just happened?' Nick asks.

'I think she got embarrassed about forgetting the lines,' I say.

That gets a snort from Laney. 'I don't know where I am half the time. If I let that bother me, I'd never leave my room.'

Chapter 18

June and I wait till book club is finished to go up to Maggie. She was obviously upset to have fled the scene like that, and we can't let her backslide into hermithood again. Not that she wants us pestering her in her room, either. But we've got to at least try, for her sake and – selfishly, I'll admit – for mine. I'm still holding on to a shred of hope that eventually she'll eat with everyone else and save me the daily deliveries.

Most of all, though, we want to make sure she's okay.

'Go away,' she says when we knock. 'I don't want to talk to anyone.'

'Should we go?' I ask June.

'It's my responsibility to make sure she's okay. If she's in there topping herself, Max won't be pleased.'

'He wouldn't like to lose the income,' I say.

'You don't have to stay, though.'

'I'm not leaving you.'

'Maggie, I'm sorry,' June calls through the door, 'but I need to talk to you. I won't take much of your time, I promise.'

'You're going to use your key, aren't you?' Maggie says.

We look at each other. How does she know that June's just taken it out of her pocket? 'I could, but I'd rather you let me in,' she says. She's always been the diplomat between us.

Maggie saves us the trouble of letting ourselves in. 'As this isn't going to take long, I won't invite you inside,' she says, going back to her sofa. 'You can conduct your conversation from there.'

Now that I look around Maggie's room, it's so obvious that she's a bookworm. Not like Dot, though, who's got entire shelves lined with Danielle Steele, Jilly Cooper and other racy romances. Maggie's books are nearly all hardbacks and lots of them have leather spines. They look real too, not like the cardboard sets Mum bought to give some old-world ambiance to the great room.

'We just want to check that you're all right,' June says. 'You seemed upset when you left.'

'I'm fine, thank you.' She smooths the front of her silk cardigan. It's the paisley one that I know is amongst her favourites. She dressed up specially to make an impression. In spite of the glare she's giving us, my heart goes out to her. She wanted to be at her best when she joined in with the other women.

'Then why did you leave like that?' June asks. That's a lot bolder than I'd have dared, but I guess she's got to get an answer one way or another. Even if it will be dripping with abuse.

Maggie draws herself up even straighter. 'I am sorry, but I was under the impression that we're free to come and go within our own home. Is the book group not voluntary? I wasn't aware I needed to *punch a clock*.'

'Yes, of course, Maggie,' I say. 'But you have to admit that you seemed upset.'

'How should I know how I *seemed* to you, Cook, when I am not you?'

'So, you're all right, then?' June asks. I guess if she's not clutching a handful of pills or a razor blade to an artery, then June has done her job.

'Perfectly.'

'Knock knock,' comes Laney's voice as she squeezes though the doorway between June and me. She goes straight to the chair beside the sofa and throws herself into it. 'Please don't be upset, Maggie. I'm sure it's not that bad, whatever it is.' Laney snatches Maggie's hand from her lap. 'What is it? Please tell me.' Her golden eyes search out Maggie's.

I'm just about to turn to go when June stops me.

'I used to know those quotes as well as my own name,' Maggie says quietly, still holding Laney's hand. 'They're only throwaway lines, silly party tricks. If I can't even remember those... everything I've ever worked for really is slipping away.'

'But Maggie,' June says, 'it's not a big deal. So what if you've forgotten a few lines. Nobody minds, really.'

'*I* mind, and it is a very big deal,' Maggie says. She's swallowing hard and her eyes are glistening. 'I was an expert in literature, I lectured all over the world. I've had dinner with Nobel Laureates. Doris Lessing and Beryl Bainbridge were my friends. I used to be someone. Now what have I got?'

'I understand,' says Laney. 'Everyone tells you it's not a big deal. They're only trying to be nice, but it is a big deal when it's happening to you. It feels like bits of yourself are getting lost. You watch piece after piece fall away and wonder how long before you disappear altogether. But, Maggie, you're still you, even if you're forgetful.' Her laughter tinkles through the bedroom. 'Look at me! I'm not even seventy and I'm not fit to live on my own. I'd forget to feed myself or turn on the gas and set the house on fire. Maggie. You don't have to be your old self here. None of us is perfect. We like you the way you are.'

June taps my shoulder and, quietly, we leave Maggie's doorway. Laney's friendship will do more for her than we ever could.

Max is lurking again, and by now we know what that means. It's only a matter of which flavour poison he'll try to convince us to swallow this time. He's never been here this often. He wouldn't even come when Terence was at his worst. He sent his poor wife instead. I'm sure she was thrilled that her marital duties included keeping her father-in-law from wandering around the garden in his Y-fronts.

We never see Max's wife now that money is involved instead of underpants, but maybe she should come back again to knock Terence into line. Someone needs to do something. He had a go at me this morning about the amount of meat in our menu.

'What's the matter with you?' he'd snapped. 'Are you afraid to cook real food? Hello?! Are you listening?'

I was listening. I also happened to be cutting the potatoes for chips, and knew better than to take my eye off the slicer. The scar from two years ago still sometimes hurts if I bang it.

'We want to eat like men, not old spinsters watching their figures.'

Where to start? At one end he was rubbishing my cooking. At the other he was insulting the women, and in between he was a sexist pig who claimed to speak for all mankind. 'The meals are always well balanced, Terence, with enough meat, carbohydrates and vegetables.' That is my job.

'Bullshit,' he said. 'In the last week we've had quiche. No meat. That rice with the tiddly little bits of salmon. And bean stew with weeds.'

'That was Tuscan bean soup with kale, Terence, and there is meat in it. It's made with bacon.'

'What'd you do, wave a slice over the pot? What about the lasagne? You're not going to try to claim that was meat too. You're feeding us like hamsters.'

Not enough like hamsters, according to Sophie. She was in here last week lobbying for a vegan option at every meal. Not that she, or anyone else here, are vegans. I can't win.

'I happen to know that we need more meat as we get older,' he continued. 'Don't try to deny it.'

'I will deny it, because it's not true. There are studies that say we need more *protein* to help keep muscle mass healthy. Protein doesn't have to come from meat. It's also in dairy, eggs and, sorry to say, beans. For the record you also need iron, and dark leafy veg like kale is a good source of that. It doesn't always need to come from beef. You should be happy to eat those weeds. They're a superfood.'

'They're super shite,' he said, and stalked out just as my phone buzzed with a text from Tamsyn saying she'd overslept and wouldn't be in till Nick could come get her.

So, I've had it up to my back teeth with the Greenes by the time Max calls his meeting. I'm not sure why he makes me attend anyway. My job is to cook, not to enforce his management decisions.

'Right, I'll be short and sweet,' says Max. 'The advertising is working great. We've had… how many new applications is it, June?'

'Sixteen as of yesterday. I haven't added the new ones yet today. You're not going to keep running the adverts, are you? Because we haven't got room for many more residents.'

Max flashes his crooked-toothed vampire smile. 'Thus, the reason for this meeting. We're going to expand.'

'I thought you wanted to reduce costs?' June points out. 'Renovations are expensive. Unless you're thinking about putting a few residents into Terence's old cottage?'

I raise my hand. 'Wouldn't there be safety implications for that? It'll be harder keeping an eye on things in a separate building. Plus, they'd have to walk across the lawn to get to the dining room. In the dark sometimes.'

Max shakes his head. 'I'm not talking about the cottage. That should be sold soon anyway. There is more room here in the house. You've just got to think laterally.' He waits for us to do this. 'No? Well, here's the plan. We offer a discount to the women to share a bedroom.'

From the look on his face, you'd think he's just told us the secret to spinning gold from straw. 'Great idea or what? The women pay less, which is always helpful, and we free up their rooms for new residents.'

'Who will pay more,' says June, sussing out the punchline before me. 'You're talking about subsidising the women with the men's fees. I get it, Max, but I doubt the women are going to want roommates at this stage. It's not really fair for you to ask them.'

'I'm not asking them,' he says.

He's leaving that to us.

By now they know that when we interrupt *Judge Judy* for a meeting in the living room, they're not going to like what we say. This time they don't even wait for us to start.

'Don't tell us, you're inviting a mass murderer to come live here,' Dot says. 'And he'll be replacing the community nurse.'

'You're turning our occupational therapy into piecework?' Rosemary asks with a smirk. 'And we'll be paid in biscuits.'

The others banter around their guesses, which are only a bit more outlandish than what we're about to tell them.

'It could be good news,' June tells them, though no one believes that. 'Max is offering a twenty-five per cent discount to all the residents. That's not bad, eh?'

Sophie narrows her eyes. 'Why?' The others wait for June to explain the catch.

'For sharing a room.' She soldiers on over the women's objections. The faster we can get through this, the faster we can tell Max that everyone thinks his idea is terrible. 'It would only be for the biggest rooms, obviously, and it's completely voluntary, so if you'd like to share with a friend, you'll both get twenty-five per cent off your fees. Look, don't shoot the messenger, I'm only telling you what Max has told me.'

That stops most of their talking. They know June is caught in the middle. 'Thank you for telling us, June,' says Dot. 'We understand that you've got to do your job, but you can probably tell from the response that this isn't something we're interested in. Speaking for myself, in any case.'

'Twenty-five per cent off would come in handy, though,' Laney says.

'Laney, darling, aren't your fees covered by the council?'

'Oh, right,' she says. 'I forgot that.'

Then Rosemary says, 'I've got council support too. I think a lot of us do. Why would Max want to give us a discount? Not out of the goodness of his heart.'

June glances at me. She's got no choice but to tell them. 'We're getting a lot of new applications. Max wants us to be able to accept them, but there are only a few empty rooms now.'

'More men!' Dot and Sophie say at the same time. Though their expressions are very different. 'Isn't it bad enough now?' Dot says. The discussion moves on to all the ways the men aren't welcome. Sophie, as usual, is the only one defending them.

We haven't been back in June's office thirty seconds when she says, 'Okay, don't be mad. I did something.' Her look is worried and excited all at once.

'Oh, no, you didn't ring Callum again? Because, June, if you leave him alone for a few weeks then there's a chance of being in touch again later. If that's what you want.'

Such a look of sadness crosses her face that straightaway I feel bad. I shouldn't bring it up again unless she does. 'Of course that's what I want, but I didn't ring him. It's about you. You've only gone and won an award! We nominated you for it, and you've won!'

'What award?' I'm already grinning. Even if it's nothing more than a Tesco Club Card competition, an award is an award!

'Have you heard about the Social Superheroes honours list? It awards the best areas of social care in the community. And you've won, Phoebe! We didn't want to tell you about the nomination because you'd only say you weren't worth it. And, obviously, you are. You have no idea how hard it has been not to tell you. Remember when you rang me that Saturday and I was here? I had to get the testimonials and everything when you weren't around. Otherwise you'd have sniffed us out. Believe me, none of our residents could hold down a job in the Secret Service. Are you happy? You're not cross, are you?'

'No, no, of course not! I can't believe you did that.'

'Me and all the others,' she reminds me. 'Wait till you see the testimonials everyone did. Even Sophie, and she was the biggest wildcard.'

'What have I won?'

'Sorry, of course!' She hurries around her desk to hug me. 'You're the government's new Social Superhero for care home catering. Phoebe, this is big. You're the Jamie Oliver of care homes!'

'Well, that's… super!' I say, hugging her back and fighting tears. Max might think I do nothing but microwave ready meals, but the others appreciate me. That's what really counts.

The Social Superhero award. Me! I don't think I've felt this proud since I got my college certificate.

So the sense of loss that kicks me in the tummy takes me by surprise. This is exactly the kind of thing I've always wanted my mum to see. Someone other than me is saying that I'm really good at my job, presumably someone important if it's a national government award. 'I wish Mum could be there.' She would have been proud of me.

'I know. But I'm sure your dad will come to the ceremony – it's in three weeks so don't make any plans for the twenty-sixth – and we all want to be there to see you get the award.'

'I'd love that, thanks. I'm going to ring Dad now.'

June nods, taking her own mobile out. She sighs and turns off the screen. She's still checking for texts from Callum.

Chapter 19

Now it's my turn to confess. I've done something and it's not award-winning, unless it's for the Biggest Bad Idea by someone who should know better. It's Nick's fault. If he wasn't so persuasive then I wouldn't now be nervously on my way to meet him.

I started out completely resolved to say no when he asked me out again. In fact, I did say no. I didn't shy away from the Tamsyn issue, either. I got right in there with my big girl pants on. He's denied again that there's anything going on between them. I double-checked there's *nothing* between them, just to be sure. He promised, and I do believe him. That's not to say she's not gunning for it, or that he's not closer to her than I'd like. Though in fairness, Timbuktu would be too close for my liking.

That might still cause problems, but I have to take this chance and hope it's the right decision. This *is* Nick: kind, funny, hot-as-a-volcano and, as far as I can prove, honest Nick. If he wasn't all of those things then I wouldn't be about to meet him.

He's already waiting for me at the pub's bar. It's an ancient country pub with exposed beams so low that they're nearly grazing the top of his head. Every flat surface is covered with milk jugs and bottles – some with candles stuck in – and fiddly porcelain figurines of chickens and dogs. Above the huge fireplace hangs a hodgepodge of copper pots and pans and I can already tell it's too dim to read a menu without the light on your phone.

In other words, it's a perfectly romantic setting. Nick's in his usual jeans and dark jumper, but as he leans in to kiss my cheek – that's a new development – I catch the citrusy scent he wore at the supper club.

'All right, one of us needs to say it,' I tell him when we've tucked ourselves away at a little corner table by a window. 'This feels weird.'

'I think it feels fantastic,' he says. 'Thank you for finally saying yes.'

'Well, you were starting to get pathetic.'

We smile into each other's eyes.

'Don't you know I've liked you for months, Phoebe?'

How long have I fantasised about hearing those words? I'd need to check Nick's employment file to know for sure, but it was from about 10 a.m. on his first day.

It's tricky to answer him, though, without risking Seth or Tamsyn popping up, and I do *not* want that. I can't say that he made his feelings pretty clear after the supper club. Or that lately he's been too busy following Tamsyn around like a lost puppy to pay much attention to me.

'Erm, it wasn't always clear,' I say.

He shakes his head. 'It's clear that I think you're amazing, though, right?'

'I'm very open to convincing, but I wouldn't want to get a swollen head.'

He leans back in his chair and stretches out his long legs. In a butcher's shop, he'd be more sirloin than fillet. 'I can't imagine anyone with a less swollen head than yours. It might even be shrunken.'

'Thanks, that makes me sound so *hot*.'

When he laughs, his eyes glimmer in the candlelight. 'I mean that you're a lot more amazing than you give yourself credit for.'

'I'm giving myself *all* the credit. You're looking at the new Social Superhero for care home catering.' I polish my fingernails on my top. 'I'm an award winner.'

'Yes, exactly. And you've been downplaying it all week. Face facts, Phoebe. You're a lovely woman, but you're possibly the worst credit-taker in the world.'

'That's my mother.'

'From what you've told me, your mother had no trouble with her self-esteem.'

'Exactly,' I say. 'That's why she was so disappointed with me.'

If only she could see me now. Dad did sound pleased when I rang him about coming to the ceremony. Especially when I told him it was a national honour, and that it'll be in London. He's disappointed that the Queen won't give it to me, though.

'What's your family like?' I ask, mainly to stop thinking about my own. 'Your mother is Greek, right? Did you ever live there?'

'No, but I spent school holidays in Crete with my grandparents. It feels like a second home.'

That sounds very romantic. I imagine wizened old villagers bobbing around the sea in their blue-painted fishing boats while their wives – wearing headscarves and peasant dresses – mend nets in the hot sun and trade feta recipes.

Crete's not like that at all, Nick says. Plus, it's the twenty-first century. His grandfather is a retired insurance broker and doesn't even like fish. His grandmother worked at the archaeological museum and only wears peasant skirts when H&M stocks them. But it is sunny and hot in summer, and as a child Nick couldn't wait to get there to be with all his cousins. His mum was the only one in the family who left. 'She couldn't wait to get off the island when she finished school,' he tells me. 'Though I swear the longer she lives here, the more Greek she gets. Her accent is stronger than any of her sisters'. Dad always thought it was cute. Maybe that's why she kept it.'

'You mean your real dad or your stepdad?'

'My stepdad was my real dad,' he says with an unusual sharpness. 'My biological father left mum when I was three.'

'I take it you're not very close?' Clearly I've hit a nerve.

'He was around a lot till he remarried and his wife had a baby. We're okay now, but I know exactly what it feels like to want more from a parent.'

Then he tells me about the birthday parties and the sports days when he waited for his biological father while his mum made up excuses. The time he promised to take Nick camping during half-term, then cancelled an hour beforehand while Nick sat on the front step with his little backpack. 'He always blamed work, but he just didn't have time for me with his new family,' he says matter-of-factly. 'If it wasn't for my stepmum I probably wouldn't have any relationship with him at all. She used to ring Mum, see, when important stuff was coming up, and between them, sometimes they'd get him there.' He smiles. 'She's not the typical step-monster. I feel sorry for her sometimes. She's got a lot to deal with.'

'We're similar,' I tell him, 'though I didn't get the step-parent to make everything okay.'

His fingers brush mine as he says, 'It can't be any easier now that your mum is gone.'

When I realise he's saying exactly what I've been thinking all these months, I weave our fingers together. His hand is so warm. It fits mine perfectly.

'Remember the last time we did this?' he asks, glancing at our hands on the table. 'I'm not really sure what happened that night, but, Phoebe, I'm just happy that things seem to be... back on track?' His voice goes up about two octaves by the end of his question.

'So am I.'

Without taking my hand from his, he moves around the table, then pulls me to my feet. I breathe in his citrusy scent. If I touch my tongue to the soft skin on his neck, will he taste of limoncello too? It takes all my willpower to keep my tongue to myself.

When his lips press to mine, they're as perfect as I've always dreamed. It's not turn-the-firehose-on-them snogging, but still a wonderful hint of things to come. 'That's nice,' I murmur.

He pulls back. 'I was going for a lot better than nice.'

'You'll get us thrown out of the pub.'

'Maybe we should try again somewhere more private?'

As he leads me from the pub, my tummy begins to flip with excitement.

Chapter 20

Nick's flat is sparsely furnished, with a weight bench in one corner of the living room that actually looks like it gets used. There's no laundry hanging from it.

But there is a bloke slouched on the sofa watching TV. 'Ben, this is Phoebe. Phoebe, my flatmate, Ben.'

Ben sits up enough to shake my hand. 'Do you want me to?' he asks Nick, pointing to what must be his bedroom down the hallway.

'No, no, that's okay. We can go into the kitchen.' He turns to me. 'Is that okay?'

'Sure, fine,' I say. Maybe I've misread things. This doesn't feel like the seduction I was hoping for.

The kitchen is small but there's room for a table up against the wall, with two chairs on the long side and one on each end. The flat isn't too grubby for two blokes. 'Who takes his coffee so seriously?' I point at the fancy coffee pod machine that gleams on the worktop.

'Oh, my father gave it to me for my birthday. Not my dad, my father. It's over the top, but it has won me over to the dark side. I admit I love that cup first thing.'

'I thought you were a morning tea drinker.'

'I am. With you.'

We let that hang in the air for a moment.

'Now that I know what you really like, I'll have to up my game.'

Nick smiles. 'Your game is just fine. Besides, I don't get home-made biscuits here.' He pulls a bottle of red wine from under the sink. 'Our impressive wine cellar.'

When he pours me a glass I say, 'I'm getting a hint of Dettol on the nose.'

'We're saving the bleachy Malbec for a special occasion.' He clinks my glass and our banter ambles on like this while we sip our wine. There are no lulls in the conversation. There might be a few spaces, but they're comfortable, with no need to rush to fill them. It feels a bit like being at work, in that there's no awkwardness between us. But there is a tinge of something else, something in the way Nick and I are watching each other. I hope that kiss in the pub was an amuse bouche, because it definitely piqued my appetite.

Our chairs have crept closer as we've been talking. Now our knees are nearly touching. 'This has been a really nice night,' he says. When his palm brushes my knee, a delightful jolt shoots up my leg. The warmth of his hand radiates through my jeans. 'I usually get nervous on dates,' he says, 'but I'm not now. Thanks for that.'

'But I haven't done anything,' I answer. 'It helps that we're friends.'

His hand is still on my knee. 'Could we be more, do you think?'

He doesn't wait for an answer. When his lips meet mine, they're so warm and soft that I want to stay that way all night.

Nick guides me closer and cups my face in his hands. 'I've wanted to do this for such a long time,' he says.

'Me too.'

When his lips find the space where my neck meets my shoulder, a delicious shiver runs through me. My face is inches from his neck. I give an exploratory lick.

Definitely not limoncello.

'I wouldn't want to embarrass Ben, if he came in here,' Nick murmurs. 'Shall we?'

I nod and he leads me to his bedroom.

I've imagined sleeping with Nick, of course. In my head it has always been full of fiery, acrobatic passion – what with him being so sporty – and me trying to keep up. But the reality is different. We take our time. That doesn't make it any less passionate. But amongst the gasping joy of feeling completely free with this man, there's also a lot of gentle exploration and easy laughter. You'd never think it was the first time we've been together. There's no I'm-so-sorry fumbling. It's not that we instinctively know what the other wants, only that we're not afraid to ask. I've been with blokes for months who couldn't find a clitoris with a satnav, but never said anything. It's different with Nick.

I'm not often thrilled to be naked with the lights on, either. The bonus of Nick being able to see my wobbly bits is that I get to see him in all his weight-benched glory. It's even better than I imagined. He's slender without being slim, and has a six-pack that I could probably grate cheese on.

If there are any whispers of doubt about this, it's only that I wish we weren't so uneven. Even if Nick likes me – and I'm sure he's being honest when he says he does – I've been in love with him for months. It's going to be hard for us to draw even when I've had such a head start. I've already thought about our whole relationship when he probably hasn't thought any further than breakfast.

I can feel myself smiling when I drift off to sleep with Nick's arms around me and my head on his chest. I'll pay for it in the morning with a cricked neck, but it's so worth it right now.

All I want to do at work the next day is stay loved-up in some secluded corner with Nick. But he's in no position to be loved-up with me. He's been down at the greenhouse with Terence and the other men all morning. Tamsyn has been his shadow. As if she cares about compost.

He's building a long potting table to go alongside the greenhouse, while the others haul the contents out on to the lawn. Terence is shouting orders and deciding what's still useful and what they should toss.

I wouldn't normally make deliveries – except for Maggie's meals, and you know how I much I love doing that – but since the mountain can't come to Mohammed, I've brought tea to the mountain.

'Not the pots, for God's sake!' Terence shouts at Mr Campbell, who's just thrown them into the rubbish pile.

'But they're all broken,' he says.

'Exactly, so why would you throw them away?! Put them in one of those bags. Hopeless.'

Nick glances my way with a complicit smile, and the world shrinks to just the two of us. The feeling goes way beyond my usual skipping heart or skittery tummy when we've shared a joke, because this isn't only the hope of things to come. It's the knowledge that this is real. It's happening. Nick and I are really happening. In amongst the excitement, there's a calm certainty about it all.

He gently explains to Mr Campbell that they'll use the broken pots for soil drainage. That seems to be part of Nick's job description now too: smoothing over Terence's spikes so they don't catch on the other residents.

'What should we do with these?' Nick asks, aiming his question at Terence. He must know the answer, given that he's holding up a stack of mouldy gardening magazines with stuck-together pages. They're good for nothing but the bin. He's just cosying up as usual, though seeing it doesn't make me as annoyed as it did before last night. Ha. One little orgasm and suddenly the man can do no wrong.

I can't stop smiling. That is, until Tamsyn opens her mouth. She's standing uselessly beside Nick with her face tipped to the sun, while he nails together the table frame out of the old scaffolding boards we found piled behind the greenhouse.

If she's going to be underfoot like that, she could at least help him instead of sunning herself. I'd much rather that she just trot along so that I can have Nick to myself. I might be sure about him now, but I still don't want Tamsyn around.

'Nicky,' she says eventually. 'How much longer? I'm bored.'

As if we're all here to entertain her.

She tosses her hair, which gives me envy because it does shine coppery in the sun. 'You can go set the tables for lunch if you like,' I say. I shouldn't have made it sound like a choice, though, because she ignores me. Instead of the pay cheque she gets at the end of every work week, Max should just hand her the allowance from his wallet. Then at least she wouldn't be underfoot to annoy those of us who have to work around her.

'Why is she here?' Terence snaps. 'You're a waste of space.'

Sometimes I do love his cranky honesty.

'To keep you company, Grandad!' She honestly seems to believe this. 'We should spend as much time together as we can and now that I'm working here—'

Working here, ha! Hardly.

'—we can spend all day together. That'll be nice.'

'Nice as piles,' he grumbles. 'Same pain in the arse.'

But Tamsyn just laughs. Nothing's going to put her off when there's his inheritance to play for. Because that's what this is, and she's ruthless enough to cut her own father out if she can. Then she'll probably sell the whole place off to developers for flats.

It's nearly lunchtime before Nick and I can get any time alone. 'I've been dying to do this all morning!' he says, sweeping me up into his arms as soon as the kitchen door closes.

'Me too!' Between kisses I get a whiff of mould and fertiliser. I never thought I'd find that so sexy.

'Am I boring you?' he jokes when he catches me stifle a yawn.

'Not at all! I just didn't sleep that well. I'm not used to your pillows.'

'Would it help to stay at your flat next time? If there's a next time...? I hope that's not being too presumptuous.'

There's a next time! 'Definitely. I mean definitely that there's a next time, not that you're being presumptuous.' As much as I want to suggest tonight (and every night for the rest of our lives), June pops into my head. I'd never cold-shoulder Nick the way she did Callum, but it's probably best to let him suggest the next date. 'I'm just so glad this is happening!' I tell him. 'What with Callum dropping June like that, I was starting to lose faith in l— in relationships.'

'She's getting over that now, though, isn't she?' he asks. His arms are still around my waist, his hands clasped together behind me.

I sigh. 'It's still killing her. Did he seem weird to you at dinner? June says she didn't notice anything, but then he didn't go on with us after, and he's not the type to put work before fun.'

Nick shakes his head. 'So, can we see each other tonight? We could have a drink when you've finished with the dinner service.'

'Yes, please, I'd love that!'

I'm floating through the rest of the day, so happy that even Tamsyn can't bring me down.

Chapter 21

June now calls us her dirty little HR secret. Not that we're in a real company where Nick and I could pass sensitive information to each other or collude in fraud. What are we going to do – get Nick's favourite dessert on the lunch menu a bit more often?

We're not technically a secret, either. We just haven't come around to making any big announcements yet. Plus, this *is* our workplace. It's important to stay professional.

If only everyone had as much decorum as we're managing. I'm talking about Terence, who roams around the home leading the new residents like schoolboys in the playground.

We never know what they'll get up to next, only that it's guaranteed to annoy the women.

'What happens in DIY club stays in DIY club,' he stubbornly tells June. His geriatric posse is standing behind him.

'Will you stop saying that?' she retorts. 'It doesn't even make sense.'

'It makes perfect sense to us, because we're in DIY club.'

'Look, Terence,' I say. 'All June needs to know is whether you're planning anything that could disrupt the other residents.' I came into work the other day to find drop cloths covering the front hall's floor, the men in painter's dungarees and a white base coat already drying on the walls. Dot said they were crashing around down there from 4 a.m. Terence claims they only wanted to make an early start to avoid disruption. We all know he did it before June got in.

'Or anything that needs planning permission,' she adds. 'Or that's going to cost us money to fix. That little stunt with your bedroom was expensive, you know.'

The builders had to reinstate the wall that Terence knocked through. Luckily, he didn't get to any of the structural beams before we heard the commotion, or the whole upper floor might have come down. 'I know you own the property, Terence. You remind us about it every chance you get.'

'That's right,' says Terence. 'If I want to spend my money on it, I will.'

June's voice is barely above a whisper when she answers. 'But I run this home, so don't start making changes without clearing them through me. End of discussion.'

I bite down a smile. June is formidable if you try crossing her. Even Terence will have to think twice about that. 'Tea break?' I ask her once Terence leads the men back out to the greenhouse. They've turned it into their clubhouse, though they'll have to come back inside soon. There's no electricity out there, and the little camp stove they use to brew their tea won't keep them warm once the weather really turns.

'You mean can we go back to the kitchen so you can fall all over Nick,' she says as we go.

He'll have just finished up his occupational therapy in the dining room and put the coffee pot on. 'Am I that obvious?'

'Totally. But I also want some of your biscuits,' she says as she opens the kitchen door. 'Oh, look, here's Nick.' She raises her eyebrows at me. 'What a surprise.'

'Sarcasm is the lowest form of wit.' I push past her to flip on the kettle for us. 'Hi,' I say to Nick.

'Hi.'

'Look at the two of you,' she says. 'Will you please stop undressing each other with your eyes?'

'Sorry,' we both say. Try as we might not to do anything that could compromise June at work, it's harder to control our thoughts.

She waves the apology away. 'Oh, don't mind me, old misery guts. I'm only jealous that you're actually talking to each other. Though I might have come up with a plan about Callum.' She throws the teabags into our mugs as the kettle finishes boiling. 'What do you think of this? If I ring his work, I know he'll answer, and then I can explain everything. If I tell him how I feel, and apologise for whatever's put him off, he'll have to at least hear me out, right? He might... I don't know, change his mind?'

I'm nodding like a mad thing. Wasn't I talking about doing the very same thing myself not long ago?

She heaves a big sigh. 'It gives us a chance, at least. I've got nothing to lose. It's not like I've got any pride left anyway.'

She sounds so sad. 'It is worth a try,' I tell her. 'Like you say, there's nothing to lose.' I'll back any plan that might cheer her up.

But Nick is shaking his head. 'It's really not a good idea, June. Think about it. You do still have your pride right now, because you haven't been in touch. You're better off leaving it rather than make it worse.'

Now I'm shaking my head. 'It can't be any worse,' I say. 'They're already not together and she's obviously miserable over it. I'd do it if I were you.' I appreciate Nick's concern, but I don't think he grasps how badly June feels. 'Put yourself in June's shoes, Nick. Or think about if it was us and I suddenly stopped answering your calls for no good reason. Wouldn't you try anything to talk things through? Why shouldn't June?'

'Because I'm not— You're not— Really, seriously don't, June. Just trust me, it's not worth it.'

'How can it not be worth it?' she asks. 'If it means we could get back together, then of course it's worth it.' She laughs. 'What's a little dented pride, right?'

Nick's look is pure misery. 'You're much better off without him. Please believe me. I know what he's like. Callum isn't worth you wasting any more time on. I know the guy. He's bad news.'

We both stare at Nick. What does he mean: he knows Callum?

Then he says, 'I didn't realise I knew who he was until dinner, otherwise I promise I'd have said something way before that night and saved you all of this.'

Little warning bells are sounding off all over the place. 'What's that supposed to mean: that you'd have said something *before that night*?' Because he didn't say anything to June that night, did he? This is the first she's hearing of it. That means… 'Who did you say something to that night? What did you do, Nick?'

'How do you know him?' June asks.

'It doesn't matter. I just do, and he's horrible to women.'

'What did you do?' I ask again, fighting down the sick feeling building inside me.

'I had to… talk to him,' he mumbles. 'It was for your own good, June, please believe me. He'd have dumped you later anyway. That's what he does. It would have hurt more when he did it later.'

'You put him off me?' June says, with tears building in her eyes. 'All this time I've been blaming myself, obsessing over what I did wrong. I thought maybe I'd said something, or that he got tired of me not ringing him back. I thought maybe Phoebe was right and he thought I'd tricked him into liking me.'

I flinch. 'I'm so sorry, I shouldn't have said that.'

She waves away my apology. 'But you're the one who ruined my relationship? Nick? You?'

'I'm so sorry, June,' he says. 'I should have told you.'

'No, Nick, wrong,' she says. 'You shouldn't have meddled in my relationship!'

He goes towards her, but freezes mid-step when she glares at him. 'June, please understand. I did it for your own good.'

'That was not your call to make.' Then she crosses her arms. 'Can I assume that whatever you said means that my ringing him now will do no good?'

'I'm sorry,' he says. 'That's exactly the wrong thing to do.'

She deflates. 'Because it'll just prove what you told him. Because you knew I'd spent months convincing him that I wasn't clingy.'

Any other time, the anguish in Nick's face would make me desperate to comfort him. 'No,' he says. 'Because he hates anyone who actually likes him. That's what pushes his buttons.'

And thanks to Nick, he pushed the ejector button on June.

This can't be right. Nick can't have hurt my best friend like this. It's a mistake.

'Then I proved you right by ringing him a million times.' She shakes her head. 'Well done. You're an effective assassin.' With that she heads for the door. 'No, thanks, Phoebe,' she says when I start to follow her. 'I don't want to talk right now. Later, yes, just not right now. Though you might want to talk to Nick,' she adds ominously.

Oh, yes, I definitely do.

'I know this sounds really bad,' he says as soon as I start to speak, 'but I was only thinking about June. I should have told you as soon as it happened, but June was with us in the pub after.'

I stare at him. 'Just so you know, that sounds like such B.S.,' I tell him. 'What would you have said to me if June hadn't been there? *I've just scuppered your best friend's relationship and oh, by the way, shall we get some crisps with our round?* You might have ruined my best friend's future. How could you do that to her and then go ahead and… do this with me?' I still can't believe that this is Nick. Nice, caring, sensitive Nick who, let's face it, I am definitely in love with.

He makes a what-are-you-talking-about face. 'But my feelings for you have nothing to do with that! Except that I was watching out for *your friend*. Phoebe, I wouldn't have said a thing if Callum wasn't such a horrible man. He was going to hurt her.'

'All right, let's say that, in theory, you really did have June's best interests at heart. Then why didn't you tell *her* and let her make the decision to dump him if she wanted to? At least then she wouldn't have blamed herself all this time, thinking she'd done something wrong.'

He closes his eyes. 'Because then I'd have to get into how I'm so sure about him, and that's... complicated. But I am one hundred per cent sure, Phoebe. I wouldn't have said anything otherwise. I couldn't tell June directly. I just didn't want you to find out I'd done it, to be honest.'

I glare at him. 'It seems to me, Nick, that being honest is the last thing you've been. Now please get out of my kitchen. I don't want to see you.'

'What does that mean?'

'Please just go away.'

June and I have our heads together, whispering in her office, when Sophie knocks. 'What's going on?' she says, seeing our pitiful faces.

June hasn't been shy about her feelings over what Nick has done, but she's not making it personal, or even suggesting that I have a go at him. She'd never ask me to punish someone because of her, even when he deserves it as much as Nick does.

'Nothing,' we both answer Sophie. The residents shouldn't have to listen to us go on about our sad love lives. That's why we've got each other. Nick's convinced I'll never speak to him again, and he's totally miserable about it, which might give me some satisfaction if I could stop feeling so sick.

It's at times like these that I really wish Mum was here. She was never great on the empathy front, but she knew what to do in a crisis. Mum was a doer, and I need some of that right now.

'How can I help?' June asks Sophie. Ever the professional, even when everything is crumbling.

'Yes, thank you,' says Sophie. 'I want to join the DIY club.'

She's hardly about to do any renovations dressed like that. It looks like a new frock, or at least one I've not seen before. That's possibly because we haven't had any tea dances here. On her short frame, the burgundy taffeta flows past her shins, and its nipped-in tailoring even gives her a bit of a waist.

But it's not our business what the residents wear in their own home, so neither June nor I make any comment. 'Oh, well, it's not an official club, through me, I mean,' says June. 'I haven't got anything to do with it. It seems to be Terence's brainchild.'

Sophie nods. 'Can you please come with me to ask Terence? I think I'd be an asset to them.'

Only if you define an asset as someone getting in the way while trying to flirt.

'You mean, officially? I can't.'

'I mean unofficially, as my friend.'

'Of course we will,' I say. 'Right? Unofficially.' Despite Sophie's motives, the more we can encourage the women and men to mix, the better it will be for the home. They're still acting like they're living on the border between the Koreas.

But not everyone wants to see barriers come down. 'You!' Dot protests as she spots us heading for the French doors to the garden.

'Damn it,' Sophie mutters. 'Ignore her.'

As if we could.

'Where are you going?' she demands. 'To join the He-Man Woman Hater's Club? That's quite an outfit for the garden. Unless you've been invited to the Queen's.'

'You look lovely,' Laney says, stroking Sophie's silk-clad arm. 'Are we having a party?' Her look becomes troubled as she stares at her high-tops. 'I'm afraid I don't have any dresses. Maybe I could borrow one of yours?'

Dot might be snippy to Sophie, but she's ever-so patient with Laney. 'No, remember I told you? This–' she points an accusatory finger at Sophie '–is all for the men.'

'Shame on you,' Sophie exclaims. 'You claim to be a feminist. Can't a woman dress the way she likes? And, not that it's any business of yours, but I happen to be very good with tools.'

'I'll bet you are,' Dot snaps. 'Sophie, you must see that you're being ridiculous.'

Sophie wheels around on her heel at that. Her pale powdered face is very close to Dot's, but the older woman isn't giving an inch. 'No, Dot, *you're* the one being ridiculous. You're acting like the men are your sworn enemies when all they've done is be born with a Y chromosome.'

Dot looks like she's about to say more but clamps her lips shut. 'You're making a fool of yourself.'

'We'll see about that,' says Sophie.

Dot is right about Sophie's outfit. Her heels aren't a good idea on the soft lawn. She only manages to make it to the greenhouse by mincing on her tiptoes. The men see us coming, of course. They *are* sitting in a building made of windows.

A few stand up when Sophie reaches the door, but Terence's look lands them back in their folding chairs.

They've cleared nearly the whole space inside, piling the bags of compost neatly along one wall to make room for the half-dozen chairs arranged in a circle. There's a narrow table pushed against the long side for seeding and potting and the makeshift kitchen. The teapot is still steaming on the camp stove. And Nick has fashioned a rack to hang all the tools above the lawnmower.

'Can we help you?' Terence asks.

Sophie must have used up all of her nerve on Dot, because she's surprisingly meek when she answers him. Her lashes flutter behind her thick glasses. 'I just wondered if there's anything I can do for the DIY club,' she nearly whispers.

'No, thank you,' he says.

'Oh.'

'But didn't you tell me this was a voluntary club, Terence?' June says. 'Sophie is volunteering.'

'We've got enough volunteers,' he says. 'See? No more chairs.'

'We could easily bring one from the house,' I suggest. Sophie might be about as useful to them as a hammer made of noodles, but I'm not about to let her be bullied away if she wants to join them.

Terence puts his hands in his pockets. Now I know he's about to be horrible. 'The thing is, you wouldn't enjoy it. It's not only looking at paint swatches, you know. It's electrical and plumbing and demolition.'

'No demolition, Terence,' June reminds him.

'This is man's work.'

I'm about to tell him about our resident, Ann-Marie, who was a plumber for thirty-five years, but Sophie is nodding like that's a perfectly sane statement. 'Well then, maybe you could use some of my tools? Some are quite technical. They're just collecting dust.'

June and I look at her. I've never seen Sophie use anything more complicated than a hairdryer.

Terence laughs. 'I think we're fine with our own hammers.'

'Shame,' she says, 'it's all just sitting in self-storage. I should probably sell it. I understand that Makita has a good resale value.'

'They were your husband's?' Mr Campbell asks.

'No,' she laughs. 'I loved him to bits, but he was hopeless. He wouldn't know which end to plug in. I did all the work in our houses. Not the building work itself. I was never good at bricklaying, but the first- and second-fix plumbing, electrics, conduits and cabling, dry-wall... drains and pipes, doors and windows... built-in shelving, kitchen installation. I did all those. Let's see.' She's run out of fingers. 'Decorating, of course, that's easy.'

'You did all that?' June says. 'Well done, Sophie!'

She smiles. 'These muscles didn't only come from aerobics, you know. It's cheaper taking the courses to do it yourself than paying someone else. Hey, do-it-yourself. I guess that's exactly what I did. So, you might be able to use the tools? You'll know how to use them all, won't you?'

There's an embarrassed rumbling amongst the men as they admit that Sophie might actually be quite useful in the club.

'By the way, your windows need a good cleaning,' she says as we go. 'You can hardly see through them.'

'Feel free any time you like,' Terence calls out.

'Not flipping likely,' she mutters. 'I'll be too busy doing the work that you lot can't.'

Chapter 22

If only I could get over what Nick did to June, then I know (I hope!) it would stop this sick feeling in the pit of my tummy. He thinks I'm only being snippy to hurt him, but I'm not doing it on purpose. It's hurting me too. Every time I think about it, the rage wells up inside me. How could he have sabotaged June like that?

The hardest part about the whole sorry situation is having the disappointment of dashed relationship hopes piled on top of all this fury. The weight of that is what hurts most: the idea of everything that could have been, if Nick hadn't torpedoed my best friend's happiness.

Don't think I can't hear myself. I know it sounds like an overreaction. After all, June is a big girl. She can take care of herself and fight her own battles. I know that, but it's how Nick went about the whole thing that, no matter what I tell myself, I can't let go. What a monumental lapse in judgment to put off Callum instead of warning June. If only he'd done that instead, then June could have made up her own mind and she wouldn't have felt like such a loser when Callum ghosted her. It was disloyal, and that's so out of character that I never thought I'd say it about Nick.

There's something else too. Maybe it's because I'm doubting everything now. I did believe Nick when he told me that there's nothing between him and Tamsyn, but watching them through fresh eyes, I'm not so sure. After all, he didn't tell me what he did to June until he had to. How do I really know he's been truthful about Tamsyn? Especially when she's constantly hanging on him? Maybe I've been deluding myself all along. I wanted so much to believe him.

How I hate these suspicions.

I know what Mum would say. *Just ignore him.* She had an incredible ability to pretend that tricky situations didn't exist. She could blank a person until they not only started wondering whether she really saw them, they also started wondering if they were actually there at all.

I might have to deal with Nick invading my kitchen for more coffee – he's going to develop heart palpitations if he keeps up this schedule – but at least in the book club it's easier to ignore him with the others around.

We're getting to the really juicy bit in *Pride and Prejudice*, when the secrets are starting to come out. June is skipping this week, which is a relief since Mr Bingley has just thrown Jane over in the story and it doesn't take an Austen scholar to see the parallels with June's very own Mr Bingley. If I were Nick, I'd be squirming.

He might be. I don't know because I'm definitely not looking in his direction.

'This is the sad bit!' Laney says. 'I don't like it when Lizzy rejects Darcy. He's so obviously in love with her.'

'That's a brilliant scene, though,' says Sophie. She's wearing her gown again, though I'm glad to see that she gave up on the heels. 'I love when Lizzy listens to Darcy putting his foot in it. "His sense of her inferiority – of its being a degradation – of the family obstacles which judgment had always opposed to inclination, were dwelt on with a warmth which seemed due to the consequence he was wounding, but was very unlikely to recommend his suit." As if anyone would give him the time of day after *that*! It's an empowering scene, not a sad one at all. You can't feel sorry for Darcy after he's been such a, a—.'

'Wanker,' I say. Although I'm not sure I'm talking about Darcy.

'I do feel for him, though,' Laney objects, 'because he's so tortured. Even though I know it'll be a happy ending.' She clamps her hands over her mouth. 'Am I allowed to say that?'

Dot laughs. 'We've all read it many times before.'

'Or seen one of the films,' Nick adds, which just makes me think of Tamsyn.

Maggie half raises her hand to speak. 'It's a well-used literary tradition to put impediments in the way of the protagonist's goals. If it was easy for her to get what she wants, then the reader wouldn't be invested in the story.'

Maggie keeps glancing at her notebook as she speaks. Sometimes she flips through the pages to make her points, but mostly it seems enough just to hold the notebook.

That was Laney's idea. 'You'd never give a lecture without jotting down some notes, would you?' she had asked when Maggie resisted. 'You're expected to come prepared for those things. Well, we have to be ready for book club too, otherwise we can't talk about the book. It's just common sense.'

That's what convinced Maggie to come back.

I'm glad that none of the others know what happened between June and Callum (and Nick). It's uncomfortable enough picking apart Darcy's meddling in Jane and Mr Bingley's affair without having to talk about how much like real life the book is turning out to be.

Everything was going along fine for Jane and Bingley, or so Jane thought, until, one day, Bingley scarpered off to London and out of her life. That was Darcy's fault. He'd warned off Bingley over Jane's feelings (though for indifference rather than neediness), leaving Lizzy rightly furious at Darcy for it.

Add a couple of corsets and some flickering gaslight and the Happy Home for Ladies might as well be the Bennets' house.

I won't be saying any of that to June, obviously.

Maggie is in the middle of talking about the symbolism of Darcy's home when we all start to notice that Dot's not paying attention. Instead, she's glaring into the hallway. 'What are you doing here?' she finally says.

'Am I late?' Terence holds up a worn hardback. 'It's book club, right? This was Patricia's favourite.'

'Very late. And Patricia didn't have a favourite,' Dot declares. 'She loved them all the same. You can't stay, so don't bother sitting.'

'What's the big deal, Dot? This isn't a women-only club, is it? Because we're not allowed to have those, you know. House rules, right, Sophie?'

Sophie titters.

'You can see very clearly that Nick is here,' Dot says, 'so it's not women only. It is, however, my club. You might not have any appreciation of ownership, but I do. Terence, leave. Please.'

'Come on, Dot,' he says. 'Can't you drop it?'

'Please.' There's real sadness in her voice.

Terence shrugs. 'I hope you change your mind one day. It has been long enough. It's not fair.'

'Don't you dare try to tell me what's fair,' she says. 'You of all people. Now go.'

When the door has closed, I ask, 'Dot, please tell us, what is going on with you two?'

We're not about to let her brush us off as easily as she seems to be able to do to Terence. Not when something is so obviously upsetting her.

Maybe she's tired of keeping it all inside. Or maybe she's just tired of us pestering her. Either way, finally she does tell us why she's been acting so strangely since Terence turned up here.

'It's still so hurtful that I can't ever forgive him,' she starts. 'You know that Patricia, his wife, and I were best friends. Since we were six years old. She was like my sister. Better than a sister, because we didn't have to compete over things. Or so I thought.'

Dot tells us that she and Patricia met Terence at the same time. But it wasn't Patricia who fell head over heels for him. It was Dot.

'Terence?' I say. 'Sorry, I don't mean to sound so surprised, but Terence?'

She laughs. 'He's nothing now like he used to be. He was fun, and nice, and handsome. He's always been smart, if a bit of a smart-arse.'

He and Dot were going strong, but then she got her job at the boy's school in Oxford. 'It's only three hours by car, but neither of us had one. The trains from Ipswich were expensive. It sounds so trivial now, that something like that would have kept us apart, but I was just starting my career and Terence wasn't rich. The distance didn't seem like it would be a problem, given how we felt about each other.'

'So Patricia moved in on him?' I say. What a cow. And she looks like such a nice woman in the painting.

Dot shakes her head. 'It was the other way around. Terence admits that it was he who first had feelings for Patricia. This was a year or more after I'd moved. We saw each other when we could, during half-term and summer and sometimes on a weekend. But it wasn't like being in the same place all the time. He didn't tell me when things started to change. Of course, he wouldn't. I could tell something was wrong, but what could I do? I wasn't about to leave my job just because I thought my boyfriend was going off me. It was Patricia who finally told me. It sounds strange to call her a good friend when she ended up with my boyfriend, but at least she told me face-to-face. By then it was getting serious between them. I was devastated.' She shrugs. 'I don't blame Patricia. Believe it or not, Terence could be charming then. I blame him for shifting his affections like that. Then she got pregnant and they got married.'

'But it was the sixties,' I say. 'She could have had other options. She could have raised the baby herself.'

'Oh, no,' says Dot. 'I wouldn't have wanted Patricia to have to go through that. Besides, I knew she loved Terence. Maybe I made the wrong decision, but eventually I forgave Patricia. It's him I've always hated.'

'But Dot, don't you think you'd feel better if you could get over it?' Laney asks. 'It must take a lot of energy to hate someone. You could be using that to be happy instead.'

Dot smiles at Laney. 'If only it were as easy as deciding to do it. I wanted him to suffer like I did. That's petty of me, I know.'

'I understand,' I say. 'We can't help the way we feel. Your feelings are valid, whatever they are.' I can tell that Nick is watching me, but I keep my eyes trained on Dot as we all try to make her feel better. I'm not sure if we're helping. It's hard to change emotions.

Mr Campbell is waiting in the corridor for Sophie when we finish book club.

'Hi, Billy,' she says, beaming. 'Sorry, that went on longer than I thought.'

'That's all right,' he says, holding up a bottle of wine and two glasses. 'I didn't have any other pressing engagements. Certainly none as nice as this.' He gallantly offers Sophie his arm and, without daring to look at Dot, they head for the garden. Even in her flat shoes she's as tall as him, and the top of his head shines from the recessed lighting. He's more George Bush than Clooney, but he does seem very nice. I wouldn't dare say that to a tight-lipped Dot, though.

'Did she tell you what she's done now?' Dot asks me. 'The DIY club has become the DIY and gardening club. She's expanded their remit. They're doing flowers!'

'Well, the borders could do with some TLC. Maybe it needs to be a more formally organised thing.'

'But we've always done it,' she says.

'And you still can. There's nothing stopping you.'

She harrumphs at that. 'Apparently, Terence is putting together a garden design. I know him. He'll have a fit if any of us dares go off-plan. Well, I've got news for him. They can cut the grass and pull all the weeds they want. We'll be doing our own flowers, to our own plan, and they will be gorgeous, like they always are.'

She starts muttering to Laney about aphids on their agapanthus.

Good lord. It's shaping up to be the Great British Plant Off around here, but with none of the witty puns or comforting nans. These nans are cutthroat.

Then the sight of Tamsyn makes me do a double take. She's sitting in one of the wingback chairs by the door. She doesn't even willingly come in during work hours. What's she doing here now?

Clearly, Nick's not expecting to see her, either. His eyes dart between Tamsyn and me. It's a very guilty look.

'Nicky!' she says, leaping up.

'What are you still doing here?' he asks.

'I went the pub after work. I told you, remember? Everyone's still there, but I'm wiped out. Take me home, Nicky?' she whines.

But Nick doesn't answer right away. His questioning gaze searches my face.

I turn away from them.

'Sure, come on,' he finally says.

I feel such a tug of sadness as I hear them leave together.

I know I could reel Nick back in to me. Telling him I'm not angry anymore would probably be enough.

It's torture watching them together. They're so cosy, so intimate that I want to scream, but I cannot – *will* not – lie, even if it is the only way to keep Tamsyn's claws out of him. I can't betray myself like that. My feelings are perfectly valid. If I overrule them to hang on to a bloke, then what does that say about me? I'll still be miserable, plus a traitor to myself.

I can thank Mum for my principles. And I'm not being snarky. I mean that. She might have bashed the life out of most of my decisions, but she also taught me to stick to what I believe in. She was one of the most principled people I knew. It's nice to have something good rub off from her.

Tomorrow is Saturday, visitor's day, and with all the new residents, it'll be even more hectic than usual. So instead of going home after lunch, I'm still here, making as much ahead of time as I can. Plus, I've had Sophie in here distracting me with her menu demands again. She wanted to debate whether kale or broccoli would win, nutritionally, in a vegetable fight club.

'I've also been thinking about our meals,' she'd said once we'd exhausted the veggie cage fight conversation. 'Now that we've expanded, shouldn't we expand our meals too?'

'But I'm cooking nearly twice as much.'

'I don't mean volume, Phoebe. I mean your dishes. They should be more manly now that you're not only cooking for women.'

I had to check her expression to see if she was kidding. 'More manly. What, like stewed bear? Bull's bollocks soup? Meat with a side of screwdrivers? Sophie, what's manly food? There's no such thing.'

257

'Less salady,' she said. 'And not so much lentil.'

This, coming from Sophie! It had Terence's fingerprints all over it, so we bickered about that for a while, delaying me further.

I guess that's why Tamsyn and Nick don't expect me to still be in here when they start talking in the dining room. I don't mean to be eavesdropping. It's not my fault that they're sitting at the table closest to the kitchen door. They're only making idle conversation anyway. So far, so boring. That is, until Nick mentions me.

'God, Nicky, you'd better do something about that,' Tamsyn says. 'It's bad enough that she's acting like a lovesick teenager.'

'She is not.'

'You're blind,' says Tamsyn. 'She is and, honestly, it's pathetic. You've got to put her out of her misery.'

There's silence. Only the ringing in my ears. I don't want to hear any more. I feel vomity enough as it is. So maybe I should stop pressing my ear to the door.

'If you don't,' she says, 'then I'm going to tell her about us. For all our sakes. She has to find out sooner or later anyway.'

'Don't you dare, Tamsyn, I mean it,' Nick nearly shouts. 'I've told you, I will never forgive you if you say a word to her. There will be no *us* if you do. Stop smiling, it's no joke. I will never speak to you again.'

'Then do it,' Tamsyn says with a laugh in her voice. 'And you know you're bluffing. You don't want me out of your life. You love me too much.'

With a shaky hand, I set the chopping knife down so that I don't accidentally stab myself. Humiliation? Fury? Misery? Take your pick, it's all there.

Us, she said. Nick and Tamsyn are an *us*. He loves her.

Tamsyn is right. I am being pathetic, though not only for the reason she thinks. If she knew that Nick's also been cheating on her, she wouldn't be so calm.

Though maybe she's ignoring what she suspects too. I have been, just because I wanted so badly for Nick and I to be an 'us'. Love really is blind. It has only cost me every shred of my self-esteem. Because I did suspect that there was something between them. It's my own fault that I've conveniently ignored that so that I could justify a relationship with him. I was that desperate to be with him that I've been living in la-la land ever since, as in la-la-la-la I don't hear the truth.

Nick is a total wanker for playing both me and Tamsyn. And I am pathetic for letting him, when in my heart of hearts, I've known better all along.

MICHELE GORMAN

Chapter 23

It's awards day – arguably the most important day in my entire career, achievement-wise – and instead of being excited I've got this cloud hanging over me, fat with humiliation and gloom, blotting out all the brightness.

When I told June about what Tamsyn had said, she loyally offered to sack them both for me. For what, though? There's no HR rule against bringing one's personal life to work. Or even for two-timing. There should be one, though, for making a colleague cry into her dishcloths for days on end.

Even though I hate the idea that Tamsyn thinks I'm pathetic, I can't deny that she's right. More than she even knows, given how I've trailed after Nick since day one, long before she turned up. She's only judging recent events, and she doesn't know the half of that, thank goodness. I feel awful enough as it is. I couldn't face having her tell me off for sleeping with her boyfriend too.

So, I'm taking Mum's advice, putting on my happy face, and my best dress, and I'll accept that award as if my heart was in it.

The rest of the house is excited enough to make up for me anyway, and I can't blame them. They might get regular outings to Ipswich, to the cinema if there's something big-screen-worthy that they want to see, or to shows or for shopping at Christmas. But getting to go all the way to London is a real treat. And some are a lot keener than I imagined they'd be.

I brought Maggie's meal up to her as usual this morning. While the other women were trying on dresses and doing each other's hair or, in Dot's case, plotting a tragic accident for Terence, Maggie was in her room, calmly reading. I have to admire her ability to exist above all the melee of the mundane. 'I know you wanted your usual,' I said, holding the tray in front of me, 'and you've got it. But I also brought you a slice of spelt toast. Sophie says we should be eating less wheat.' I wasn't sure how trendy grains fit into her idea of manly food. She claims that because it's an ancient grain, it's what cavemen used to eat.

'I think Sophie should worry about herself and leave the rest of us to eat what we like,' Maggie said. 'Thank you, I'll try it.'

I was just about to go when Maggie cleared her throat. 'Congratulations on your award, Phoebe.'

She said my name! My actual name, not just my job title. 'Thank you, Maggie. It was so nice of everyone to nominate me.'

'What time will you leave for the ceremony?'

'Around three, I guess, in case there's traffic. It doesn't start till six. Nick's driving us.'

She nodded, rubbing her flower brooch.

'Would you… Would you like to come, Maggie? There's plenty of room in the minibus. Only if you want to.'

Then she smiled broadly. 'I'd like that, thank you. I always found that one should have as many familiar faces as possible in the audience when receiving an award. It can be daunting otherwise. I'll be ready at three.'

Everyone is already in the hall when June and I emerge from the downstairs loo in a cloud of hairspray. She's done my make-up – demure drag queen, which apparently photographs well – and blow-dried my hair to swingy perfection. I even let her take me shopping for a dress that I have to admit, I love. It's got a boat neckline (I'm told) and a nipped in middle that gives me a waist.

'Wow, gorgeous!' Sophie says when she sees me. 'You should dress like that more often.'

'It's not very practical for the kitchen,' I tell her. 'I'll stick to my whites at work, but thank you.'

I can feel my cheeks go hot over all the compliments, and this is only in front of my friends. What will I be like when I have to accept the award onstage with strangers looking at me?

Then Nick pitches in his opinion and completely stalls my mood. I don't want to hear that I'm beautiful from him. I did once, but not now that I'm so *pathetic*.

I give him my best put-down glare.

If there was another way to get everyone to London comfortably, he wouldn't be taking us in the minibus, either. But it seemed selfish to make my elders trudge across station platforms or maybe even stand on the train just because I don't want to be around Nick. He actually had the cheek to act hurt when I told him I don't want him to come into the ceremony. And he still denies that there's anything between him and Tamsyn. Even though I heard it straight from their lips.

That word: pathetic. It keeps ricocheting around my brain, painfully bumping against everything else in my life. Whenever I have to talk to Nick now, I wonder whether I sound pathetic. Is it in what I say? Or the way I say it? Or maybe there's some kind of pitiful look that I'm giving off. It's too humiliating to think about, yet I can't stop.

For completely different reasons, Nick has made June and I feel exactly the same way. Thanks to his little talk with Callum, now every time she thinks about how she rang him after our dinner together, she burns up with the mortification of knowing what he thinks of her. And his illuminating chat with Tamsyn means that every time I think about him, now so do I.

Fragile doesn't even begin to describe how I feel around him. He can't very well blame me for not wanting him there when I get my award.

Despite the occasion, the mood is subdued as we make our way to London in the minibus. I suppose having Maggie with us could be making everyone less silly than usual. She is still frightfully proper, though she does smile more now. It's probably just me giving off the killjoy vibes.

Finally, Nick pulls up in front of the hotel. Naturally, the women want to know why he's not coming into the ceremony when it becomes clear that he's only dropping us off.

I'm just about to stutter some lame excuse, when he says, 'I'd love to, but I have to meet my mum now. I hardly ever get to London, with working on the weekends, so it has been ages since she has seen me. When I found out about the award I thought I'd better take the chance. You understand. I'll be here, though, to drive you back when you're finished. Good luck, Phoebe! I'll be thinking about you.'

I smile tightly. Just when it seems he can't get any saintlier in the women's eyes, he adds Good Son to his credits.

'I've been here before!' Laney cries as we step into the opulent foyer where the organisers are handing out name badges. 'I came for a charity ball.' She smiles at the memory. 'It was called the Snowball. So magical. Everyone was glamorous and there were even princesses, and such beautiful dancing and dinner and champagne and I wore a pale blue silk dress with silver diamante shoes.' Then she glances down at her dress, which is a very nice deep blue. 'But this isn't...' She looks around.

Dot takes her arm. 'It's the award for Phoebe. But it sounds like you had a wonderful time at the Snowball.'

June spots my dad right away. He's already at the table as we make our way through the ballroom. He looks so handsome in his suit that I can't stop grinning as I introduce him to Sophie, Laney, Dot and Maggie. We do make a good-looking group. June is gorgeous as usual, with her blonde curls shining in the overhead lights of the ballroom. Her dress is deep green and fitted and definitely not too show-offy, which she was worried about.

'All right, Phoebe?' Dad asks. 'You look nice.'

'I feel nervous!' I say. 'I don't know how Mum did this.' She always made acceptance speeches look so easy. A few words, a little self-deprecation and a lot of thanks. That's what I'm planning. 'I'm glad you're here.'

'I wouldn't miss my daughter's big night,' he says, and I nearly fall off my chair. He's never said anything like that to me. It was always Will's big night, big game, graduation, whatever.

It's his turn nearly to fall off his chair when I throw my arms around him. 'Thanks, Dad.'

But I'm too nervous to enjoy any of this, really. At least it's not like all those televised award shows, where all the finalists have to sit in the same room to hear the winner announced, and then pretend to be happy when it's not them. I couldn't manage that. It would be just my luck that a camera would catch my expression just as I'm sneering.

Listen to me, like I'm going to get photographed at the Social Superheroes awards. These are all charity people and care-home workers, not the princesses that Laney was rubbing elbows with at the Snowball.

'Remind me to give you something after,' Dad says.

'What is it?' A congratulations gift!

'Not now. After your award. Just remind me so I don't forget.'

The dinner seems to take ages, with the women assuring me that I cook better than the chefs at the five-star hotel. I love their loyal lies. The excitement of the night, and free-flowing wine, must be going to their heads. At least they're keeping me distracted from what's ahead.

That Mum is missing this seems unfair to both of us. Mostly to me, if I'm being honest. I can tell myself till I'm blue in the face that it shouldn't matter what another person thinks of my choices. Even my mum. As long as I know I'm doing my best, and I'm happy with where I am in the world, that's what matters. Nobody but me can really make me happy. I know all that.

I just wish I'd stood up for myself more, instead of being struck mute by her judgment. I spent way too much time trying to appease her instead of telling her how proud I am of everything I've done, first at the bistro and now at the home. If she were here, I'd tell her that there is more than one way to be successful, and it doesn't have to be measured only in pay cheques and other people's estimation. That knowing I'm keeping an entire care home healthy and happy makes me happy. And yes, that I'm proud to be getting an award from intelligent people with enough sense to recognise everything that she was too blind to see.

Mostly, though, I wish Mum were here to see all this for herself.

Finally, the awards begin, and I can feel my shoulders tensing up. I'll probably still be able to recite my little speech in fifty years. I've practised it enough. And I've mentally mapped my route to the stage, around the two sets of tables in front of us. I'm as ready as I'll ever be.

Yet when the presenter announces the Care Home category, it sends the women, and my tummy, into a flutter. Dad grabs my hand, and when his big, warm one envelops mine, I couldn't be more grateful. 'Thanks, Dad,' I murmur.

'Next is the award for excellence in care-home catering,' says the woman onstage. Her voice has the deep timbre of someone used to being listened to. 'This award recognises excellence in providing meals that are not only nutritionally balanced and tailored for the clientele, but consistently delicious. I like to think of this as the yummy award.' That gets a laugh. 'I only wish we'd been able to judge by sampling all the nominees' best efforts. Never mind. Maybe the winner will let me come and have lunch one day.'

I laugh and nod.

'I'm delighted to announce that this year's winner of the award for excellence in care-home catering is…' She pauses, exactly like they do at all the big movie awards. 'Phoebe Stockton of Framlingham's Happy Home for Ladies.'

Everyone applauds, none louder than our table. Even Maggie is enthusiastic. There's no going back now. As I weave my way to the stage, I'm surprised that I'm not more nervous. I can't stop grinning. The presenter shakes my hand while handing me the small glass award (crystal? Mum would know) and moves aside for me to stand in front of the podium. 'Thank you so much,' I start, then remember my script. 'It is such an honour to be recognised officially for my cooking. But I feel like I'm thanked every day by the Happy Home residents, some of whom are here tonight: Dot, Sophie, Laney and Maggie, you and every one of the thirty-three residents make me love my job. I also want to thank our manager, June Cole, for hiring me in the first place. Your support and friendship mean the world to me. My parents, Simon and Barb Stockton, are the reason that I am who I am, so thank you. And of course, a huge thank you to the Department for Social Welfare, for recognising the contributions that the charity sector makes to our society, and having these awards, and this great party! Thank you.'

Then I hold my award in the air, just like actors hoist theirs, because, sod it, this is my night!

Everyone wants to hold the gong when I get back to the table, but we have to pass it around quietly because the rest of the awards are still going on. It's hard work to keep my clapping as enthusiastic as it was before I went onstage. Look at me, already resting on my laurels.

I haven't forgotten what Dad said. 'You have something for me?' I remind him when there's finally a break.

'Ah, right.' From the bag-for-life by his feet, he takes a big album. 'I found this a few weeks ago. Tonight seems like the right time to give it to you. I know you'll be thinking about Mum.'

My eyes meet his at the mention of Mum. He's smiling as he hands me one of those fake leather photo albums with loose binder pages. Deep green, a colour Mum always preferred. My heart is thudding as I open it. It must be photos I've not seen before, maybe of Mum and me. I'm touched that he wants me to share the night with Mum in this way, but this will definitely reduce me to a puddle. Everyone is watching me as I open the cover.

'I don't understand. What is this?' I say, leafing through the first few pages. They're not photos. First is a cut-out page of course listings. It takes me a second to notice that it's from my catering college. 'These were my courses,' I say. My first year. There's a business card from the school's careers placement counsellor with a number handwritten across the front. A mobile number. And my commencement invitation and the receipt for the cap and gown we hired for it.

'Your mum was proud of you,' Dad says with tears in his eyes. 'I know she didn't show it in the best way, but she was. Always.'

'Oh, Dad.' Then I flip the page. 'My menus!' I remember typing up those first ones. We used that horrible scrolly font, until we had to change it because the waitress kept getting asked to read out the dishes. Every single menu I made is in Mum's scrapbook.

And all my awards, or at least the newspaper and magazine clippings about them. And that article for the bistro's five-year anniversary where I went on about Mum's kitchen. She saw it.

Dad is smiling at me. 'You see?'

I do. I think, finally, I do. *Mum,* I tell her, *you would have loved seeing this tonight. I've 'stamped my mark on the world', just like you always wanted.*

Finally, I feel like I know my mother. She was too harsh and often hurtful. She didn't easily praise and always found fault. What I didn't understand till now is that I shouldn't have taken her words at face value because, even though she went about it in completely the wrong way, she was trying to encourage me to be the best person I could be.

I only wish I could tell her now that I understand. That although she did it all wrong, now I know it came from a good place. It's all right here in my hands. My mum was proud of me all along.

Chapter 24

It's times like this when June would rather be the home's cleaner than its manager. She's been pacing the office floor for the past ten minutes mumbling to herself as she works out her strategy. I know better than to try interrupting her. She'll only shush me and have to start over.

Terence has asked officially for a meeting with Dot. He didn't use the word mediation, but he wants June there to referee. 'I suppose it's nice that he trusts you.'

'I'm not a bloody social worker, am I? Dot's never going to agree to it. She hates his guts. I don't blame her, the bastard. Imagine doing that to someone you're supposed to love, and with her best friend. I think Dot's shown remarkable restraint. He's lucky she hasn't stabbed him already.'

I know she's thinking as much about Callum as Terence. Or maybe it's Nick she's imagining assaulting. Things are frosty between them. At least he's got the sense not to push her. Every time they have to be in the room together, he acts like she's got a gun pointed at his temple. In a way, she does. She makes all the sacking decisions around here.

Finally, she says, 'You've got to be there too. If she tries to kill him, I'm not sure I can stop her alone. I'm not sure I want to. After what he did? He doesn't deserve anything.'

But I've been thinking about that in light of Mum's scrapbook. It's sitting on my coffee table in the flat, and I get quite teary every time I look at it. I don't think I'll ever put it away. I want it there to remind me that even though I saw her criticism as disappointment, it wasn't that. It was a monumentally misguided way of trying to encourage me to reach for the stars. How many other parents think they're helping their children by pushing them harder, when all the child hears is *You're not good enough?* Hopefully not many, because not everyone will be handed a scrapbook to clear things up.

I do wonder if it's possible that Terence is misunderstood too. I can't imagine how groping our waitresses or insulting the residents can be misunderstood, but that scrapbook is making me see everyone's actions in a new light.

'Will they want me there?' I ask. 'It sounds quite personal. Of course, I'll come if you want me to.'

'You have to be there,' she says. 'It'll take two of us to keep them apart.'

She's only half kidding.

'I have nothing to say to him,' Dot says when we tell her about Terence's request.

'You don't have to say anything,' June says. 'He's only asking that you listen.'

'It might make you feel better.'

She gives me her over-the-glasses look. 'How, exactly, is that supposed to make me feel better? It seems to me that Terence wants to make himself feel better. It has nothing to do with me.'

'I'm sure he wants to apologise properly,' says June. 'Wouldn't it be a little bit nice to hear him grovel?'

'Mmm, I suppose, though who knows what rubbish he'll come out with. You'll be there?'

'Of course! Both of us, if you like.' I, for one, can't wait to hear what rubbish he comes out with.

So that's how the Happy Home for Ladies got its very first mediation. News spreads through the home faster than when I'm serving home-made custard with apple crumble. By the time the meeting is due to start – in the office, where there's at least a door to give Dot and Terence some privacy – nearly all the residents have gathered in the living room. The atmosphere in there isn't tense so much as expectant. Battle lines have been drawn by gender (unsurprising), except for Sophie, who can sympathise with Terence's point of view. That peeved Dot.

But Sophie's soppy romanticism means that she's not so much Team Terence as she is Team Love. Or at least Team Please Stop Fighting.

The men and women might be on opposite sides of the Terence/Dot debate, but there has been some softening lately in other areas. Sophie joining the DIY club definitely helped. That's because she's got them doing all sorts of work that the women want, from making 'feature walls' in their rooms with gorgeous rolls of vintage wallpaper to building alcove shelves. Plus, they're pretty good with flat-pack instructions. It's a good thing Max had the driveway widened when he took over, because it would be a tight squeeze for all the Ikea deliveries otherwise.

Of course, Sophie could have been helping the women with their home makeovers all along. I guess it took the added prospect of romance amidst the building supplies to get her back into her designer tool belt.

Dot comes into the office looking much like she always does, in her flowery day dress and with her glasses hanging on a chain around her neck. It's the way she smells that makes June and I glance at each other. 'Chanel No. 5?' June says.

'My signature scent.'

Hmm. If so, then I've never run across her signature before.

She peers at the old sixties industrial wall clock. 'I do hope he isn't going to be late now that he's got me here. Because I won't stay.'

'I saw him just a minute ago,' I tell her. 'How are you feeling?'

'I'm not looking forward to it, if that's what you're asking.' She gives a small shake of her head. 'Patricia and I made our amends years ago. She's the one I cared about. This isn't necessary.'

'You're good to do it,' June says, just as Terence appears in the doorway.

He's wearing a suit that I haven't seen before and his hair is neatly combed over to one side. Heart surgeons are probably more relaxed doing a triple bypass than Terence looks about speaking to Dot.

'What's *he* doing here?' I say when I see who's standing behind him.

Nick falters, I'm pleased to see.

'He's not involved with this,' I add. His brown-nosing really does know no bounds. Tamsyn has probably put him up to it. They're a perfect pair. I bet Terence doesn't know where her nose ends and Nick's begins.

'I want him here,' Terence says. 'If you get backup, then so do I. Nick is my second.'

June scoffs. 'What are you talking about, Terence? This isn't a duel.'

'Not yet,' murmurs Dot. 'I don't mind if he stays. He'll see through your nonsense. He's got common sense.'

Now it's my turn to snort disbelief. 'Sorry.'

'It's you who wanted to talk, Terence, so be quick about it and stop wasting my time.'

As there aren't enough chairs for everyone, and Terence and Dot are our elders, we let them sit, with Dot in June's office chair and Terence in the one opposite the desk. Terence leans in towards her. She leans back. 'I remember that perfume,' he says. 'I loved that.'

She holds him in her steady gaze.

When Nick makes a move to lean beside me against the extra desk, I say, 'Sit on your own side.'

'There are no sides.'

'Aren't there? You *are* with Tamsyn's family, so...'

The look on his face is pure shock. With a sinking heart I realise that that's what a bloke looks like when he knows there's no point trying to deny the truth. There's no point in me denying it, either. Nick and Tamsyn are together. Why is that so hard for me to accept, even when the evidence keeps bashing me over the head? No matter what happened between us, she's Nick's girlfriend, not me. She thinks I'm pathetic, and you heard what she said. At some point he's going to tell me about them. Well, there, I've given him the perfect excuse.

Dot's got her arms folded in front of her, not giving one millimetre as we wait for Terence to start. He clears his throat. 'Dot, you know I've always had the highest regard for you.'

'Hmph.'

He waits for more, but she says, 'I'm saving my comments for the end.'

'She always did like to get the last word,' he says to the rest of us.

'You're here to talk to Dot,' June reminds him.

That makes him sit up straighter. 'When I look back at what happened between us, it's the single biggest regret of my life. Dot, I shouldn't have let you go to Oxford.'

Uh-oh.

'What?!' Dot says. 'Shouldn't have *let* me?'

'That's not what I mean,' he hurries to add. 'I mean that I shouldn't have let you go alone. I should have gone too. I could have found work there instead of in Ipswich, but I was a fool. And to be honest, it's only with hindsight that I can see that. At the time I really thought, in my heart of hearts, that you should have stayed with me. I didn't think your job was as important as mine. That was the biggest problem.'

She glares over her glasses. 'No, Terence, the biggest problem was that you cheated on me with my best friend.'

'You're right,' he admits. 'But the reason that I was idiot enough to do that was that I had such stupid ideas about you being away. I'm not excusing what I did. I never could. I'm only trying to explain it, because you never gave me the chance.'

'Why should I have given you anything? You presented me with a fait accompli. What would I have gained by talking about it? It was only Patricia who offered to step aside for me. You never sounded like you regretted it for a moment.'

'I didn't know that Patricia did that.'

'You don't know a lot of things,' Dot says. 'Like how it felt to be betrayed by your best friend and the man you love. Who was I supposed to talk to? Who was there to help me get over it? Nobody, because you took my best friend from me. I might have eventually forgiven you for what you did to me, but I hated you for making me lose her.'

'But you made up,' he says, 'with Patricia.' His look is so earnest that I can hardly remember the Terence who defiantly weed in the rhododendrons.

'Eventually, yes. But she couldn't be there when I most needed her. I went through that alone.'

'I'm sorry. I'm sorry, Dot, for being such an arsehole then, and for pushing you to forgive me over the years, when what I probably deserved was a punch in the mouth. It doesn't make up for what I did, but know that I truly am very sorry.'

'Thank you.'

'I'm glad that you and Patricia were able to make up. She loved you so.'

Dot nods. 'I know.'

'If you can bear it, I'd like the chance to try to make it up to you too, Dot. I know I can't erase the damage I did, but do you think you might at least let me try?' He takes a deep breath. 'I think the world of you.'

We're all staring at them. What I see mostly is sadness in both their faces. Finally, it seems, they agree on something.

'I'm tired of hating you,' she says at last. 'It used to make me feel… I don't know, like I was doing something about it. Like I was empowered. But it takes so much energy. Someone clever told me that.'

'Then we can be friends?' Terence nearly whispers.

'Friends? Oh, I don't know. It might be too late for that. Besides, you have a lot of making up to do first. I mean a lot.'

Terence reaches across the table. Dot hesitates, but eventually she reaches too, and they shake. 'Understood,' he says. 'Thank you.'

Then we hear voices coming from the other side of the office door. 'Why don't we just knock? I can't hear anything.'

'Because we're supposed to be quiet, remember? Put your ear to the door, you'll hear better.'

Dot laughs. 'Open the door, Nick, will you please? Put them out of their misery.'

Laney and Sophie nearly fall through it. 'Oh, we were just—'

'Being quiet so you didn't hear us,' Laney says. 'Or was it so we could hear you?'

'Both!' snaps Sophie. 'Sorry. Are you friends now?'

Terence and Dot look at each other. 'I think it might be a fragile truce,' he finally says.

Chapter 25

It's always bittersweet when we're close to finishing a book in book club. Bitter because we're not quite ready to stop talking about the story, but sweet with anticipation for the next read. We'll pick something contemporary next. We always do that after a classic. But I won't forget everything we've discussed about *Pride and Prejudice* any time soon.

We're all here for the finale. Now that Mr Campbell is officially Sophie's hot younger man (or at least lukewarm at seventy-two), she has relaxed her dress code. She's even wearing her signature legwarmers tonight. Laney and Maggie have their heads together over Maggie's notes. Laney likes going through them before we start, to give her a chance of remembering why we're here. Not that any of us minds if she does forget.

I don't recognise Maggie's cardigan, but her brooch is pinned to the left side as usual. 'Maggie? You always wear the same brooch. Does it have a special meaning?'

As her hand finds the lapis lazuli poppy, she smiles. 'It was given to me by my faculty. It reminds me of who I once was. I treasure it above everything else I own.'

It's no good telling her that, even retired and sometimes forgetful, she's still as smart as she always was. She's still Maggie. It only makes her cross, so instead I say, 'It's beautiful.'

Dot's not acting any differently since her truce with Terence, and she's tired of everyone asking if she's okay. I've got to keep reminding myself that just because a person looks frail doesn't mean she's weak. Dot's probably been through more in her life on an average weekend, and come out the other side, than I have in my whole life so far.

June and I are pretending that Nick's not here, which would be much easier if the women would stop fussing over him. If they only knew what he was really like. But he's got them fooled. He had us all fooled.

No one's surprised that Tamsyn's a no-show. If she can't watch it on YouTube from her phone, then she's not interested.

'Let's start,' Dot says, opening her book to the passage she wants. 'This is just after Elizabeth gets the letter from her aunt explaining how Mr Darcy got Wickham to marry Lydia.' She reads the long passage aloud.

June says, 'It's the final thing Lizzy needs to hear to know that she was wrong about Darcy. Which might be fine for her and Darcy, but I've got to question why Darcy would want to saddle Lydia with Wickham after what he did to his sister?! The poor girl is going to be miserable. He should have let Lydia get dumped. She'd have found someone better.'

But Nick is shaking his head. 'In different circumstances he probably would have. But she'd already gone off with Wickham, so finding a suitable match would have been too hard. Her social position was the most important thing.'

Well, he'd know all about that, wouldn't he? I'm surprised he doesn't need an oxygen tank with all the social climbing he's been doing. He might as well attach handholds to Terence or Max every time the talks to them, and don't get me started on his motives for being with Tamsyn.

'Oh, bollocks to social position!' I say. 'June is right, and Austen was poking fun at those norms by exposing them. She thought they were just as ridiculous then as we do now.'

'But what about the women who only had enough money to live on if they married well?' Nick says. 'Don't you feel sorry for them? The five Bennet women, for example.'

'Why are you saying it's only women? That's exactly what Wickham was doing in trying to elope with Georgiana. And Mr Collins with Lady Catherine de Bourgh, though he was sucking up to her rather than marrying her.'

Sound familiar, Nick? The only real difference between Terence and Lady Catherine is that she wouldn't pee in the bushes.

'It's not only money-grabbing women, Nick, despite what you seem to think. Some men are just as bad.' I glare at him. 'Just because people do it, marrying for money or power or using their attributes to get them, doesn't mean it's not disgusting.' Tamsyn springs to mind. 'You can give me any excuse you want, Nick, but it's a betrayal of yourself. It's selling out, and even more sickening when they're pushed into it by their family, like Mrs Bennet did with her daughters. It's *hard* to go against your entire family, even if you know what you really want to do instead. A person shouldn't be expected to choose status over their own happiness, especially when it's not even about them, it's about their parents and making *them* look good or fit in or have something to brag about to their friends, when maybe their daughter is just fine doing what makes her happy and she doesn't want to follow some pie-in-the-sky path to become CEO or president of the boardroom or whatever will make her mother proud, even though she'll hate it and be miserable for the rest of her life.'

Whoah. That wasn't about the book. 'But, luckily, we don't have to do that today,' I finish lamely. I guess knowing Mum was proud of me doesn't yet make up for all those other feelings. It's a good start, but I am a work in progress.

Nick corners me straight after the meeting, asking for a quick word. As much as I really, really want to tell him where to get off, it would look weird in front of the other women. They don't know that anything is wrong between us.

'Let's go outside. It's not too cold.' When I start to grumble he says, 'Please, Phoebe, it's important. I have to talk to you.'

His words take a steel-toed boot to my tummy. This has to be about him and Tamsyn. He's finally worked up the nerve to *put me out of my misery* – will her words ever stop haunting me? – and tell me they're together. He looks like he's about to have a heart attack. That's the guilt. Good. He was the one who asked me out, the two-timing rat. And he lied to me. Repeatedly. Her too, at least by omission.

Ugh, god, I'm disgusted thinking about being in the same bed where he and Tamsyn have been sleeping together. And what must his flatmate have thought when he saw me? He was probably laughing, or high-fiving Nick behind my back.

'So? Talk before I get cold,' I say with my arms crossed in front of me. I will not show him how much this is hurting me. I want to salvage any tiny snippet of self-esteem that I can.

It's pretty dark out here, but not too dark to see the worry on Nick's face.

He sighs. 'There's no easy way to say this, and believe me, I know I should have told you a long time ago, because now everything is so messed up.' His eyes search mine in the gloom. 'Do you already know?'

'Just say it,' I snap. 'And let me get on.' He's not going to get away without at least telling me to my face.

'Tamsyn's not my girlfriend.'

'Oh my God, please, Nick, give me some credit for intelligence. All right, I might have been stupid for not wanting to believe it before, but don't insult me now. You owe me more than that.'

'I'm not insulting you.'

'Aren't you? Even after everything, you're still lying to me. You've been in a relationship with her practically since the first day she arrived,' I scoff. 'Will you please just stop denying it?!'

'I'm not denying that,' he says, 'though you're wrong about the timing. It has been a lot longer.'

I didn't think I could feel any worse. Wrong. 'Well, then why don't you just go ahead and get married and be done with it? Or are you already? Is that what you're telling me? Thanks, Nick, for being an even bigger arsehole than I thought you were. And that's saying something.'

He makes a face. 'I wouldn't marry Tamsyn.'

'Oh, great, be an arsehole to her too.' I have no idea why I'm standing up for her now.

'And she wouldn't marry me, either. It's illegal, for a start. Because she's my sister.'

…

'Did you hear me?'

'I'm not sure. Say it again.'

'Tamsyn is my sister. My half-sister, actually. My complete pain-in-the-arse little half-sister. I couldn't let anyone know because… I should have told you.'

'That makes Max your…'

'Right, Max is my father,' he says, which – extremely inappropriately, given the gravity of the moment, reminds me of Luke Skywalker talking about Darth Vader. It's all I can do not to make heavy-breathing noises.

Nick rubs his face. 'Everything got so screwed up because I couldn't let anyone know about Max. It would have looked like nepotism that I got the job.'

I think about that for a second. 'No, nepotism is when you're favoured by your relative.' Max treats Nick like anything but the favourite. 'This is—'

'Fascism,' he says. 'I know. Ironic, isn't it? June doesn't know, obviously, or she probably wouldn't have hired me. Plus, there's something else. Which means she definitely wouldn't have hired me. I'm so sorry, Phoebe, that I didn't tell you all this before. Are you all right?'

It's hard to take in what he's telling me. I'm still stuck back on Tamsyn not being his girlfriend. 'Go on.'

'I'm not trying to justify anything. I just need you to know the truth. I need you to know why I did what I did.'

He takes a deep breath. 'Max is my father, and he can be a complete arse, but he is smart and did well at uni and he's a success. Same with Terence.'

'Oh, God, Terence is your granddad.' Max is bad enough, but Terence too? Talk about bad genes.

He grimaces. 'I know. And he acts like an arse even though he's actually just grumpy and not a bad person underneath. But the point is that he was successful. And my Granny Patricia, the same with starting the home. Then I come along. Phoebe, I barely made it out of school. I've never been smart. Max says I take after my mum. He doesn't mean it as a compliment, but I do take it that way, because she's one of the savviest people I know even having left school at sixteen. I haven't exactly been a success to Max and the rest of the family.'

It's not like I don't know what that feels like. It's not pretty to say it, but part of me is glad that my brother has lost his job. I know that I should feel bad for him, but Will's had all the success so far. A kick in the pants won't kill him. 'You may not be book smart,' I tell Nick, 'but you are smart.' I've seen him with residents. He wouldn't be that good at his job if he were dim. 'You went to uni, which is more than I can say.'

He swallows hard. 'Barely. I failed my first year. I was just lucky that I eventually found a reception job for a practice of physical and occupational therapists. Otherwise, I'd probably still have no idea what to do with my life. I went back to uni as a mature student.'

'So that's good,' I say. 'It's what Max wanted.'

But Nick shakes his head. 'I barely got through. I only graduated with a pass. I couldn't find a job, and I looked for over a year.'

Something sparks in my memory. 'June told me you had a first.'

He shrugs. 'See why I couldn't tell anyone? Aside from the embarrassment, this whole thing, my job, it's a lie.'

'You *lied* on your CV?' He's right. He shouldn't tell anyone that.

'Not technically.' He flinches when he says this. 'I am certified to practise. I never claimed to have a first. I'd sent Max my CV to pass along to June. He made the change. He always wanted a first-class son. I didn't find out about that until after I was hired. By then everyone hated Max over the changes he was making here, and you couldn't stand Tamsyn—'

'Because she's useless,' I remind him.

'She is hopeless,' he agrees. 'So, I couldn't very well hold up my hand then and say, "Oh, by the way, I'm related to everyone causing you all such problems and my CV is a lie too." Who wants to be that underperforming loser with bad genes?'

I guess that's something. At least he wasn't the one who lied on his CV. Only about everything else. 'You're right, June definitely wouldn't have hired you if she'd known. She might overlook the connection to Max, but not the grades.'

'I know,' says Nick with a shrug. 'I was only looking out for myself. It was selfish. Pride too. I wanted to be hired on my own merit. Or at least for everyone to think I had been. I was too embarrassed that it took me so long to get my qualification. And if June knew about the connection, she might have... rightly suspected that I got the job because of who I am. Then all she'd have had to do was check with my university to see that my CV was a fraud.'

'So why are you admitting this now, when it probably means you can't keep working here?'

'Because, Phoebe, telling you the truth is more important than keeping my job. I'm so sorry for the way I treated June. The last thing I wanted to do was hurt either of you. But I had to do something when I met Callum and realised who he was. Even if it was the wrong thing.'

'... Who is he?'

'He used to be Tamsyn's boyfriend. The love of her life, actually, if you can imagine Tamsyn loving anyone more than herself. I'd never met him so I didn't realise it until he started talking about the yurt business. Two yurty Callums in the area would have been a big coincidence. Phoebe, he's a really bad guy.'

'What did he do?' Maybe he killed someone and buried them in a field. Then put a yurt over the grave.

'They met at a wedding when she was still in uni. He did everything he could to get her to fall for him. As soon as she did, he backed off. But he didn't end it. He kept stringing her along, pulling her in just enough to keep her there, then ignoring her. It went on for months, until Max and my stepmother started to worry that Tamsyn was going to do something drastic. It got that bad. But it's all just a game to him. He pretends that the woman is the centre of his world, until she really likes him, then he loses interest. It would have been kinder if he'd just dropped her, but he wouldn't do that for some sick reason. Maybe the family money, I don't know. People see the home and they make assumptions. Maybe just because he likes the attention. He likes having someone need him. I could see he'd done the same thing to June, being all keen as long as she kept her distance. As soon as she let her guard down he would have started the same game with her, pulling her in and backing off. I couldn't let him do that to her too. He would have, eventually. I'm sorry, I should have told June instead or, I didn't think it till it was too late, had Tamsyn tell her.'

'Yeah, it would have been smarter to have Tamsyn tell her.'

'I told you I'm not smart.'

What a stupid choice of words, Phoebe. 'It has nothing to do with being smart, Nick. You acted as soon as you realised who Callum was to keep June from getting hurt.'

His laugh is grim. 'Yeah, that worked out well.'

'Only because June doesn't know the story yet. She'll forgive you when she does.'

But Nick shakes his head. 'No. She'll fire me when she does. My fake CV, remember?'

'Oh, right.'

Telling me all this means he's putting his future in my hands. It's probably best if I'm careful with it. 'I won't say anything to her if you don't want me to.'

'Thanks, but you don't need to hide anything from her. I'll tell her anyway. I owe her a huge apology. It's nice of you to offer, but I'm so tired of secrets.'

My head is spinning. 'I need a minute,' I tell him, gesturing to the door, 'to take this all in. Can you…? Just for a minute.' Obediently, he goes inside, though he's still staring at me through the French window.

Let me see if I've got this straight. Nick never lied about having a girlfriend. His protests whenever I accused him over Tamsyn were genuine. And probably made him feel icky given that she's his sister. Which means he wasn't two-timing anyone, or snogging me, etc., under false pretences.

So that's good. And presumably he really did like me, rather than just wanting to sleep with me. Also good. Very good.

But, in a way, he did lie by not telling me who Tamsyn really was. And that's bad, because the basis of any relationship has to be trust. He could have trusted me with that knowledge. I wouldn't have said anything to June if he didn't want me to. Not even about Max rewriting his CV.

Although it would have put me in a sticky position to withhold something that affected June's job. In any other situation, I would have let her know that she had a management issue. We're not just talking about our personal lives here.

Speaking of being personal, I think back to everything we've said about Max and Terence. It's easy to see why Nick wouldn't mention that he's related to the tyrants. Would I have judged him for it? I'd like to think not, but the fact that I hope he's got his mum's genes instead of his dad's probably means I would have.

All of which is to say that I understand why he kept his family connection secret from me, even with the strife it caused. Of all people, I know how it feels not to measure up. It's almost more insulting that Max rewrote his CV to give him those grades. He was embarrassed by his own son. That's just wrong.

What's still hard to overlook, though, is what he did to June. That was a boneheaded move. Plus, it was selfish. He should have told the truth and let June decide how to handle Callum. He should have taken those consequences.

Yet he did just confess to flunking at life. It's not like I haven't felt that way too. And he will come clean with June. I suppose if she can forgive him, then it's a bit pointless for me to hold a grudge on her behalf.

He's still watching me through the window. 'Come out,' I tell him.

When he steps back into the garden, he looks like he's facing a firing squad. 'Can I please say something?'

'Yes.'

'Phoebe, I'm not even sure whether I'd forgive me if I were you. I'd love to tell you that of course I would, and try to convince you. But I don't know if what I've done, with the way I've made everyone feel, is forgivable. I guess I just want you to know that it seemed like such a miracle when we got together. I've been mad for you, but I never dared dream you'd feel the same. Especially after the supper club.'

I wince at that.

'I've been so afraid of losing everything,' he goes on. 'My job, everyone's good opinion, but most of all, you.' He laughs, but there's no joy in it. 'Ironic, isn't it? Because that's exactly what I'm afraid I've done. I was stupid, and wrong, not to mention unfair. To you and to June.' When he grasps my hands, I let him. 'I'm not asking you to forgive me, but I hope that you can at least understand why I hid the truth.'

I inspect his expression in the glow of the moonlight. There's no hope in it. There's only sadness, in the downward turn of his lips, in his lined brow and glistening eyes. I realise that I'm barely breathing.

He waits.

Finally, I say, 'As long as we're being completely honest, you need to know a few things.'

He braces himself.

'What you did was wrong. The way you treated me was wrong and I don't deserve that. I deserve honesty and respect. That's not to say I don't understand your reasons, just that I didn't deserve your actions.'

'I know.'

'So you'd better not even think of treating me that way again.'

His face brightens the tiniest bit. 'I promise I won't.'

'You should also know that I can't stand your sister. I mean I really hate her.'

'I've gathered that from every word you've ever said about her.'

'Even aside from her personality,' I go on, 'and that's bad enough, she's the most useless person I've ever had to deal with. Plus, she's rude. I'm surprised she didn't just tell me that she's your sister. She'd have enjoyed spilling your secret to watch you squirm.'

But Nick shakes his head. 'She probably enjoyed making you jealous to watch you squirm more.'

'What an absolute nightmare! That little—'

'Sister,' he quickly finishes for me. 'I know. She's been that way her whole life. If it helps, she'll be gone soon. She's talking about going to London to live with a friend. Framlingham is too small for her ambitions.'

I nod. 'She's better off in London. There's probably better bandwidth there for her phone… but you don't have any plans for London, do you?'

His eyes search mine. Then he allows himself a tiny smile. 'I'd like to think I've got too much keeping me here to even think about leaving it. Do I?'

'I hope you do.'

We're both grinning at each other now. It feels so *good* to do that again.

Chapter 26

The joy is short-lived, though, because when June hears Nick's explanation, she's not nearly as forgiving as I was. 'His entire job here has been a lie,' June says. 'This is a valid HR issue.' We've been going round and round about it.

'Yes, but he didn't know what Max did until after he started, did he, so he didn't lie to get the job. It's Max you should be angry with.'

'I am angry with Max,' she says. 'Don't worry, I've got enough to go around the whole family. I'm not sacking Nick because of the lie. I'm sacking him because he's not qualified. I would never have hired a candidate with only a pass. That's the issue.'

'And you're sure it has nothing to do with his talking to Callum.'

'Give me some credit for being professional, Phoebe. That's a reason to dislike him personally, not to sack him.'

'Sorry, I was only checking. What about extenuating circumstances, like how good he actually is at his job? You can't deny how much he's helped the residents. He got Dot back on her feet in record time and that's not even part of his job. He's not a physical therapist. Look at what he's doing for Laney. And for Sophie. That man does Zumba. Talk about going above and beyond. Who cares if his grades weren't great? … I didn't even go to uni and you hired me.' This is playing dirty. June knows how sensitive I am about it.

She shakes her head. 'Nice try, but that's completely different. You did get your qualification from catering college, and did well, if I remember. I hired you fair and square, based on a true account of your qualifications, not because you're a mate. Unlike Nick.'

Nick's not expecting to keep his job. He's resigned to his fate. I'm the one who can't let it go. So far, June's not budging.

I can't even use the weekend to try softening her up over drinks because I've got go to Dad's. He rang yesterday – 'Phoebe, this is your father' – just to see how I am. That's a sure sign that he's lonely.

My brother is at the house when I get there. He's sitting with his phone on the arm of one of the chairs in the great room.

'Hey.' Will looks up from his screen. 'What did you bring for dinner?'

'Nice to see you too. I've got chicken stuffed with ham and cheddar or aubergine lasagne.'

'There's cheese in both. I'm trying to stay away from dairy.'

Glad to know I'm running a restaurant for my brother. 'Then scrape the cheese out of the chicken or get takeaway.' Dad didn't mention that Will would be home too. Not that I mind. It's just unusual. Nice, actually.

'How's the job hunt going?' I ask him.

'I've got a few options. Nothing solid yet, but I'm not worried.'

'You know, Will, you don't have to act tough with me. You can be yourself.' When he raises his eyebrows, I go on. 'I do know what it's like to be out of work. I know how that feels.'

But he shakes his head. 'It's different for me.'

I bristle at that. 'Why, because your job is so important and mine wasn't?' I may as well be talking to Mum.

His mouth drops open. 'No, Phoebe! You don't really think that, do you? I'd kill to be in your shoes, to get to do whatever you wanted. You never let their opinions bother you. Just try being the one who's always got to be perfect.'

That makes my mouth drop open. 'Just try being the one who's never perfect enough! And you're delusional if you think our parents' opinions never mattered to me.'

'You've always stood up for yourself.'

'Hmph, not always. It wasn't worth fighting over the same thing all the time.' Then I tell him all about how angry I've been at Mum since she died. 'I might have stood up for myself, but I should have done it more. I should have made her stop making me feel like a failure just because I didn't measure up to *her* ideals. It's not my fault that she wanted to go to uni and be CEO of a huge company. It's not fair to foist that on me, on us, just because she didn't manage to live her own dreams.'

'It was bloody unfair! Though now you know she was proud of you,' he points out. 'Or else she wouldn't have kept that scrapbook.'

'Sure, now I know that. But what about all the years when it would have mattered more? Or these past months when I've been so furious with her? She could have saved me a lot of angst if she'd just told me while she was alive.'

His tiny smile is wry. 'At least she screwed us both up. I thought it was just me. I'm glad it wasn't. Sorry.'

'Don't be sorry. I know exactly what you mean.'

This might be the first time in my life that I feel close to my brother. I guess, in a roundabout way, that's thanks to Mum.

Dinner passes easily around the dining table. It's too chilly now to sit in the garden. Will even remembers to ask about my award. I like this new, unemployed brother of mine. 'My sister's a superhero,' he says. 'Does that mean you wore your pants on the outside when you collected the award?'

'Only because I was wearing my cape. Otherwise it would have looked stupid.'

'Mum would have loved seeing that,' he says. We share a smile.

'She would have been proud of you that night,' Dad adds.

'Are you saying she wasn't proud of me all the time?' I'm half teasing. It's new territory to think she was proud of me at all.

'No,' he says, 'she wasn't.'

'Wow, harsh, Dad,' says Will. 'Tell it like it is.'

'She wasn't always proud of you, either, so get down off your high horse. Sometimes she was frustrated by your decisions. Both of you. Mum was a complicated person. Nobody is as cut and dried as you like to make them. We're not all one thing or all another. That shouldn't be expected of us.'

He's talking about Mum, but it applies to everyone. 'I'm just glad that she was proud of me sometimes.'

Dad shakes his head. He's making the same face he does when anyone mentions his football team's biggest rival. 'How can you think she wasn't proud of you? You're her daughter. She encouraged your cooking all your life. She always wanted what was best for you. You're the one who mistook encouragement for criticism. She pushed you and your brother, and me, and herself to be the best we could. It's because she believed we could, not because she thought we couldn't.'

'I didn't mistake it, Dad. She *was* critical of me. I can see now why. She thought she was motivating me, but seriously, don't deify her just because she's not here to remind us what she could be like. I loved her too, but she wasn't known for her compassion.'

At first Dad just stares at me. He's offended. No one should speak ill of the dead. Especially to someone who loves them.

'She could be blunt,' he finally says.

Okay, we'll call it blunt.

'Knock knock!' comes a call from the hallway, startling us. The dishes are cleared from the table but we're still sitting there. Without Mum to move us into the great room – *At least use the sofas that I went to all that trouble to find* – we can't be bothered.

It's Dad's neighbour.

'Hi, Valerie,' says Dad, who's clearly not as surprised as we are to see her. It takes a nanosecond to evaluate her, from the top of her dark blonde head – with a haircut that's so like Mum's that she must use the same salon – to the tips of her pointy-toed leather boots and all the red lipstick, skinny jeans, trendy top and jewellery in between. I'm like the Terminator, scanning for a match.

Identity confirmed. She's got keys in her hand. 'You remember Phoebe and Will?' says Dad.

'Of course, hello,' she says. 'Did you have a good journey?'

'Yes, thank you,' we both politely tell her. Will's got the same look on his face that I probably do.

'I just wanted to drop these off,' she says, holding up a carrier bag. 'For the fundraiser. If we can get them in the post on Monday, there'll be plenty of time. Have you dry-cleaned your tux? If you give it to me, I can drop it off. I need to put my dress in anyway.'

Obediently, Dad goes upstairs to fetch his dinner jacket. Mum wouldn't have liked hearing it called a tux.

'It's nice that you can stay the weekend,' she says. 'Your dad misses you.'

Will is quicker than I am. 'It's nice that he's got you to keep him company.'

She appraises us both. 'Yes.'

Dad does offer Valerie a drink, but she doesn't stay. Good, because we need to talk.

'She's had a key for years,' Dad says when Will brings it up.

'Yes, in case you or Mum accidentally left the gas on,' I say. 'Has she been using her key to let herself in for years?'

'It's not a big deal,' he says.

'No, Dad, I know it's not. I'm only teasing. I don't care if you have a... friend. If you want to spend time with her, then I think that's nice.'

'She's not a friend.' He sounds tired when he answers.

'Friend, date,' I say, 'whatever you want to call her is fine with us.'

Dad squirms. 'I don't know. I can't really see it now. It has not been that long.'

'Well, over six months, actually,' Will says. 'Not that there's a time limit on these things. What would Mum say?' He doesn't mean it as a challenge, and Dad seems to know that.

He laughs. 'She'd tell me not to be such a sentimental old goat. She'd want the best for me. She always did.'

'Well, then, that seems like your answer,' I say.

'Maybe.'

Nick rings me before bed. 'How's it going? Having fun?'

'It has been illuminating. I think my dad has a girlfriend, though he won't admit it to us. The signs are all there.'

'Is that good?' Nick asks. 'Do you feel weird about it?'

'Not at all. I want him to be happy and it'd be a shame if he was alone for the rest of his life. I don't know the woman very well, but she's a neighbour, so he's known her for years. People need to move on to be happy.'

'Speaking of which, have you got plans when you get back tomorrow?'

I know he can hear me smiling when I answer. 'Nope. Just doing laundry.'

'Can I see you?'

'You want to help with the laundry?'

'If that's how I get to see you, then I'll bring my fabric softener.'

'I'm sure we can find something more fun than watching a spin cycle.' Although with Nick, I'd even enjoy that.

It's after eight by the time I pull up in front of my flat on Sunday. Will left first thing this morning, but Dad was happy to have him there for a few hours at least, and he claims he's going to stay the whole week between Christmas and New Year's. We'll see if this new, sensitive brother disappears again when he finds a job. For now, I'm enjoying it.

Nick's car is already out front. 'Have you been here long? Sorry, I should have rung to say the traffic was bad.'

'No, not long. Well, only an hour or so. I didn't want to be late.'

Just like his interview at the home. That seems like so long ago now.

He gallantly takes my overnight bag and the empty cool bag. He doesn't need to. It's not like I haven't carried my own bags nearly my whole life.

I like that he wants to do it, though.

'Do you want to go out for a drink or something?' I say. I've no idea why. I'm too nervous to drink.

'It doesn't matter. I really just want to be with you. I hope that's okay? It's that—'

'It's okay.'

'I've waited a long time.'

'An hour, I know.'

'That's not what I mean.'

Why am I so nervous? This is Nick. *Nick*. I was about to say that I know him nearly as well as myself. At least I hope I do now.

He takes my hand as soon as we throw ourselves on to my squashy sofa. I always mean to fluff up the pillows on the back but never get around to it. Now, though, when they're squeezing Nick and I closer, I'm glad I haven't been house-proud.

'I need to ask you something, officially,' he says.

'That sounds serious.'

'It is.' He takes a deep breath. 'I need to know whether you can completely forgive me for lying to you about Tamsyn and Max.'

'It wasn't a— it was a lie of omission. But yes, I understand why you did it, and I forgive you. I'm not sure that June will, though.'

'That's okay,' he says. 'I'm prepared to take whatever consequences come. You're the one that I care about, Phoebe. I can probably find another job. I couldn't find another you.'

He smiles deeply into my eyes as he leans closer. Our lips meet over the squashy sofa cushions, and I feel like I've sunk into the most luxurious, perfectly warm bath imaginable. With bubbles and bath salts and scented candles and a cold glass of champagne within reach. It's perfect.

'There's something else,' he says, breaking off our kiss. 'I shouldn't say this, but you may as well know, and I'm done with keeping things in. I'm not saying "I love you" now, because I know it's too soon and I don't want to scare you. But I'm telling you that I will say it to you in the future. Just so you know.'

I was wrong before, about the bubbles and bath salts and scented candles and cold glass of champagne being perfect. *This* is perfect.

'And just so *you* know, I'm not telling you now that I love you, either, but I'll be telling you in the future.'

As our lips meet again, I've never been so happy in my life.

Chapter 27

June is getting a worrying amount of satisfaction from feeding old paperwork into the shredder and hearing the whirring scrunch as it has turned into streams of confetti. 'I could do this for a living,' she says as the pile grows.

I'm keeping her company, even though it's our Saturday off and it's probably only encouraging her weekend work habit. 'So, you're telling me you're in love,' she says. 'Both of you. That's quick.'

I have to inspect her comment carefully, though I don't find any judgment in it. It's hard enough talking about this to her at all, what with the Callum situation. But if we don't, then there'll only be a Nick-sized elephant in the room to avoid. 'Not yet,' I say. 'We've just said that we will be telling each other in the future. I know, it sounds stupid now saying it.'

'If it's so stupid, then why can't you stop smiling?'

'I don't know!' Maybe because my heart might actually burst with the excitement of Nick and I finally being together. What I didn't dare to hope for is actually happening.

'You know this puts me in a difficult situation,' she says, and suddenly we're not joking anymore. 'I've always kept my personal life out of work. It's one of the most important things about my job. I can't get emotionally involved, and I've never let myself. You know that. Even with us, and we're best friends.'

'And you shouldn't get emotionally involved now, June. Nick shouldn't have said anything to Callum, I agree, but that has nothing to do with work.'

'You think this is about Callum? Phoebe, please give me more credit. It's about Nick's CV. Specifically, lying on it.'

'But he didn't lie, Max did!'

'It doesn't—'

Her protest gets cut off by Nick, who bursts through the office door. He's here doing some therapy with Laney. Which *might* also be why I'm keeping June company. 'Come out front, you've got to see this!' he says.

The chill between June and me pulls him up sharply. 'What's happening?' He's between us. 'Did I interrupt something?'

'Come in, Nick, I've been wanting to talk to you anyway,' says June. 'We may as well do this now.'

With a sick feeling, I start to get up.

'No, stay, Phoebe.'

'But this is an HR issue,' I say. The last thing I want to do is watch my boyfriend get sacked by my best friend.

'It is, but stay. Please.' Then she turns to Nick, who has obediently sat in the extra chair. 'I was just telling Phoebe that you've put me in an awkward position. Your CV isn't an accurate reflection of your actual educational experience. Is that fair to say?'

Nick nods.

'Or, to put it another way, you've falsified your credentials in a medical position. Is that also fair to say?'

'It is.' Nick sighs. 'I could blame my father, but it's true that when I found out what he'd done, I didn't tell you. So yes, it's fair.'

'What would you do in my position? Be honest.'

'I'd sack me,' he says. 'I completely understand why you would. My only explanation, which isn't a defence, is that I love my job and I hope I'm good at it.'

June sighs. 'And that's what's so hard about this. You are good at it. I'd have sacked you already if it wasn't for that. So, this is what you're going to do.'

She rifles through one of her drawers, selects a document and feeds it through the shredder. Just before the machine crunches it, I catch Nick's name on top.

'You're going to give me your CV Monday morning, and so help me, Nick, it had better be one hundred per cent true. If you've so much as embellished an after-school club, you'll be gone before lunchtime.'

'Thank you!' I say.

'Wait, I'm not finished. Second, you will never get involved in my love life again as long as you live, because you suck at it. Promise me.'

He holds up his hand. 'I promise. I won't so much as suggest a restaurant to you.' He steals a relieved glance at me.

'And thirdly, Nick, you will not, ever, for as long as you both shall live, hurt Phoebe. You haven't seen a mad woman until you've seen one whose best friend has been messed around.'

'I can vouch for that,' I tell him, although he's felt my wrath over June, so he's had some experience already.

At that, Nick stands to grasp June's hand in his, training his intense gaze into her eyes. 'June, thank you for giving me another chance. And I won't ever hurt Phoebe. It feels like a miracle that we're finally together and I will never, ever, do anything to risk losing that.'

'Blimey!' she says. 'You weren't kidding, Phoebe!'

'What wasn't she kidding about?' Nick asks, now smiling as much as June and me.

'None of your business,' I add quickly. 'It's best friend stuff. What do we have to see?'

'What?'

'Before. You said—'

'Oh, right, I forgot. Come on!'

Most of the residents are standing outside in front of the home, all bundled up against the cold. With a sinking heart, I realise that they've split again by gender. The men, plus Sophie, are huddled around Terence near the building with the rest of the residents facing them.

'What's going on?' June calls over.

'They're showing us something,' Dot says. 'Though I do wish they'd hurry up so we can go back inside.'

'We're ready now,' Sophie says to everyone. 'Thank you for coming out in the cold. This won't take long.' She raises her voice after a few women at the back shout that they can't hear. 'This won't take long! It's no secret that this hasn't been an easy few months for us. There were some… let's call them teething pains… adjusting to the new residents. But I think we've made an admirable job of it. So, to commemorate the home that we all love, we in the DIY club have made a new sign.'

With that, the men move apart so that we can all see a long sheet-covered sign on posts sunk into the grass. 'Ready, Terence?'

Like a magician's assistant, Terence obediently gives the sheet a yank.

THE HAPPY HOME FOR LADIES AND GENTS (also FRIENDSHIP HOUSE)

'You've put the happy back!' Laney cries. 'That's wonderful!'

'Plus friendship,' Dot adds, smiling at the men.

'And it will be the Happy Home forever, right, Terence?' Sophie says. 'Go on, tell them.'

Terence, not normally bashful, actually looks like he's blushing. 'It's not a big deal, just that I made a few changes legally so that the home can't be sold off to any bloody developers for flats. It's my house, and now it has to stay as our home. That's the way Patricia wanted it. I should have done it years ago.'

'Tamsyn won't be happy,' Nick says. We all know she'd sell the home out from under the residents.

'Tamsyn can kiss my—'

'Terence!' I warn. 'Though she already does,' I murmur to June and Nick.

'Tamsyn isn't getting the home,' he goes on. 'As annoying as my son can be, he has paid his dues over the years. It'll go to him when I die. Though he shouldn't bank on that for a while, because I'm not going anywhere yet. I've still got some living to do.' At that, he smiles at Dot.

Maybe their truce is entering a new phase.

'I think we've all got a lot of living to do,' Dot answers. 'And I'm glad we're doing it together.'

'Me too,' I say, as Nick takes my hand.

The End

About the Author

Michele writes books packed with heart and humor, best friends and girl power. She is both a Sunday Times and a USA Today bestselling author, raised in the US and living in London. She is very fond of naps, ice cream and Richard Curtis films but objects to spiders.

Michele also writes cozy chick lit under the pen-name Lilly Bartlett. Lilly's books are full of warmth, romance, quirky characters and guaranteed happily-ever-afters.

MICHELE GORMAN

TUESDAY 6:30
AUGUST 27, 2019
JANET POTASY

TERRY'S HOUSE BUINZ
                        JUDY
SEVENTH
HEAVEN

6:15   ALICE
THURS   HOFFMAN
SEPT 12

Made in the USA
Columbia, SC
25 June 2019